IRVING
BERLIN

Irving Berlin in 1913

IRVING BERLIN

Songs from the Melting Pot:
The Formative Years,
1907–1914

CHARLES HAMM

New York   Oxford
OXFORD UNIVERSITY PRESS
1997

Oxford University Press

Oxford   New York
Athens   Auckland   Bangkok   Bogotá   Bombay
Buenos Aires   Calcutta   Cape Town   Dar es Salaam
Delhi   Florence   Hong Kong   Istanbul   Karachi
Kuala Lumpur   Madras   Madrid   Melbourne
Mexico City   Nairobi   Paris   Singapore
Taipei   Tokyo   Toronto

and associated companies in
Berlin   Ibadan

Published by Oxford University Press, Inc.
198 Madison Avenue, New York, New York 10016

Oxford is a registered trademark of Oxford University Press

Library of Congress Cataloging-in-Publication Data
Hamm, Charles.
Irving Berlin : songs from the melting pot :
the formative years, 1907–1914 / Charles Hamm.
p.   cm.
Includes bibliography and discography of Berlin's early songs and index.
ISBN 0-19-507188-3
1. Berlin, Irving, 1888–1989.
2. Composers—United States—Biography.
I. Title.
ML410.B499H36   1996
782.42164'092—dc20
[B]   96-6335

The following sheet music covers are reprinted courtesy of the Lester S. Levy Collection of Sheet
Music, Special Collections, Milton S. Eisenhower Library, The Johns Hopkins University:
"Pick, Pick, Pick On The Mandolin, Antonio"
"Do Your Duty Doctor"
"They've Got Me Doin' It Now"
"She Was a Dear Little Girl"
"Dog Gone That Chilly Man"

9 8 7 6 5 4 3 2 1

Printed in the United States of America
on acid-free paper

Irving Berlin and the Crucible of God

The great conglomeration of men from ev'ry nation,
The Babylonian tower, oh! it could not equal that;
Peculiar institution, where brouges without dilution,
Were rattled off together in McNally's row of flats.
It's Ireland and Italy, Jerusalem and Germany,
Oh, Chinamen and nagers, and a paradise for cats,
All jumbled up togather in the snow or rainy weather,
They represent the tenants in McNally's row of flats.

"McNally's Row Of Flats," Ed Harrigan and
Dave Braham, 1882

David Quixando, the central character in Israel Zangwill's drama *The Melting-Pot,*[1] set in New York City in the first decade of the twentieth century, is a Russian Jew who comes to America after all of his immediate family are killed in a pogrom. A violinist and composer, he finds employment as a teacher and theater musician, then sets out to compose an "American Symphony" into which he pours his vision of the United States as a land "waiting, beckoning, shining—the place where God would wipe away tears from off all faces."

Though Zangwill was British and a Zionist, his play, dedicated to Theodore Roosevelt "in respectful recognition of his strenuous struggle against the forces that threaten to shipwreck the great republic which carries mankind and its fortunes" and first performed at Washington's Columbia Theatre on 5 October 1908, offered a hopeful vision of the future to the millions of immigrants who had come to the United States over the previous several decades. Quixando often visits Ellis Island, to be reminded that "America is God's Crucible, the great Melting-Pot where all the races of Europe are melting and re-forming!"[2] The sight of a thousand Jewish children saluting the American flag is for him "the roaring of the fires of God," and he is ecstatic when he thinks that "all those little Jews will grow up Americans!" His grandmother, who speaks only Yiddish, finds ways to communicate with and then befriends her Irish maid; Quixando falls in love with a Christian woman; and a kindly German conductor arranges a performance of his symphony for an audience of "new immigrants—those who have known the pain of the old world and the hope of the new," people who can "understand [the] music not with their brains or their ears, but with their hearts and their souls."[3] After the first performance of his symphony, the composer stands at sunset on a roof looking over New York Harbor and the Statue of Liberty, imaging the scene to be "the fires of God round his Crucible."

> There she lies, the great Melting-Pot—listen! Can't you hear the roaring and the bubbling? There gapes her mouth—the harbour where a thousand mammoth feeders come from the ends of the world to pour in their human freight. Ah, what a stirring and a seething! Celt and Latin, Slav and Teuton, Greek and Syrian—black and yellow—Jew and Gentile—yes, East and West, and North and South, the palm and the pine, the pole and the equator, the crescent and the cross—how the great Alchemist melts and fuses them with his purging flame! Here they shall all unite to build the Republic of Man and the Kingdom of God.[4]

At the time of the play's premiere, Irving Berlin, like the fictional David Quixando an immigrant Jewish musician who had fled a pogrom, was also supporting himself with menial gigs while pursuing a career as a composer or, more accurate in his case, a songwriter.

What little we know of his early life has been pieced together from scattered official documentation, journalistic coverage of his activities, an early biography by his friend Alexander Woollcott, the lyrics and music of his earliest songs, and general information about life and culture in the Lower East Side.[5] Born Israel Baline in Tumen in Western Siberia on 11 May 1888,[6] the youngest of the eight children of a cantor, Moses Baline, and his wife, Leah (Lipkin), he had come with his parents and five of his siblings to the New World, arriving in New York aboard the SS *Rhynland* on 13 September 1893. The family found temporary lodging in a basement apartment on Monroe Street in Manhattan's Lower East Side, then settled at 330 Cherry Street, in the southeastern corner of the Jewish quarter, in a flat that remained the family home until 1913.

The father was able to find only part-time employment, as a kosher poultry inspector and a manual laborer, and, as in so many immigrant families, everyone in the Baline household was expected to contribute to the family income. The mother became a midwife, three of the daughters found irregular employment wrapping cigars, the oldest son, Benjamin, worked in a sweatshop,[7] and young Israel peddled newspaper and junk in the streets while attending public school and receiving religious instruction at a *cheder*. With the death of the father in 1901, matters became even more difficult for the family, and Israel decided to strike out on his own:

> [Berlin] knew that he contributed less than the least of his sisters and that skeptical eyes were being turned on him as his legs lengthened and his earning power remained the same. He was sick with a sense of his own worthlessness. He was a misfit and he knew it and he suffered intolerably. Finally, in a miserable retreat from reproaches unspoken, he cleared out one evening after supper, vaguely bent on fending for himself or starving if he failed. In the idiom of his neighborhood, where the phenomenon was not uncommon, he went on the bum.[8]

Faced with the necessity of supporting himself, the fourteen-year-old Israel fell back on his one obvious talent: singing. According to Woolcott, he was paid for singing popular songs on Saturday nights at MacAlear's Bar, not far from Cherry Street, was hired briefly in the chorus of the road company for *The Show Girl,* which had opened in New York on 5 May 1902, and briefly plugged songs from the balcony at Tony Pastor's Music Hall. Most of the time, however, he was one of the company of buskers who, having learned the latest hit songs brought out by Tin Pan Alley publishers, "would appear in the bar-rooms and dance-halls of the Bowery and, in the words of Master Balieff, 'sink sat sonks' until the patrons wept and showered down the pennies they had vaguely intended for investment in more beer."[9]

Early in 1904, Izzy, as he was now called, found a more secure position as a singing waiter at the Pelham Café, a saloon and dance hall at 12 Pell Street in Chinatown that was owned and operated by Mike Salter, a Russian Jewish immigrant whose dark complexion had earned him the nickname Nigger Mike. Salter capitalized on the location of his establishment in this sordid quarter to attract tourists, college students, and other "slummers" looking for vicarious thrills in the bowels of the city. In truth, though, "the sightseers usually outnumbered the local talent [at the Pelham], and the grand folk who journeyed eagerly from Fifth Avenue to Nigger Mike's seeking glimpses of the seamy side of life were usually in the predicament of those American tourists who retreat to some quaint village in France or Spain only to find its narrow streets clogged with not strikingly picturesque visitors from Red Bank, N.J., Utica, N.Y., and Kansas City, Mo."[10]

Izzy served drinks to the patrons of the Pelham Café and also entertained them by singing for coins tossed his way, specializing in "blue" parodies of hit songs of the day to the delight of both regular customers and tourists. In his free time he taught himself to play the piano, an instrument available to him for the first time in his life at the Pelham, and tried his hand at songwriting, his first attempt being "Marie From Sunny Italy," written in collaboration with the Pelham's resident pianist, Mike Nicholson. For reasons never fully explained, he chose to identify himself in the published sheet music of that first song as Irving Berlin, a name that he retained for the rest of his life.

His way with lyrics came to the attention of representatives of the popular music industry, who supplied him with the latest songs. Max Winslow, for instance, a staff member of the Harry Von Tilzer Company, came often to the Pelham to hear Izzy and was so taken with his talent that he attempted to place him in that publishing firm. As Von Tilzer described the episode in his unpublished autobiography:

> Max Winslow came to me and said, "I have discovered a great kid, I would like to see you write some songs with." Max raved about him so much that I said, "Who is he?" He said a boy down on the east side by the name of Irving Berlin. . . . I said, "Max, How can I write with him, you know I have got the best lyric writers in the country?" But Max would not stop boosting Berlin to me, and I want to say right here that Berlin can attribute a great deal of his success to Max Winslow. Max brought Berlin into my office one day shortly afterwards, and we shook hands, and I told him that I was glad to meet him and also said, "You have got a great booster in Winslow." Berlin told me that he had a song that he had written with Al Piantadosi and said he would like to have me hear it. I said I would be glad to hear it.[11]

Even though Von Tilzer agreed to publish the song, "Just Like The Rose," he didn't offer Berlin a position on his staff.

In 1908 Berlin took a better-paying position at a saloon in the Union Square neighborhood run by Jimmy Kelly, a one-time boxer who had been a bouncer at the Pelham, and moved into an apartment in the area with Max Winslow. Collaboration with such established songwriters as Edgar Leslie, Ted Snyder, Al Piantadosi, and George Whiting strengthened his ties with Tin Pan Alley, and in 1909, the year of the premiere of Zangwill's *The Melting-Pot,* he took a position as staff lyricist at the Ted Snyder Company. His meteoric rise as a songwriter in Tin Pan Alley and then on Broadway is chronicled in the chapters of this book.

Even though Berlin had left home as a teenager to pursue a life unimaginable to his parents and their peers, he retained close ties with his family, as well as with their community of immigrant Eastern European Jews. When he was the featured performer at Hammerstein's vaudeville house in the fall of 1911, as the wealthy and world-famous writer of "Alexander's Ragtime Band" and dozens of other songs, the New York *Telegraph* for 8 October reported that "a delegation of two hundred of his friends from the pent and huddled East Side appeared . . . to see 'their boy,' as one man among them expressed it, when he stopped the show long enough to tell the audience that 'Berlin was our boy when he wasn't known to Broadway, and he had never forgotten his pals during his success—and he is still our boy.'" The account goes on to say that "all the little writer could do was to finger the buttons on his coat and tears ran down his cheeks—in a vaudeville house!" In addition, according to the *Telegraph*, "the home [on Cherry Street] is envied by all who are invited into it from the original neighborhood where Berlin first saw the light. There his mother and sisters enjoy the benefits—all of them—of his first years' royalties." In 1913 he moved his mother into a new home at 834 Beck Street in the Bronx, in what was then a much more fashionable neighborhood, and on opening night of his first musical show, *Watch Your Step,* he shared his box at the New Amsterdam Theatre with his mother and his sisters.

In addition to maintaining his ties to his own community, Berlin was very much a part of New York City's radically multicultural milieu, which encompassed, in addition to his own group, Jews who had been in the United States for several generations; other recent immigrants to the New World from such places as Italy, Sicily, Portugal, and Turkey; Irish, Germans, and Scandinavians who had come over a generation or two ago; Americans of British heritage who had a much longer history in the United States and who had largely shaped the nation's political, educational, and cultural life; and some blacks, who were still very much on the fringes of American society. Like David Quixando in Zangwill's play, Berlin had personal and professional association with many people outside his own ethnic group: Chuck Connors, a friend and protector during his early days in Chinatown; his first collaborator, Mike Nicholson; Edgar Leslie, born in Stamford, Connecticut, and a graduate of the Cooper Union; the Irish-American George M. Cohan and the Dublin-born Victor Herbert, who became mentors and friends. He associated as freely as was possible at the time with such black musicians as Eubie Blake. And he fell in love with and married Dorothy Goetz, a Catholic, and some years after her tragic early death married another Catholic.

Berlin, then, was a product of the multiethnic and predominantly immigrant/first-generation community of turn-of-the-century New York City, of which the Jewish enclave of Manhattan's Lower East Side was merely one component. His early songs, like those of his peers on Tin Pan Alley, encode or reflect or perpetuate or shape or empower—depending on how one views the social function of popular music—the culture and values of this complex community.

Remarkably, though, despite their regional origin and character, Tin Pan Alley songs came to be accepted far beyond the community in and for which they had been created. A parallel suggests itself. At exactly the same time, a quite different community, this one of African Americans, was forging its own body of popular music, created for and performed within its home community at first but eventually finding favor elsewhere as well. This music was jazz, and its acceptance by people outside its home community, like that of Tin Pan Alley song, seems to be explainable by this observation: Although it retained important aspects of the character and the distinctive musical style of the people who created it, it also accommodated and assimilated enough external aspects of America's older and more dominant culture to make it easily accessible to those outside the community as well.

Neither jazz nor Tin Pan Alley songs of the first decades of the twentieth century can be understood as products of a "melting pot," in which all differences among various groups and their cultures have been obliterated. Both genres were, rather, products of the "crucible of God," in which the fundamental style and the inner character of a subordinate culture had been modified but not eliminated through contact with and accommodation to a dominant culture.

A school of "melting pot theorists" at the University of Chicago has described the cultural strategies of immigrants to a country with a language and a dominant culture quite different from their own. The theorists suggest that adaption to a new and often unwelcoming environment proceeds in three stages—contact, accommodation, and assimilation—bringing about a "superficial uniformity" with the dominant culture without, however, obliterating deep-seated differences in "opinion, sentiments, and beliefs."[12] Successive chapters in this book focus on these three stages in Berlin's early songs, by (1) identifying and describing the song repertories with which he came into contact during his formative years; (2) discussing ways in which these repertories represented an accomodation to a "mainstream" American music; and (3) tracing Berlin's own assimilation of various of these stylistic elements into what became a mainstream popular style itself.

Berlin was a "little Jew who grew up American," but this book argues that the "American-ness" of his songs was more a product of the crucible of God than of the melting pot.

Acknowledgments

Sheldon Meyer, Senior Vice President of Oxford University Press, encouraged me to undertake this book, gave excellent and valuable advice at many points along the way, and then, after a careful reading of the first draft, offered numerous perceptive suggestions, all of which were incorporated into this final version. Oxford's fine catalog of books on America's popular music stands as a monument to Sheldon's love for this material and his skill and enthusiasm in encouraging and promoting the writing of such books.

The editorial staff at Oxford was always thoroughly professional, helpful, and patient of my blunders and oversights. I'd like to thank, in particular, Joellyn Ausanka, the production editor for this book; Andrew Albanese, who did an excellent job with illustrations and musical examples; Jeri Famighetti, the copy editor; and Charles Gibbs, who handled trade marketing.

I'm deeply indebted to Paul Charosh. Given the emphasis in this book on contemporary performance of Berlin's early songs, it seemed important to include a discography of period recordings. An abortive attempt to assemble such a discography myself served only to remind me that I lack the necessary skills, and Paul graciously agreed to take on the job. The result of his work, offered here as Appendix 3, is the first comprehensive and professionally done discography of early recordings of Berlin's songs and might serve as a model for discographies of similar repertories.

Most special thanks go to Mary Ellin Barrett, Linda Emmet, and Elizabeth Peters, Berlin's daughters, for facilitating my access to the Irving Berlin Collection in the Library of Congress in Washington and materials in the offices of the Irving Berlin Music Company in New York, and for allowing me to quote from unpublished lyrics and letters. Robert Kimball, who together with Linda Emmet is editing a comprehensive collection of Berlin's lyrics, has helped in ways too numerous to list here from the beginning of my study of Berlin's songs. Ted Chapin, Executive Director of the Rodgers and Hammerstein Organization (which now owns the catalogue of the Irving Berlin Music Company), and members of his staff, particularly Bert Fink, were cooperative and helpful.

Eric Bernhoft and Paul Charosh generously supplied me with tapes of period recordings of Berlin's early songs, dubbed from original cylinders and disks. Ed Berlin and Wayne Shirley read an early version of Chapter 3, "Alexander and His Band," and offered useful comments and suggestions. John Graziano called my attention to several useful items. Cynthia Requardt, Kurrelmeyer Curator of Special Collections at the Milton S. Eisenhower Library of the Johns Hopkins University, and Joan Grattan, a member of her staff, furnished me with photographs of five rare sheet music covers in the Lester S. Levy Collection of Sheet Music, reproduced in this book.

A slightly different version of Chapter 3 was published in *American Music* 14/1 (Spring 1996). Josephine R. B. Wright's superb editorial skills helped polish it for publication, there and here, and I'd also like to thank her and the Board of Trustees of the University of Illinois for granting permission for the article to be published as part of this book.

Finally, I'd like to acknowledge the help of our cats, Woody and Genji, who kept me company during endless hours at the computer keyboard, and our dog, Tati, who saw to it that I took frequent exercise breaks.

Contents

Introduction

Irving Berlin and the Nature of Tin Pan Alley Song

Between 1907, when Irving Berlin wrote "Marie From Sunny Italy" in collaboration with Mike Nicholson, and December 1914, when his first full-length musical show, *Watch Your Step,* opened at New York's New Amsterdam Theatre, 190 songs for which he had written lyrics, music, or both were copyrighted and published.[1] These are listed, alphabetically by title, in Appendix 1.

These were not the only songs he wrote during these seven years. One interviewer reported that "Berlin turns out an average of three songs a week," although "the majority of them never are heard by the general public. By a process of elimination about one in ten is finally published. It is upon the basis of that average that Berlin works. . . . He is willing to waste nine efforts for the sake of evolving one good tune."[2] Berlin himself was quoted as saying, "I am merely a song-writer who has enjoyed a few successes and many failures. . . . Sometimes I turn out four or five songs a night, so you can imagine how many bad ones I write,"[3] and elsewhere, probably more accurately, "I average from four to five songs a week and, by elimination, but one out of ten reaches the public."[4]

Virtually everyone who came in contact with Berlin remarked on his obsession with turning out songs. Frederick James Smith reported that "he works practically without pause. . . . If there is one thing about his unassuming and almost eagerly alert personality, it is [a] quality of indomitable will."[5] Another writer noted that "the real basis of Berlin's success is industry—ceaseless, cruel, torturing industry. There is scarcely a waking minute when he is not engaged either in teaching his songs to a vaudeville

3

player, or composing new ones. His regular working hours are from noon until daybreak. All night long he usually keeps himself a prisoner in his apartment, bent on evolving a new melody which shall set the whole world to beating time."[6] Berlin himself satirized this preoccupation in an unpublished lyric:

> He wakes her up and cries
> I've written another song
> You've got to listen to it
> She rubs her eyes and answers
> I don't want to hear it
> I don't want to hear it
> He keeps it up all morning
> Until the day is dawning
> And when he sees her yawning
> He starts to holler louder—she takes a sleeping powder
> And then he wakes her up and cries
> I've written another song
> She has to listen to it
> She simply cannot keep him shut
> He's a nut—He's a nut—He's a nut—
> One night she went to her Mother's home.
> While she was sleeping there all alone
> He called her up on the telephone
> And cried I've written another song . . .[7]*

Evidence supports these accounts of Berlin's high rate of productivity. Appendix 2 lists the titles of more than a hundred songs that he is known to have written in addition to the copyrighted and published pieces, brought together from various sources: handwritten or typed lyric sheets, ranging from fragmentary to complete, of otherwise unknown songs;[8] lead sheets of unpublished songs; phonograph recordings of songs that were never copyrighted or published; reviews and programs identifying unpublished pieces sung in musical shows or in vaudeville; and several working lists compiled by Berlin of his own songs.[9]

Creation, Collaboration and Originality

More than a third of Berlin's early songs were written in collaboration with one or more other songwriters, raising the question of whether these pieces should be included in the canon of his work. He was clear in his own mind on this: At one point he drew up several lists of his songs, which include not only those pieces for which he was sole author but also the ones written with other songwriters, and his personal six-volume set of

early songs, bound in leather and stamped "My Songs," also contains collaborative efforts.[10]

Writing a Tin Pan Alley song was a both a complex and a corporate
process. As Berlin described his own working method, he would begin with
an idea for "either a title or a phrase or a melody, and hum it out to
something definite. . . . I am working on songs all of the time, at home
and outside and in the office. I gather ideas, and then I usually work them
out between eight o'clock at night and five in the morning."[11] He would
jot down lyrics as they came to him, on whatever material was at hand;
some of his unpublished lyrics are written on scraps of paper or on hotel
or business stationery, and others were typed out by a staff member of his
publishing house.

In the next stage, words and music would be worked out more fully in
collaboration with another songwriter and/or an arranger. Berlin's first biographer describes the genesis of Berlin's first song, "Marie From Sunny Italy":

> It was agreed that [Berlin and Mike Nicholson] must publish a song. Nick, of
> course, would invent the tune and [Berlin] must write the words, for which,
> they said, he had a knack because he was already famous in Chinatown for the
> amusing if seldom printable travesties he improvised as the new songs found
> their way downtown. . . .
>
> This masterpiece was wrought with great groaning and infinite travail of the
> spirit. Its rhymes, which filled the young lyricist with the warm glow of author-
> ship, were achieved day by day and committed nervously to stray bits of paper.
> Much of it had to be doctored by Nick, with considerable experimenting at the
> piano and a consequent displeasure felt by the patrons at Nigger Mike's who
> would express their feelings by hurling the damp beer cloths at the singer's head.
> Truly it might be said that Berlin's first song was wrought while he dodged the
> clouts of his outraged neighbors.
>
> Finally the thing was done and then the two stared blankly at the bleak fact
> that neither of them knew how to record their work. Nick could read sheet
> music after a fashion but he had no notion how to reverse the process. . . .
> [W]hen the song was finally transcribed, the work was done by a young violinist
> who shall remain unidentified in this narrative because he has since clothed
> himself in the grandeur of a Russian name and betaken himself to the concert
> platform with the air of a virtuoso just off the boat from Paris.
>
> Next the masterpiece was borne with shaking knees to Tin Pan Alley, where
> it was promptly accepted by Joseph Stern for publication.[12]

Some songwriters were primarily lyricists, writing texts to which more
musically adept collaborators added music, and at the beginning of his
career Berlin was considered to be one of these.

He was hired as staff lyricist for the Ted Snyder Company early in 1909,
and as Table 1 shows, most of his songs for the next several years were
written in collaboration with Snyder himself.[13]

Table 1

Year	Total songs	By Berlin alone	Collaborations	With Ted Snyder
1907	1	-	1	-
1908	2	-	2	-
1909	24	5	19	13
1910	30	7	23	21
1911	39	26	13	5
1912	41	32	9	3
1913	33	27	6	-
1914	20	20	-	-
Totals	190	117	73	42

Most of the forty-two songs the two men wrote together have music attributed to Snyder and lyrics to Berlin, but this is probably more a function of the respective positions and statuses of the two men in the publishing house, and of royalty distribution, than of their respective contributions to the song in question. Berlin probably drafted the lyrics for most of these pieces and Snyder came up with the first musical ideas, but distinctions between composer and lyricist almost certainly broke down in the throes of creation, and both words and music of the completed songs must represent some degree of collaboration. Berlin was quite capable of writing music for his lyrics by this time, and had in fact published several successful songs for which he had written music as well as words. Occasional disagreements between the attributions on the first page of a song and those on its cover, or between either of these and the information submitted for copyright entries, support the notion that the division of labor in writing a song was not strictly maintained. The title page of "I Just Came Back To Say Goodbye," for instance, attributes the words to Berlin and the music to Snyder, while the cover reads, "Words and Music by Irving Berlin"; similarly, the cover of " 'Thank You, Kind Sir!' Said She" attributes the piece to "Berlin and Snyder" while the title page reads "Words by Irving Berlin/ Music by Ted Snyder."

There is little beyond anecdote, such as the description quoted earlier of how "Marie From Sunny Italy" was created, to document how two or more Tin Pan Alley songwriters worked together on a piece. Typical is an account of the genesis of one of Berlin's most successful early songs:

> Henry Waterson, head of a music firm, tells a funny story about Berlin's second *[sic]* song, "Sadie Salome, Go Home." For two weeks previous to submitting the song Berlin, with a pianist [Edgar Leslie], occupied a room adjoining Waterson's, and [they] played and sang until Waterson said he dreamed of "Sadie Salome." At the expiration of two weeks Berlin called him into the piano room

to hear the song; but at the conclusion of the introduction, and before he heard a word of it, Waterson said he'd take it. "Play it a tone lower, and I'll sing it for you," he said to the surprised writers, which he did, much to their embarrassment.[14]

And Rennold Wolf gives an account of how he, Berlin, Vincent Bryan, and Channing Pollock worked together on a show song in Atlantic City:

> We assembled in Mr. Berlin's imposing suite of parlors, where there was a piano. . . . Seated at the instrument, he was not long in conceiving a melody, which immediately he began to pound out. All night, until dawn was breaking, he sat on the stool, playing that same melody over and over and over again, while two fagged and dejected lyric writers struggled and heaved to fit it with words. . . . One cigarette replaced another as he pegged away; a pitcher of beer, stationed at one end of the keyboard, was replenished frequently; and there he sat, trying patiently to suggest, to two minds that were completely worn out by long rehearsals and over-work, a lyric that would fit his melody. Mr. Pollock and I paced the floor; we sat, in turn, in every chair and on every divan in the rooms; we tore at our hair; we fumed, we spluttered, and probably we cursed.[15]

In some cases, Berlin's contribution to a song seems to have been more in the nature of tinkering with an already written song than of contributing to the piece in its early stages. W. Raymond Walker tells how Berlin was called in to revise "Oh, What I Know About You" after Walker had written the song in collaboration with Joseph H. McKeon and Harry M. Piano, but even though Walker says that the published song was "a great deal different" from the first version, Berlin's name doesn't appear on the published song.[16] "Virginia Lou" was originally copyrighted and published as a song by Eddie Leonard and Earl Taylor, then withdrawn and republished with a new lyric by Berlin. The sheet music for "There's A Girl In Havana" credits the piece to E. Ray Goetz and A. Baldwin Sloane, but the copyright deposit card in the Library of Congress adds Berlin's name as coauthor, and several other songs attributed to the team of Goetz and Sloane—"Lonely Moon," "My Heather Bell," and "Take Me Back To The Garden Of Love"—were included in a catalogue of Berlin's songs brought out in 1948 by the Irving Berlin Music Corporation. It seems that Berlin may have "doctored" these songs, then decided to withdraw mention of his input.

Despite such collaborations and team efforts, Berlin wrote both words and music for almost two thirds of his early songs, and in later years it became the exception for him to collaborate with another songwriter. He described the advantages of being both lyricist and composer this way:

> Nearly all other writers work in teams, one writing the music and the other the words. They either are forced to fit some one's words to their music or some

one's music to their words. Latitude—which begets novelty—is denied them, and in consequence both lyrics and melody suffer. Writing both words and music I can compose them together and make them fit. I sacrifice one for the other. If I have a melody I want to use, I plug away at the lyrics until I make them fit the best parts of my music and vice versa.[17]

Even when Berlin was writing both words and music for a song, he was still engaged in collaboration. Like other songwriters of the day, he depended on someone else to take down his tunes in musical notation and to work out details of the piano accompaniment; as he put it, "when I have completed a song and memorized it, I dictate it to an arranger."[18] Though he has often been criticized for this, it was in fact standard procedure for Tin Pan Alley songwriters, even those fluent in musical notation, from Charles K. Harris on.

After depending on one or another of the staff musicians at the Snyder Music Company for this sort of help for several years, Berlin hired his own "musical secretary" in early 1913. According to one account:

At the time "In My Harem" was written, Mr. [Cliff] Hess was working in the Chicago office of the Waterson, Berlin and Snyder Company. Berlin went to Chicago on the 20th Century Limited and worked out this tune in his head while on the train. When in Chicago he played it over (all on the black keys, as he always does) and Mr. Hess sat by him and wrote it down on paper as he played it. This struck the composer as a great time-saving device, for Mr. Hess afterwards transposed it into a simpler key, and arranged it in its less complicated commercial form.[19]

Berlin hired Hess on the spot and brought him back to New York.

Hess resides with Berlin at the latter's apartment in Seventy-first Street; he attends to the details of the young song-writers's business affairs, transcribes the melodies which Berlin conceives and plays them over and over again while the latter is setting the lyrics. When Berlin goes abroad Hess accompanies him. Hess' position is not so easy as it might at first appear, for Berlin's working hours are, to say the least, unconventional. Much of the night Hess sits by his side, ready to put on record a tune once his chief has hit upon it. His regular hour for retiring is five o'clock in the morning. He arises for breakfast at exactly noon. In the afternoon he goes to the offices of Watterson [sic], Berlin and Snyder and demonstrates his songs.[20]

After Berlin gave a public demonstration of his songwriting technique in London, a journalist described the two men working together:

A musician sat at the piano. Mr. Berlin began to hum and to sway in the motion of ragtime. Round and round the room he went while the pianist jotted down the notes. Mr. Berlin stopped occasionally: "That's wrong, we will begin again." A marvelous ear, a more marvelous memory, he detects anything amiss in the harmony and he can remember the construction of his song from the beginning after humming it over once. The actual melody took him an hour. Then he began on the words. While he swayed with the pianist playing the humming gave way to a jumble of words sung softly. And out of the jumble came the final composition above. This is how most of his ragtime melodies have been evolved. For one melody he must cover several miles of carpet.[21]

It would be impossible to document precisely what Hess contributed to the final versions of Berlin's songs. The piano accompaniments were, in all likelihood, mostly his work.[22] Lyrics and tunes were Berlin's inventions, and various accounts agree that he knew what harmony he wanted as well; one of his later musical secretaries reported, "I'd play [the song] back for him to hear what he'd dictated, and he'd say, 'You got one chord wrong in there.' And he'd be right."[23] But Hess was much more than an accomplished pianist with a good ear; in later years he published songs under his own name, and it's difficult to imagine that he didn't have some input into the shaping and polishing of tune, rhythm, and harmony that took place as he and Berlin worked together to transform the latter's fragments of lyrics and music into finished songs.

The point of this discussion of the Tin Pan Alley mode of song production is not merely to justify the inclusion in the Berlin canon of pieces written by him in collaboration with others but, more important, to underline that the creation of a popular song is a vastly different process from the composition of a classical piece. And the difference between popular and classical music extends far beyond the mechanical details of how a new piece within each genre comes into being to such issues as the concept of "originality" and the relationship of music and its composers to the community for which it is created.

This era in classical music, falling at the tag end of the Romantic era, was marked by the exaltation of the individual genius/composer to the position of a visionary capable of creating objects of art unimaginable to anyone else. As a result of this focus on radical individuality, a composer's music was expected to differ stylistically from the music of all earlier composers and also from that of other contemporaneous writers, and it was judged in large part by the extent to which it moved forward, breaking new stylistic ground.

> The suggestion that a new classical piece sounded like the music of another composer could be meant (and taken) as negative criticism. Audiences were often resistant to new pieces written in more complex styles than they were accustomed to, but some composers and critics viewed audience rejection as an inevitable reaction to the stylistic progressiveness of the piece in question.[24]

In contrast, a popular song was judged by its conformity to the taste and standards of the community in and for which it was created and by its reception within this community.

For songwriters such as Berlin, widespread approval by performers and audiences was the distinguishing mark of a good song, and a poor song was one no one wanted to hear again. Since mass audiences were unlikely to respond favorably to a song that sounded too different from those they already knew, writing a good popular song required, first of all, the use of musical and textual materials already familiar to audiences. Popular songwriters weren't concerned with turning out products that moved beyond the style of their peers, but in working with them in a common idiom and establishing common ground with their audiences. Thus one cannot judge their songs according to whether or not they broke new harmonic, melodic, or structural ground, and audience rejection signalled failure, not success.[25]

In order to achieve this instant familiarity, as it might be called, writers of popular songs not only conformed stylistically to the music best known to their audiences but often quoted and parodied familiar melodic material, as well.

Like his Tin Pan Alley peers, Berlin "knew all the music his audiences knew, and his songs make use of the common melodic, harmonic, and rhythmic patterns of this music and frequently offer direct quotations from one familiar piece or another"; as a result, his songs were "almost—but not quite—already known to his listeners when heard for the first time."[26] As Berlin himself once put it, "we depend largely on tricks, we writers of songs. There has been a standing offer in Vienna, holding a large prize, to anyone who can write eight bars of original music. . . . Thousands of compositions have been submitted, but all of them have been traced back to some other melody." He concludes that "our work is to connect the old phrases in a new way, so that they will sound like a new tune."[27]

Writing elsewhere, Berlin insisted that he "[knew] the danger of writing melodies that are too original" because "it must be remembered that the public is the final and supreme judge of song merit." He was confident that audiences are "getting wiser every day regarding the caliber of songs [they] desire" and predicted that "the time will come when this indirect censorship will produce song[s] that will express real human emotion in the way such emotion should be expressed." The best songs are original in some way, he observed, but the "the real originality in song writing consists in the construction of the song rather than in the actual melodic base."[28]

Berlin's songs of 1913 and 1914 are considerably different in melody, rhythm, harmony, subject matter, and expression from those of five years or so earlier, and new subgenres emerged between 1907 and 1914. Popular song, like classical music, does change; new stylistic and formal ground is broken; and I will make the case later that Berlin was one of the most "important" songwriters of the period precisely because he was one of the chief instigators of several new developments. But there's a critical distinction between stylistic and expressive "progress" in popular and classical music, a distinction that speaks to the most elemental differences between the two genres.

The aesthetic of popular music insists that there is a social contract among members of its community that demands that a piece be acceptable to all members of the group. Stylistic changes in Tin Pan Alley song in the early twentieth century took place in the context of interaction and collaboration among songwriters, between songwriters and staff pianists and arrangers, between songwriters and performers, and, most critical of all, between songwriters and audiences. The aesthetic of classical music, at least at this time, insisted that stylistic change was the prerogative of the composer alone, a choice made in artistic isolation.

During the second week of July 1911, Berlin appeared at the Hippo-drome in London in the revue *Hullo, Ragtime!,* singing a selection of his own songs. *The Encore* of London reported on 10 July that "he met with a most enthusiastic reception," and *The Times,* uncharacteristically re-viewing a show for the popular musical stage, admitted on 8 July that "[he] sings his rag-time songs with diffidence, skill and charm" and that they "sound, indeed, quite new, and innocently, almost childishly, pleasing." In curious coincidence, Stravinsky's *Le Sacre du Printemps* was given its Lon-don concert premier the same week; *The Times,* on 11 July, complained that "harmonically it is extraordinarily rough and strident. . . . There is much that is hideously and cruelly harsh, even to ears accustomed to mod-ern music, and much, too, that is exceedingly monotonous."

Berlin's songs and Stravinsky's ballet suite were both perceived as origi-nal works, by both audiences and critics. Berlin's originality was accepted and appreciated immediately by his audience; Stravinsky's was not.

The Material Form of Tin Pan Alley Songs

Tin Pan Alley songs were disseminated primarily in the material form of published sheet music. Production of such a piece began with its collabora-tive oral creation and its subsequent capture in musical notation, as de-scribed earlier, after which the song was sent off to be engraved. A small run of first-proof sheets from punch plates was sent back to the publisher for correction and also for prepublication distribution as professional copies to singers who might be persuaded to perform the piece. An artist was commissioned to design and execute a front cover, which might take the form of: 1. a pictorial representation of one or more of the song's protago-nists; 2. a portrait of the singer who had agreed to perform the piece; or, less often, 3. an "art" cover of floral or geometric design. Illustrations of each type will be found in the following chapters. A back cover intended to advertise one or more other songs in the publisher's catalogue was then designed; sometimes the first several staves of the chorus of a single song would be given, sometimes the opening measures of several songs, sometimes a list of the titles of songs recently added to that publisher's catalogue.

Unlike the later practice of depositing handwritten lead sheets to obtain copyright protection before a song had been engraved or even completely finished, two copies of the engraved song, with or without covers, were sent to Washington, D.C., for copyright. Two more went to Ottawa for Canadian copyright and two to London for Commonwealth copyright. Copyright and publication took place simultaneously, in effect.

The finished product, in large (ca. 14″ × 11″) format, was attractive and functional. Covers were often stylish and colorful examples of one of the "minor" art forms of the day, serving to attract the eye of potential buyers. The paper and ink were of excellent quality, as proved by the excellent condition of many remaining copies after three quarters of a century, and the sheet music sat well on the piano stand. The music itself was engraved in large notes, with generous space between staves and in the margins; many of the craftsmen did beautiful work, comparing favorably in artistry with published music of any period. Any mistakes made in the process of engraving remained uncorrected in subsequent runs, since the same plates continued to be used without alteration. A new cover might be designed to replace the original one if a song sold well enough to warrant further printings, however, particularly if the piece had been taken up by a popular performer or interpolated into a show.

This sheet music was available for purchase at the offices of publishing companies, where prospective buyers, in addition to browsing through the stock, could also have songs played and sung by staff musicians. Distribution also took place at retail outlets, some specializing in music and others offering sheet music as part of a larger stock. Dissemination also took place to a lesser extent through other media. In the early years of the century, newspapers such as the *Boston Sunday American* and the *New York American and Journal* included a piece of sheet music in each week's Sunday supplement, and the lyrics of popular songs were still circulated in text-only songsters. Installments of *Delaney's Song Book,* containing the lyrics of new songs brought out by the major Tin Pan Alley publishing houses, appeared from 1892 into the 1920s; most of Berlin's early songs appeared in this popular series. In addition, publishers themselves sometimes distributed the texts of their new songs on single sheets, as broadsides.

In their material form as published sheet music, Berlin's early songs appear to exhibit a high degree of uniformity, among themselves and also in relation to pieces by other songwriters. Structurally, virtually every one of them is made up of the same component parts:

Figure 1. Front cover of "Grizzly Bear."

Figure 2. Back cover of "Grizzly Bear."

1. a brief piano introduction, drawn usually from the final bars of the chorus or the beginning of the verse
2. a two- or four-bar vamp, with melodic and rhythmic material drawn from and leading into the verse
3. two (or sometimes more) verses, usually sixteen or thirty-two bars in length, depending on the meter of the song
4. a chorus, usually equal in length to the verse, with first and second endings. The first ending indicates a repeat of the chorus; the second gives instructions for either a da capo return to the introduction or a dal segno return to the vamp

The songs also appear to be quite uniform in melodic, harmonic, and rhythmic style. Texts are set in a predominantly syllabic fashion, to mostly diatonic tunes confined to a vocal range of an octave or less, with an occasional chromatic passing note. Harmonies are tonal and triadic, shaped into two- or four-bar phrases, with secondary dominants and other chromatic chords sometimes lending variety. Modulation may lead to another key for a phrase or two, and from early on Berlin had a mannerism of abruptly shifting a phrase to a key a third away from the tonic, without modulation.[29]

Most of what has been written about Berlin's early songs takes this sheet music as the primary (and often only) text, and most recent performances of these pieces are more or less literal readings from this text. But the songs were rarely performed just as they appear on the printed page. A literal reading from the sheet music results in a performance shaped as follows:

- piano introduction
- vamp
- first verse
- chorus with first ending
- repeat of chorus, with second ending
- vamp
- second verse
- chorus with first ending
- repeat of chorus, with second ending

But we know from period recordings and other evidence that this sequence was subject to change in performance. Only the first verse might be sung, or additional verses not found in the sheet music might be added. The chorus might be sung only once after each verse, "catch" lines of text might be interpolated into the second chorus, or there might be a completely different set of lyrics, not found in the sheet music, for the second chorus. The singer might alter notes in the melody or deliver the entire song in a semispoken way without precise pitches. The accompaniment might take

Figure 3. First page of "Grizzly Bear."

over for a half or a full chorus without the singer(s), the instrumental introduction might be repeated after the last chorus, or the song might end with a coda not found in the sheet music.

Beyond that, when these songs were sung on the vaudeville or legitimate stage or in the recording studio, they were accompanied by an orchestra rather than a piano, and they were frequently sung by two or more voices despite having been published as vocal solos. A period recording of a "double" version of "Alexander's Ragtime Band" illustrates how a piece notated for one voice could be transformed into a double version in performance:

Oh my honey *[Yes?]*, Oh my honey *[Yes?]*,
Better hurry and let's meander,
Ain't ya goin' *[Where ya goin'?]*, Ain't ya goin' *[Where ya goin'?]*,
To the leader man *[Ragged meter man]*,
Oh my honey *[What?]*, Oh my honey *[What?]*,
Let me take you to Alexander's **grand stand, brass band,**
Ain't ya comin' along?
   Come on and hear *[I'd like to hear]*, Come on and hear *[I'd like to hear]*,
   Alexander's ragtime band,
   Come on and hear *[Oh yes my dear]*, Come on and hear *[Oh yes my dear]*,
   It's the best band in the land,
   Can dey play a bugle call like I never heard before?
   Why, it's so natural that you want to go to war,
   That's just the bestest band what am, Honey lamb,
   Come on along *[I'm goin' along]*. Come on along *[I'm goin' along]* . . .[30]

(brackets and italics indicate the second voice, bold type
indicates both voices singing together)

The problem with taking the notated form of these songs as the primary text, then, is that, unlike compositions of the classical repertory, which throughout the modern era were assumed to be "ideal objects with an immutable and unshifting 'real' meaning,"[31] a popular song may be "rearticulated" in any given performance.[32] In other words, "dissemination of [a popular song] as printed sheet music was only the beginning of its history; it then became fair game for performers, who according to the conventions of the genre were free to transform [it] in details of rhythm, harmony, melody, instrumentation, words, and even overall intent."[33]

Throughout its history, popular music has been marked by the extraordinary flexibility with which its text has been treated by performers, and also by the variety of meanings that listeners have perceived in these songs. Stephen Foster's "Old Folks At Home" was sung by amateurs clustered around pianos in private parlors, performed on the minstrel stage in blackface, sung on the concert stage by famous performers of the classical repertory, interpolated into stage versions of *Uncle Tom's Cabin,* sung around campfires by groups of Civil War soldiers of both sides, reworked into elaborate display pieces for virtuoso pianists and trumpet players, para-phrased in classical compositions by Charles Ives and others, and quoted in Irving Berlin's "Alexander's Ragtime Band." In each instance, the overall shape, stylistic details, and the performance medium were different, as was the meaning of the song for its performers and listeners.[34]

Today's literal, note-for-note performances of Berlin's early songs have their own validity and their own meaning, and recent analyses of the music and lyrics of these pieces using their notated form as the primary text can tell us useful things about their style and structure. But my concern is not with the performance and reception of these songs today but with their meaning for Berlin and his audiences at the time of their composition and their first performances.

To recover this meaning, one must look beyond their material form as sheet music.

Meaning in Berlin's Early Songs

Berlin's early song aren't as homogeneous a group as they appear to be in their notated form. The corpus in fact includes pieces of many different genres and subgenres, each with its own style, content, and meaning.

The issue of genre has been a favorite topic of literary critics throughout the twentieth century. Earlier, when most critics were under the spell of modernist modes of thought, the chief focus was on the construction of taxonomies based on close readings of the texts of novels, plays, poems, essays, and other literary forms, in relative isolation from the contexts in which these works were conceived, written, produced, disseminated, and received. More recently, the emphasis has switched to the flexibility and overlap of genres and to the necessity of taking factors other than the printed text into consideration.

Similarly, earlier musicological writing on genre was concerned largely with somewhat simplistic distinctions among various instrumental and vocal forms, while more recent scholars have argued that one must consider semi-otic, behavioral, social, ideological, economic, and juridical dimensions as well.[35] As Jim Samson puts it, discussions of genre should "extend beyond musical materials into the social domain so that a genre is dependent for its definition on context, function and community validation, and not simply on formal and technical regulations."[36] Even more directly and radically, Robert Walser argues that "musical meanings are always grounded socially and his-torically, and they operate on an ideological field of conflicting interests, insti-tutions, and memories," so much so that "the purpose of a genre is to organize the reproduction of a particular ideology."[37]

The issue of genre is much more complex in popular songs than in literature, or for that matter even in instrumental music, and not only because both words and music must be considered, separately and together. As noted earlier, the printed texts of these songs were much more subject to change in performance than were those of so-called serious literature and music; when context as well as text is taken into consideration, it becomes apparent that popular songs were "consumed" in a far greater variety of situations than were poems and novels, or string quartets and symphonies.

Elsewhere, I've offered a comprehensive taxonomy of Berlin's early songs based chiefly on their printed texts.[38] While I'm still convinced that there's some value in classifications of this sort, this book proposes that the contemporary perception of the genre of a song, and hence its meaning, was shaped most importantly by its performance and by the venue in which this performance took place. Conversely, stylistic differences written into these pieces were more a matter of the songwriter's sense of who would perform a given song and where than of any abstract ideas about genre. Accordingly, three chapters of this book are organized around the early twentieth century's most important performance venues for popular songs: the vaudeville house, the home circle, and the legitimate theater. The other two chapters discuss songs that make reference of one sort or another to African Americans and their culture, a critical component in the evolving style and content of American popular song that cut across performance venues.

In an attempt to understand how these songs were performed and received in their own day, I've made use of various materials in addition to printed music. First, and most important, I've listened to period recordings made on cylinders and discs by the performers who first sang these pieces and who were sometimes coached by Berlin himself.[39] There are far more of these than I first thought; in fact, almost half of Berlin's early songs were recorded, some of them more than once. Appendix 3 is a list of period recordings, compiled by Paul Charosh. These recordings bring the songs to life and shed light on performance style and contemporary meaning, in ways to be discussed in the following chapters.

I've examined the sheet music covers of these songs for whatever clues they might contain about the intended meaning of the piece. Often the relationship between a song and its cover isn't clear. Sometimes the title of a song and the name(s) of its author(s) are given in precisely the same form on the cover as on the first page of the music; at other times there are differences in the details. Sometimes it's apparent that the cover artist must have known the identity of the characters in a given song and how they were portrayed in the lyrics and the music; in other cases there are apparent contradictions between the sense of a song and what appears on its cover. There's no hard evidence one way or the other as to whether songwriters had anything to do with the covers of their songs, but there is a clear pattern in Berlin's songs—the correspondence between the content of a song and its cover increases over the years. From what we know of his determination to control every aspect of his songs, from composition to production to performance to marketing, once he was in a position to do so, it seems likely that he was increasingly involved in decisions about the covers for his songs after early 1912, when he was made a partner in the publishing company that brought out his music.

Sadly, a vast store of other material that would have helped us understand how these songs were done in their own day apparently has been lost. Like other Tin Pan Alley publishing houses, the Ted Snyder Company—renamed Waterson, Berlin & Snyder in early 1912—made various materials, prepared by staff musicians, available to professional musicians who performed pieces from its catalogue. These included copies of songs transposed to fit the voice ranges of different singers; extra verses and choruses; "catch" lines to be inserted into second choruses; "double" versions to facilitate performance by two singers; quartet arrangement of song choruses; and orchestrations of songs for use when they were sung on stage or in the recording studio.[40] None of this material has been recovered, with the exception of a few double versions of lyrics that remained in Berlin's possession, published orchestrations of "Alexander's Ragtime Band" and "Spanish Love," and a manuscript orchestration of "Opera Burlesque."[41]

Even while locating and studying such materials, I've continued to examine the sheet music itself for additional clues to the meaning of these songs. In particular, I've pursued the notion that the lyrics of a popular song are always perceived as being in someone's voice, and the identity of this person can be a key factor in a listener's perceived meaning of the song:[42]

• If a song lyric written in the first person is in the nature of a soliloquy ("I" speaking to himself), the voice will appear to be that of the songwriter, engaged in musing, reminiscing, meditating, philosophizing, or moralizing. If the piece is sung by the songwriter himself, this perception will be intensified, and the audience will be in the position of overhearing him as he speaks to himself. If it's sung by someone other than the songwriter, this performer may assume the role of a "reader," a passive intermediary conveying the voice of the author to the audience. However, if the singer convinces the audience that she has internalized the song's content and expression well enough, the voice may be heard as her own, in which case it's the singer whom the audience will overhear talking to herself. As Edward Cone puts it in a discussion of nineteenth-century art song, the persona of the composer of the song and the singer may seem to collapse into a unitary protagonist.[43]

• If a first-person lyric is addressed to a second person ("I" speaking to "you"), the voice will again appear to be that of the songwriter, now addressing someone else. In performance, the singer (if someone other than the songwriter) may project this one-way dialogue so that the voice remains that of the songwriter, or she may preempt the voice herself, in which case the audience will find itself eavesdropping on *her* remarks to another party.

• If a first-person lyric is addressed to the second person plural ("I" speaking to "you all"), once again the implied voice will be that of the songwriter speaking to the collective "you," narrating an event or a story or engaged in lecturing or haranguing. In performance, the singer will address the audience directly, either as an intermediary conveying the voice of the author or making a public utterance herself.

• Although texts in first person plural ("we" speaking to "you" or "you all") are common in choral music, they are virtually unknown in Tin Pan Alley songs, at least in their published form for solo voice with piano accompaniment.

• If a first-person lyric is written in such a way that the person speaking is clearly not the songwriter but someone else ("he" or "she" speaking as "I"), then the voice will be perceived to be that of this other person. In performance, the singer's job will be to represent or impersonate this person who is neither the songwriter nor the singer. If she's successful enough in doing this, the audience may in fact take the voice of the song to be her own.

• By the very nature of language, a song cannot have a second-person protagonist ("you" or "you all" speaking to someone). Although lyrics are sometimes *addressed* to "you," the voice will be heard as that of the songwriter, the performer, or of a protagonist in the song, speaking these words to a second party or to the audience.

• Third-person lyrics function as narration (an implied "I" describing persons, objects, or events). By casting a lyric in the third person, the songwriter establishes an expressive distance between himself and the content of the song. That is, the emotions or attitudes expressed in the lyric are heard not as his own but as those of a character in the song. In performance, the singer will assume the role of narrator.

All of this changes if a song is part of a theatrical production. If performed by a singer in the role of a specific, named character involved in a dramatic scenario, a piece will be perceived as being in the voice of that person, rather than that of the songwriter or the performer, whether the lyric is in the first or the third person. Also, lyrics written in the first person plural addressed to the second person plural ("we" speaking to "you all") are common in songs for the stage, where they are heard as the voice of the ensemble (the collective cast) addressed to the audience.

These remarks in this introduction are offered as a conceptual framework, in preparation for the more detailed discussions of individual songs and their meanings that make up the bulk of the rest of this book.

Chapter One

Berlin's Songs for the Vaudeville Stage

The majority of Berlin's earliest songs were written for performance in vaudeville, a theatrical form with roots in the mid-nineteenth-century concert saloon, a venue for working-class entertainment. As an observer described an evening in one of these places, which were clustered by the dozens in and around the Bowery section of New York City:

> We drew our knees under a roughly made round table. Our seat was a hard-bottomed chair, or perhaps it was a bench. We scraped our feet on the sawdust floor, and signalled a waiter to bring a mug of beer and plate of pretzels—those twisted things with great pieces of salt sprinkled over them, in case you don't remember. Through a haze of blue smoke, an odor of stale wine or something alcoholic filling our nostrils, we focused on a makeshift stage, across the front of which ran a row of flickering gas jets. From the wings of that stage stepped an oddly dressed comedian and his partner, one with face glowing under burnt cork, the other in caricature of a son of the Ould Sod. They sang and danced and chattered too. . . . Next came a girl in a short skirt—short in that day for it was just inches above the ankles—who sang something sentimental about "My Mother Was A Lady." Following our song lady came a green-tighted, all silver-spangled young man who walked a slack wire. Others in turn brought laughs and hurrahs and sometimes a catcall or two.[1]

Within a few years, similar entertainment was being offered in larger and more formal performance spaces, soon called vaudeville houses, which like the concert saloons were "far more open, generous, and egalitarian than most cultural institutions" of "the socially stratified theatre world of

mid-nineteenth-century New York, where immigration and indus-
trialization had created audiences divided by race, class, gender, and ethnicity."

> Vaudeville entrepreneurs attempted to reverse this fragmentation and create a
> kind of theatre that could appeal to all New Yorkers and gather them, together
> under one roof. The challenge was not just providing acts that would amuse
> profoundly different groups of people, but fitting into one building people with
> profoundly different cultures and ways of behaving.[2]

As a "distinctly urban form of popular theatrical entertainment," vaudeville
"drew the residents of the modern city together and gave them a glimpse
of themselves."

> The show dramatized the spectrum of humanity in the city and the diversity of
> urban life through its subject matter and variety. Consequently, it attracted the
> entire range of city people and, after exposing them through comedy and song
> to a diverse set of human problems, provided them with a fleeting measure of
> harmony. During these hours the audience also distilled models for everyday
> behavior and guides for living in the modern city from the stage routines, the
> etiquette, and the ambience of the vaudeville house.[3]

Crowd behavior and sometimes the acts themselves were sometimes inclined to be informal and even rowdy, in keeping with the character of the
predominantly working-class, mostly male audience, in which New York
City's immigrant and first-generation populations were well represented.
Ticket prices were geared to this audience; the best seats were priced at
half or less what it cost to attend the legitimate theater, seating in the
gallery was available for a dime, and even these prices were lower for matinee performances.

Some entrepreneurs attempted to increase their profits by reaching out
to a more varied and hence larger audience, including the middle classes,
women, and even entire families. Tony Pastor, who first performed in and
then owned and operated vaudeville houses in the Bowery, on Union
Square, and finally at Fourteenth Street and Third Avenue, was one of the
first to make his house more "respectable." As Lillian Russell recalled the
theater, many years after her first performance there in 1881:

> Everything in Pastor's was clean and fresh and new. The seats were priced at a
> dollar and a half—the same as those in theatres which had drama or comic
> opera as their attractions. There was no smoking permitted in the theatre and
> the audience was usually in full dress. In an age when "variety" was considered
> just a little too daring for women to attend, Tony Pastor's Theatre set a stan-
> dard that was unique and drew as many women as men. Every act was scrupu-
> lously clean and free from suggestiveness; the performers were fine men and
> women and great artists did not hesitate to appear there.[4]

Even though attempts by Pastor and like-minded entrepreneurs to "clean up" vaudeville succeeded in attracting some people who had previously stayed away, class distinctions persisted between audiences for the popular theater and those who patronized the legitimate stage. According to an ethnographical study made in 1911, 60 percent of the vaudeville audience was working class, 36 percent "clerical," and 4 percent "vagrant," "gamin," or "leisured." Sixty-four percent of the audience was male and 36 percent female; youths under age 18 made up slightly less than a fifth of the audience. By comparison, only 2 percent of those attending the legitimate theater were from the working class.[5]

Although its history began in New York City and its cultural roots remained there, vaudeville soon spread to the entire country, with provincial houses opening in America's larger cities and then in its towns. Starting with a theater in Providence in 1888 and adding houses in Philadelphia (1889) and then Boston and New York itself, B. F. Keith and Edward F. Albee built "a show-business empire that dominated big-time vaudeville in New York City and much of the eastern United States"[6] by the turn of the century, with a central booking office in New York controlling the selection and scheduling of acts in all theaters in the Keith-Albee chain. Martin Beck built a similar circuit, the Orpheum, based in Chicago and extending into the South and the West. By the second decade of the twentieth century, more than a thousand vaudeville houses were operating in the country. As a contemporary observer described the institutional structure of vaudeville at its peak:

> The "Big Time" is so divided that Keith's controls all houses east of Chicago; while Orpheum functions in Chicago and all points west. . . . The practically absolute control exercised by Keith's and Orpheum in "Big Time" does not extend to the "Small Time" field. Here the circuits owned by [Alexander] Pantages and [Marcus] Loew offer real competition. . . . Though there are relatively very few big-time theatres as compared with small-time, this division of vaudeville bears an importance quite out of proportion to its numerical strength. It includes all the big acts and the finest theatres, draws the largest audiences and commands the highest admission fees.[7]

There were also independent houses, ranging from Oscar Hammerstein's famous establishment in New York City to small-time operations scattered through the country's towns and villages. And in addition to the vaudeville houses proper, there were countless other places—dime museums, bars, restaurants, variety and burlesque theaters—offering the same type of entertainment as that found on the vaudeville stage, if not the same quality and quantity.[8]

A vaudeville show was made up of a succession of unrelated acts or "turns," as they were called, each lasting between ten and thirty minutes. The larger theaters opened around noon and offered continuous entertainment well into the evening. Usually the featured bill of eight or more turns was presented twice each day, filled out with as many secondary acts as necessary to keep the show going without break. Since a single admission ticket admitted the holder for the entire day, some of these filler acts were "chasers," deliberately chosen for their poor quality to encourage turnover in the audience. By the first decade of the century, the featured part of a vaudeville show had evolved into a more or less standardized nine-act bill, usually beginning with "a so-called 'dumb act,' a dancing routine, an animal group, or some other proven attention-getter that latecomers seeking seats could not ruin." Following this,

a typical vaudeville act filled the number two position—at times a ventriloquist, more frequently a man and woman singing to settle the audience and ready it for the show. The following comedy sketch, holding "the audience every minute with a culminative effect that comes to its laughter-climax at the curtain," began the actual build-up of the show and had the audience anticipating what was to come. The fourth and fifth spots produced the "first big punch of the show," a "corker" in the argot of the trade, succeeded by a big dance act or a rousing musical number, both guaranteed successes that fully occupied the conversation during the intermission.

The opening of the second half presented a unique problem. The sixth act had to restore the attitude of expectant delight and excitement, yet it had to stay at a level just below that of the subsequent routines. Comedy pantomime, jugglery, or magic often answered the need, while allowing the spectators to get back to their seats without unduly disrupting the house. Very likely a big playlet, the single problem of a story's chief character compressed into a single impression, hastened the show to its climax. That came with the grand comedy hit in the number eight spot, usually done by a great star for whom the audience had been waiting. A big "flash" closed the performance, such as the showy sight of a troupe of white-clad trapeze artists fying [*sic*] on a black background.[9]

Some sense of the range and variety of the entertainment offered on the vaudeville stage can be gained from the reviews of individual acts published each week in *Variety*. The issue for 25 June 1911, chosen at random, included critiques of the following acts playing in one house or another in New York or Chicago:

• Stella Morrison's Dogs and Ponies (animal act). "The routine is similar to many other acts, and includes a jump from a tall ladder to a net, made by a small fox terrier. A pony drill by two animals has been well arranged."
• Tom Mahoney (monologist). Mahoney tells a succession of Irish stories "bristling with wit," held together by a courtroom setting.

- Kingston and Thomas (piano and songs). Miss Thomas is "a 'rag time' piano player of exceptional ability" who offers keyboard solos and also accompanies herself and Mr. Kingston in songs.
- Felix Adler (singing and talking). "Opening with a song with no sense to it, but going big, Adler delivers his rapid-fire talk, after which he has a song in a German accent, about beer. A 'drunk' impersonation and a 'Dago' song follow. For a finish he brought out a song about a goat, accompanied by goat language. Between verses he 'kids' himself, the orchestra and the audience, without becoming offensive, and at other times swings into a few limericks, or rumbles through the chorus of an old song."
- Mlle. Rialto, "The Artist's Dream" (posing and singing). "Mlle. Rialto appears in a frame in different poses, while the artist (William Gordon) sings an appropriate song in a fairly good baritone voice. After several poses the artist tries modeling, while Mlle. Rialto reappears, this time with less clothing on. She has a good figure and looks rather pretty in the frame. In the last half of the act . . . she gives them what they want in one picture, coming pretty close to nothing in the way of garments."
- Aleta (dances). Her program includes a serpentine dance, a fire dance, a number entitled "The Dance of the Gods," and she finished with a "rag-time Salome," which the reviewer found quite amusing.
- Advance Musical Four (musical selections). "Strings and a piano with a couple of good voices, and the four ought to get along."
- Edna Mae Spooner and Company, "An Obstinate Family" (drama). A six-person comedy troupe offers a seventeen-minute comedy sketch revolving around flirtations and quarrels involving three couples: a butler and maid, their master and mistress, and the wife's mother and father.
- Mario Molasso and Company (pantomime). "To give four people a chance to do some excellent whirlwind dancing at the end of his act, Molasso forces the audience to sit through seventeen minutes of nothing more than very silly pantomimic nonsense, with a mirror effect not new, probably put in with the idea to interest."
- Moran and Tingley (dancing). The two "boys" end their act attached by the waist to a bar, dancing while hanging head down. According to the reviewer, they are "suspended for over a minute; it was easy to see the strain they were under," and "the difficulty in connection with this act is how long the boys can stand doing the upside-down dance."

Other types of vaudeville acts included banjoists, male quartets, trick cyclists, veterans of the Civil War playing old-time fiddle music, female impersonators (or "wench acts"), recitations or jokes by professional boxers

and major-league baseball players, clog dancers, ballad singers, comedy jugglers, one-person bands, male impersonators, rope skippers, bag punchers,
sharpshooters, contortionists, iron-jaw acts, "mental acts," quick-sketch artists, ventriloquists, illusionists, piano sextets, trick roller skaters, Chinese
baritones, and Japanese jugglers.

As noted earlier, some vaudeville managers made an issue of the respect-
ability of their houses and the entertainment offered in them. B. F. Keith
often boasted of his "fixed policy of cleanliness and order" and his insistence that "the stage show must be free from vulgarisms and coarseness of
any kind, so that the house and entertainment would directly appeal to the
support of ladies and children"; he claimed to have brought vaudeville to
the point of being "patronized and enjoyed by the most intelligent and
cultivated people, who flatter me by the assurance which their presence in
my theatres brings that they have confidence in my pledge that therein
nothing shall be given which could not with perfect safety be introduced
to their homes."[10] The Keith-Albee chain, sometimes referred to as the
"Sunday School Circuit," posted backstage notices to performers: "You are
hereby warned that your act must be free from all vulgarity and sugges-
tiveness in words, action, and costume, and all vulgar, double-meaning and
profane words and songs must be cut out of your act before the first performance. . . . Such words as Liar, Slob, Son-Of-A-Gun, Devil, Sucker,
Damn, and all other words unfit for the ears of ladies and children, also
any reference to questionable streets, resorts, localities, and barrooms, are
prohibited under fine of instant discharge."[11] Performers on the major
circuits were required to sign contracts containing similar admonitions:
"No suggestive remarks or vulgarity in dress, words or action, or intoxica-
tion will be permitted in this theatre. A violation of this clause by the
Artist will mean instant dismissal, and this contract will become null and
void."[12]

As one writer puts it, vaudeville "gained legitimacy by bowing (with a
wink) to the dictates of Victorianism." But despite management's determination to distance vaudeville from "the old Bowery rowdiness that had
been an important part of the first variety shows," this very rowdiness
continued to be "far more attractive to audiences than they had antici-
pated." An ongoing subtext of vaudeville's history was the struggle between
the attempts by management to impose a sheen of gentility and nineteenth-
century morality on the product, on the one hand, and an equally stubborn
determination by performers and audiences to maintain a "newer, more
expressive culture, one more concerned with release than with discipline,
self-improvement, and self-control."[13]

Tabloids, trade journals, and even the establishment press recorded this
struggle. Some crusading journalists supported management's attempts to
maintain vaudeville as a respectable institution by deploring what happened

if performers and audiences were given free rein. "Vaudeville, in the last five or six years, has done more to corrupt, vitiate and degrade public taste in matters related to the stage than all other influence [sic] put together" complained an anonymous contributor to *American Magazine* in April 1910. "The only limit is what the police will allow," the writer continued, "and the police apparently draw the line only at indecent physical exhibitions, and not always there. The far more pernicious evils of suggestive songs and lewd, lascivious jests goes quite unheeded by the authorities." With predictable regularity, performers were reported as being reprimanded or even punished by civil authorities, civic or religious groups, or management itself for using suggestive language or engaging in inappropriate behavior while on stage. A typical episode was reported in *Variety* for 12 November 1911:

> While appearing at Pantages' [in Portland, Oregon] Saturday, Sophie Tucker was arrested through her singing of "Grizzly Bear" and "The Angle Worm Wiggle." The complaint was made by the Department of Safety. Bail was furnished and Miss Tucker released. At the next performance she sang the numbers again and was re-arrested. At the hearing Miss Tucker was dismissed. She left town Tuesday night for California. She scored a big hit in this city.

"Knockabout" duos whose acts revolved around verbal and physical assaults were popular throughout the history of vaudeville; Weber and Fields were a classic team of this sort. Some performers, such as Eva Tanguay, were notorious for their uninhibited and provocative stage demeanor and behavior. And disorder of another sort was apparent from published reports of scuffles and other aggressive behavior among members of the audience; of arguments and altercations between performers, on stage and off; of frequent suicides of aging or unsuccessful performers. One history of vaudeville devotes an entire chapter to two theaters, the Boston Colonial and Hammerstein's Victoria, which the author insists on calling "nut houses" because of their reputation as places where bizarre incidents occurred frequently, on stage and in the audience.[14]

As a member of a working-class immigrant family in New York, Berlin grew up in a social environment from which a substantial part of the audience for vaudeville came, and also many of its performers. With his natural talent for music and his instinctive pull toward performing, he gravitated easily and seemingly inevitably toward vaudeville. He was a street busker and then an underage house entertainer at the Pelham Café and at Jimmy Kelly's and a "boomer" at Tony Pastor's vaudeville house, paid to sing along from the audience. Several of his earliest songs were sung with considerable success in vaudeville, earning him a position as staff lyricist at the Ted Snyder Company, where in addition to writing songs for the vaudeville stage his duties included demonstrating the firm's latest songs for potential performers, supplying extra verses and choruses for these pieces, and coaching singers who agreed to perform them. Eventually he performed several times on the vaudeville stage himself, with great success. As will become apparent from the following discussion, he was an enthusiastic proponent of treating vaudeville as a "newer, more expressive" cultural form, rather than as a relic of the Victorian era.

The Novelty Song

The majority of the songs written for performance on the vaudeville stage were known as novelty songs. Designed for performance on stage by professional singers and entertainers, novelty songs "lend themselves to action, to mimicry, to histrionic effect. They are, unlike the ballads, songs that we listen to rather than sing ourselves, and usually the emphasis is comic." [15]

Also unlike ballads, with their first-person, hegemonic expression of romantic, nostalgic, or moralistic sentiment, novelty songs were intended to amuse or titillate. Their lyrics are most often written in a third-person narrative mode, developing a comical, satirical, or suggestive scenario. Addressed from the stage directly to the audience by the singer, the voice of such a song is taken to be that of the performer rather than of the author(s). For instance, when "Becky's Got A Job In A Musical Show" was done in vaudeville, it was the singer of the moment, not Berlin, who was perceived to be relating the adventures of the protagonist, Miss Becky Rosenstein:

> Becky's got a job in a musical show,
> She's showing off her figure in the very front row;
> The fellows raise the dickens, when Becky starts a-kickin';
> And all the boys are calling her a "Yiddisha chicken."
> Becky's getting twenty dollars a week,
> And how she does it no-one seems to know;
> She's got a coat made of seal, corsets with steel,
> She comes to the theatre in an automobile. . . .

Often the lyric of a novelty song begins as a third-person narration, but at some point, most often in the chorus, one of the protagonists speaks in the first person. Here the voice of the piece becomes that of this protagonist, but that voice as conveyed to the audience by the singer, whose function switches from narration to the impersonation of that protagonist. In Berlin's "If I Thought You Wouldn't Tell," the singer must first narrate the developing drama, then take the role of Cousin Percy in the chorus.

> A maiden pretty, from Jersey city,
> Paid a visit to some cousins out of town;
> She answered "Mercy" when cousin Percy

Said, "I'd dearly love to show you all around."
Like bees a-buzzin' she and her cousin,
Were together ev'ry minute of the day;
One night he kissed her, she shouted "Mister,"
But he answered in a cute and cunning way.

"If I thought you wouldn't tell your mother,
I would try and take one more;
Promise not to tell your father or your brother,
And I'll make it three or four,
If I thought that you could keep a secret,
I would keep you busy, Nell,
I'd forget that I'm your cousin,
And I'd take a half a dozen,
If I only thought you wouldn't tell."

The songwriter remains in the background. His role is to construct a miniature drama in which one or more protagonists work their way through a scenario; the narration of this drama and the impersonation of the protagonists are the business of the performer. But the selection of characters and of the circumstances in which they find themselves and the way in which they resolve matters constitute an indirect statement by the author, as with a playright.

Berlin and the Ethnic Novelty Song

From the early days of vaudeville through the first decade of the twentieth century, it was common for the protagonist of a novelty song to be a member of one or another of America's marginalized ethnic populations, including but not limited to the Irish, Germans, Jews, African Americans, Swedes, and Chinese.

Songs that present foreign-born or first-generation protagonists in a comical or demeaning light could be taken by America's older, English-descended population as evidence of their own cultural superiority. Much more important, though, was the meaning of these pieces for immigrants and first-generation Americans, who were increasingly their authors, performers, and audiences.

The ethnic diversity of America's population, particularly in the nation's cities, reached an unprecedented level in the last two decades of the nineteenth century and the first of the twentieth. The millions of new immigrants who arrived in those years were forced to cope with life in a new and radically different society, one made up on the one hand of an older population that wasn't sure that it wanted them and on the other hand of other immigrant and first-generation peoples whose ways were equally alien but who were in a situation similar to their own vis-à-vis more established American society and culture.

Many writers have argued that the popular stage played a useful and positive role in helping these new Americans to negotiate their situation in the New World. Irving Howe, for one, has written that "the popular arts came to serve as a sort of abrasive welcoming committee for the immigrants."

> Shrewd at mocking incongruities of manner, seldom inclined to venom . . . they explored the few, fixed traits that history or legend had assigned each culture. They arranged an initiation of hazing and caricature that assured the Swedes, the Germans, the Irish, and then the Jews that to be noticed, even if through the cruel lens of parody, meant to be accepted.[16]

Robert Snyder echoes essentially the same sentiment: "Stereotypes [in the popular theater] provided simple characteristics that roughly explained immigrants to native-born Americans and introduced immigrants Americans to each other. They were identifying markers on a bewildering cityscape of races, nationalities, and cultures."[17] And Gunther Barth emphasizes the role of the vaudeville theater more specifically:

> It presented cultural traits, real or imagined, of certain groups. But this expression of many people's prejudices actually brought some people closer to each other, because the blatant stereotypes paraded on stage contradicted the experience men and women acquired daily in their encounters with members of other groups on the streets, in the store, or on the job. Further, the ridicule heaped mercilessly upon the fist-fighting Irishmen, lazy blacks, beer-drinking Germans, sharp-witted Jews, tight-fisted Scots, ignorant farm folks, and song-loving Italians fortified the individual spectator's self-esteem sufficiently to enable him or her to accept the elements of a common humanity in other life-styles.[18]

Two descendants of Lew Fields, an important figure in America's popular theater from the early days of variety and vaudeville to the years of musical comedy and film, see matters in a harsher and more pragmatic light:

> Close scrutiny of the era reveals that the familiar metaphor of the melting pot does not accurately describe the relations between ethnic groups in the Bowery; it was probably more like tomcats tied in a sack, trying to claw their way out. Not surprisingly, the encounters between ethnic groups trying to succeed in their strange new homeland quickly became the favorite subjects for the popular stage. . . . Variety's shifting gallery of stereotypes—the loutish Irishman, the slow-thinking German, the lazy black, the conniving Jew—all shared their audience's interest in the pursuit of material success, and, implicitly, assimilation. It was not the complicity of "we're all in this together"; rather, it was the momentary bond formed by their aggressive laughter at the plight of a harrassed minority. No matter what your background was, variety gave you a target to laugh at.

The variety theater itself was a neutral ground—a demilitarized zone—where the competing ethnic groups sat side by side in an uneasy truce. Outside the theater, the prejudice and exploitation experienced by the immigrants meant suffering and despair. Inside, the clever and outrageous exaggerations by variety artists transformed the prejudice and suffering into popular entertainment— ethnic humor, knockabout comedy, topical songs, and burlesques. At heart, the ethnic humor of this era was a coping strategy, best summarized in modern terms by comedian and activist Dick Gregory: "If you can laugh at me, you don't have to kill me. If I can laugh at you, I don't have to kill you."[19]

Audiences never confused the singers in vaudeville with the characters they were representing on stage, nor was it necessary for the performer's ethnicity to match that of the song's protagonist.

According to the conventions of the period, anyone could play any nationality. All that was needed was a convincing presentation of stock traits (down to skin color: sallow greasepaint for Jews, red for Irishmen, and olive for Sicilians). The Jewish Ross Brothers of New York City did Italian dialect impersonations. Lee Barth advertised himself as "the man with many dialects/I please all nationalities and cater to originality." In 1920 and 1921 a Californian of Spanish descent, Leo Carillo, performed Chinese and Italian dialect stories on the Keith circuit.[20]

Joe Weber and Lew Fields, both Jews, alternated among blackface, Irish, and German acts early in their careers. Sam Bernard, the most famous "Dutch" comedian and singer of the era, was born in Birmingham, England. The German-born Emma Carus, equally famous for her Irish and her "coon" songs, once remarked that "I'm the human dialect cocktail. A little Scotch, considerable Irish, a dash of Dutch and a great deal of Negro, together with a bit of British."[21] When Irving Berlin first took to the stage, he sang an Italian novelty song ("Sweet Italian Love") and a "coon" song ("Oh, That Beautiful Rag)," and his first commercial recording was of "Oh How That German Could Love."

Ethnic novelty songs could be sung by a vaudeville entertainer in the context of a comic ethnic skit, as when Sam Bernard inserted German novelty songs into one of his "Dutch" acts, or they could be included in a group of songs of various types. For instance, according to *Variety* for 30 December 1911, Amy Butler's turn at the Majestic in Chicago included an unnamed Irish piece and four songs by Irving Berlin—"I Want To Be In Dixie" (a "coon" song), "Pick, Pick, Pick, Pick On The Mandolin, Antonio" (a "wop" song), "Becky's Got A Job In A Musical Show" (a Jewish novelty), and "Ragtime Violin" (probably also done as a "coon" song).

"Even when a real Irishman played a stage Irishman," claims one writer, "the ethnic characterizations were treated as comic masks donned by the performer."[22] Singers did everything possible to make this mask seem convincing, by assuming the appropriate stage accent for the protagonists they were representing, whether or not it was already present in the song's lyric, and by the use of stock gestures, costumes, and makeup. The same tricks would be used even when an ethnic novelty was written in the third person, as sometimes happened; that is, a novelty song about an Italian-American would be sung in stage Italian dialect, with "Italian" hand gestures and costume.

The following discussion of Berlin's ethnic novelty songs, many of which were written in collaboration with Ted Snyder, is organized according to the protagonists' ethnicity. The earliest ones were very much in the style and spirit of the genre as he received it, but within a few years he began to explore some quite different directions, particularly in those songs for which he wrote both text and music.

Berlin's Italian Novelty Songs

Between 1880 and 1920 more than four million Italians emigrated to the United States. New York City was the port of entry for 97 percent of them, and although some of them eventually settled elsewhere in the country, the majority remained in New York, where in the first decades of the twentieth century the Italian-born population grew larger than the populations of Florence, Venice and Genoa combined.[23] Immigrant Italian families clustered first in the Lower East Side, where Berlin grew up, and in neighboring areas of Lower Manhattan. Most of them came from "the underdeveloped provinces of Southern Italy, where they worked as landless peasants," a background that inevitably shaped their new life in America.

> As a peasant, unable to perceive things *in abstracto*, and as a man of the soil, [the Italian immigrant] perceived education in association with material benefits. He saw the need to educate his children only insofar as the school provided means for bettering one's economic condition, or for breaking through the caste system. But since few precedents existed where a peasant's son became anything but a peasant, the *contadino* almost never entertained the possibility of his son's becoming a doctor, a lawyer, or embarking on some other professional career.[24]

The Italians whom Berlin knew in his childhood and youth, as neighbors and as street rivals, were poor like his own family but different in that they appeared to have less ambition for upward mobility than did members of his own ethnic group.

The protagonists of Berlin's earliest Italian novelty songs speak in stage "Italian" dialect, have such stock names as Tony and Marie, and behave in ways supposedly characteristic of people of their ethnicity. The male protagonists of these songs, who are usually barbers, manual laborers, or street organ grinders, are lazy but impulsive; they lord it over their wives, and they chase other women. The women are willing and passionate lovers when young and single; after marriage they bear large families and grow resentful of their husbands. Caught up in New York City's ethnic mix, these protagonists often come into conflict with other immigrant groups. Sheet music covers sometimes give visual reinforcement to the stereotypical images offered in the songs themselves; the men have drooping black moustaches, and the women are dressed in peasant costumes.

The protagonist of "Dorando" sells his barber shop and goes to "Madees-a Square" (Madison Square Garden) to bet the money on Dorando, an Italian runner, who proceeds to lose the race because he ate Irish stew rather than "spagett" beforehand. "Sweet Italian Love" offers observations on love, Italian style—"When you squeeze your gal and she no say, 'Please stop-a!' When you got dat twenty kids what call you 'Papa!' Dat's Italian love." The humor in "Sweet Marie, Make-a Rag-a-Time Dance Wid Me" revolves around Tony's attempts to persuade Marie to dance to ragtime music, which is obviously alien to both of them, and to speak the lingo of ragtime—"Hey you wop-a, nunga stoppa, kiss-a Tony call 'em poppa; One, two, three, I'm-a feel-a like-a 'Hully Gee.' " The protagonist of "Dat's-A My Gal" extols the physical virtues of his sweetheart, whose father, a "nice wop," has a "much-a swell-a barber shop":

> My gal, she's-a got-a such-a figure,
> So big, maybe it's a little bigger;
> Small feet just-a like-a Japaneese-a,
> Big waist, it take me seven days to squeeze 'er.

Antonio buys a mandolin to serenade his girlfriend in "Pick, Pick, Pick, Pick On The Mandolin," but his singing annoys an Irish policeman, who breaks the instrument over the suitor's head.

As insensitive and offensive as these songs might seem according to today's sensibilities, they were very much in the tradition of ethnic comedy in America's turn-of-the-century popular theater, and vaudeville audiences took them to be humorous. When Berlin sang a collection of his own novelty songs on a vaudeville bill at Hammerstein's Victoria Theatre in early September 1911, for instance, audiences and critics alike found his ethnic novelties, which included Italian, Jewish, and "coon" songs, to be "extremely funny," and "Sweet Marie, Make-a Rag-a-Time Dance Wid Me" was singled out as a "rapid, humorous Italian dialect song."[25]

As will become apparent later in this chapter, the image of Italians offered by Berlin is no more negative or mean-spirited than his portrayal of any other ethnic group, including his own. And although most of these

Figure 4. Cover of "Pick, Pick, Pick, Pick On The Mandolin, Antonio." (Lester L. Levy Collection of Sheet Music, Special Collections, Milton S. Eisenhower Library, The Johns Hopkins University)

pieces are intended to be humorous, a few of even the earliest ones are underlaid by a hard edge of social reality unusual for the genre. In "Angelo," a Lower East Side melodrama, the distress of the protagonist coupled with the reality of the Catholic position on divorce must have struck home to many who heard it.

> I feel-a da blue, and I tell-a to you,
> Up-a stairs in da head I'm-a craze,
> I make-a divorce wid my husband for course,
> He's-a sleep-a too much he's-a laze.
> He make-a me work like a big-a da Turk,
> While he sleep-a just like-a da King;
> He thinks he's-a boss, just-a, just-a for course,
> He's-a give me da wedding-a ring.
> But I nunga can stand-a for that,
> So I tell-a the good-a for not.
>> Angelo, Angelo,
>> Too-a much is-a plenty you know,
>> I make-a you fat like-a dis, like-a dat,
>> But you loose-a da fat when I leave-a you flat,
>> Angelo, Angelo,
>> When I say I'm-a gone-a I go;
>> You make-a me sick, and-a next-a da week
>> I'm-a run away quick, wid the Irish-a Mick,
>> Nunga more-a you kick wid your meal-a da tick,
>> It's-a just what I speak-a for you.

The music of Berlin's Italian novelty songs contributes to the characterization of the protagonist(s). "Angelo" is written "in a rapid, accelerating 6/8 with shifts between major and minor," invoking the tarantella, a folk dance originating in the south of Italy.[26] "Pick, Pick, Pick, Pick," with its staccato accompaniment and sequenced melody, resembles one of the commercialized Neapolitan serenades so popular at the time.

Sustained notes alternating with quick syllabic passages in "Sweet Italian Love" suggest something of the character of Italian opera, as do the patter dialogue and the "Rossini crescendo" of the chorus of "Hey Wop."

In performance, singers tended to emphasize the text at the expense of the melodic line, as was the case with other ethnic novelties, using a semi-spoken delivery with a marked "ethnic" accent. Rhoda Bernard's recording of "Hey, Wop" on Pathe 39396-A, for instance, is much more inflected, rhythmic speech than it is singing.

By 1912, Berlin's songs with Italian characters were taking on a different, less humorous, character. Both text and music of "Antonio," which a reviewer writing in *Billboard* on 18 July 1911 found to be "the best wop

song ever written," are more evocative of Italian *verismo* opera than of the vaudeville stage. A woman swears revenge on her husband for running off with "the Irish gal that live-a next-a door," and with "all the money what I hide under the floor," to boot.

> Antonio, don't you think that you can treat me so,
> Because I sharp-a da stilletto till she look-a much-a new,
> And pretty soon the people walk-a slow behind-a you.
> Antonio, don't you think that you can treat me so,
> I'm gonna give-a you a close-a shave,
> So close-a that you shake-a hand-a with the grave.

Musically, the chorus has the melodic sweep and the chromatic pungency of late-nineteenth-century Italian opera.

And "My Sweet Italian Man" (II)[27] is a bittersweet vignette of a young Italian immigrant who has left his "nice fine sweet-a gal" back in Italy and now wishes for some "nice kind fairy queen" to change him into a fish so that he can "swim right back to Italy" to "help her raise a family." Berlin underlines the pathos of the scenario with a direct quote from the famous climactic aria in Leoncavallo's *Pagliacci*.

Although the young couple in the act of waving farewell to each other on the sheet music cover are dark-haired and were probably intended by the artist to have Italianate features, they are pictured as attractive and sympathetic, with no trace of caricature, unlike the Italian protagonists on earlier covers.

These later pieces suggest a changing sensibility on Berlin's part toward ethnic stereotyping. He was never again to publish a song in which an Italian protagonist was portrayed in what could be taken as a demeaning or ridiculous—even if supposedly comic—manner.

Dorando (1909)
Sweet Marie, Make-a Rag-a-Time Dance Wid Me (1910)
Angelo (1910)
Sweet Italian Love (1910)
Dat's-a My Gal (1911)
When You Kiss An Italian Girl (1911)
Pick, Pick, Pick, Pick On The Mandolin, Antonio (1912)
Antonio (1912)
My Gal In Italy (ca. 1912) (unpublished lyric)
My Sweet Italian Man I (1912)

My Sweet Italian Man II (or, "My Sweet Italian Gal") (1913)
Come Back Antonio (1914) (unpublished lyric)
Hey Wop (1914) (unpublished, but two commercial recordings, lyric
sheet in IBC-LC)

Berlin's Jewish Novelty Songs

Jewish immigration to America was continuous but small-scale between
1654, when twenty-three Jews arrived in New Amsterdam, and 1880. As
a result of the Jewish diaspora, these immigrants came from various countries, some from the Iberian Peninsula and then many more from German-
speaking regions. Matters took a dramatic turn in the late nineteenth
century. In a period of four decades, beginning in 1881, more than two
million Jews arrived in the United States, most of them from Eastern and
Central Europe, and the vast majority of them stayed in their port of
disembarkment, New York City, where they eventually made up more than
40 percent of the city's population.[28]

With scattered exceptions, the American popular musical stage had ig-
nored the Jew before the last decade of the nineteenth century,[29] but "Hebrew" acts, often incorporating "character" songs, had become common in
vaudeville by the time Berlin began his songwriting career.

None of Berlin's Jewish novelty songs was a collaborative effort, even
though many of them were written at a time when most of his songs were
coauthored with Ted Snyder. The protagonist of "Sadie Salome (Go
Home)," Berlin's first song of this genre, leaves her "happy home" intending to become a famous actress, but she ends up doing a Salome strip-
tease in a variety show. Her boyfriend, Moses, is mortified when he sees
her performance, and shouts from the audience:

> Don't do that dance, I tell you Sadie,
> That's not a bus'ness for a lady!
> 'Most ev'rybody knows
> That I'm your loving Mose,
> Oy, Oy, Oy, Oy, where is your clothes?
> You better go and get your dresses,
> Everyone's got the op'ra glasses.
> Oy! such a sad disgrace
> No one looks in your face;
> Sadie Salome, go home.

The protagonists' names and the song's dialect, including such details as
the rhyme of "dresses" with "glasses," identify Sadie and Mose as Jewish,
and the minor-key beginning of the verse is intended to give the music a
"Hebrew" flavor. Nothing in the scenario or in the actions of the characters

suggests the stereotypical image of the immigrant Jew, however, and in fact the song is quite similar to and was probably inspired by "My Mariutch, She Come Back To Me" (1907) by Harry L. Newton and Mike Bernard, which has Italian protagonists in a virtually identical scenario:

> I think my Mariutch she go-a back to It,
> But one day at Coney I-a threw de fit,
> I see my Mariutch do the hooch-a-ma-cooch,
> And she make a de big-a big hit.

Berlin's second published song of this subgenre, "Yiddle, On Your Fiddle, Play Some Ragtime," not only begins in a minor tonality but features an augmented second as well.

Again, there's no hint of the stereotypical "Jewish" behavior so often represented on the popular stage,[30] and in fact the protagonists' ethnic identity is a bit confused, at least in the published sheet music: At one point Sadie addresses Yiddle as "mine choc'late baby," and it's not clear if her request that he play some ragtime is intended to elicit humor at the thought of a Jewish fiddler playing music associated with African Americans. There are no period recordings to help clarify the contemporary meaning of the song, unfortunately.

Becky Rosenstein of "Becky's Got A Job In A Musical Show" is obviously Jewish, from her name, from the fact that "all the boys are calling her a 'Yiddisha chicken,'" and from the minor tonality of the song's verse. But once again nothing in her character or behavior is necessarily specific to any one ethnic group. Becky, who has parlayed her figure and her willingness to "accommodate" her manager into diamonds, Turkish cigarettes, a "coat made of seal," and an automobile, could just as well have been

Italian-American, or even an "Anglo" from some small town in the Midwest. The stereotyping in the song is of the chorus girl, not the Jewish-American.

Although the Jewish protagonists in these three songs seem to represent "the embodiment of the immigrant Everyman, and not of a particular ethnic group,"[31] Berlin did write other songs with "Hebrew" protagonists who exhibit one or another of the "fixed traits that history or legend had assigned to the Jew," particularly in matters having to do with money and social status.

• There is Benny Bloom, in "Yiddisha Eyes":

> Oi, oi, oi, those Yiddisha eyes!
> Benny had those Yiddisha eyes,
> That shone so bright, with an Israel light;
> Eyes that could tell a diamond in the night.

Meeting Jenny Golden Dollars, he "took a look in her bankbook, with his Yiddisha eyes," courts her, and buys her a ring. But her father "got wise," knowingly tells Benny, "That's how I got mine," and Benny "saw the ending with his Yiddisha eyes."

• In "Business Is Business," Abie Bloom, who wants to marry Rosie Cohen, is acceptable to her family because of his status as a "bus'ness man" who owns a clothing store. But when her father begins taking a suit from his store every month, saying "charge it to my future son-in-law," Abie protests to his fiancée that "Bus'ness is business, Miss Rosie Cohen" and asks her to tell her father that "C.O.D. don't mean, come on down to my store."

• An unpublished lyric by Berlin describes the "Yiddisha Wedding" of Rebecca Klein and Abie Rosenstein:

> Jakie Bloom from Birmingham
> Sent the groom a telegram:
> "I wish you happiness for ages,
> Make heavy wages."
> Oi, such a supper,
> Chicken and potatoes, stuffed up tomatoes;
> Oi, such presents,
> Everything was sterling silver;
> Cohen sent them dishes,
> I sent my best wishes,
> At that Yiddisha wedding Sunday night.[32]*

• In "Abie Sings An Irish Song," business in Abie's clothing store in an Irish neighborhood is poor until he adopts a new strategy:

When an Irishman looks in the window,
Abie sings an Irish song,
When a suit of clothes he sells,
He turns around and yells
"By Killarney's lakes and dells";
Any time an Irish customer comes in the place
Thinking that it's owned by some one of the Irish race,
If he looks at Abie with a doubt upon his face,
Abie sings an Irish song.

• Abie Cohn wants to marry his "Yiddisha Nightingale," Minnie Rosenstein, whose singing voice was so "fine" that when you heard it, "you'd think of real estate seven blocks long." He woos her with promises of a home "made of marble," so expensive that "people will be saying, as they pass, . . . some class!"

• Abie Cohen, the "Yiddisha Professor," went off to Paris and Germany to study piano and now he's "making money out of sight, giving concerts ev'ry night." His hair is long, "like an actor," he wears a diamond on his hand, and "just to see that gent, makes you think of seven percent."

But even in these songs, which could be taken to suggest the stereotypical image of the sharp-witted, conniving Jew, the behavior of the protagonists boils down to attempts to better themselves financially and socially, goals of other immigrant groups as well.

As in his other ethnic novelty songs, Berlin's music underlines the identity of the "Hebrew" protagonists: The verses are in minor keys, without exception, and melodic figuration often invokes the Yiddish theater, or even the synogogue.[33] (See excerpt on p. 44 from "Yiddisha Nightingale.")

But in their material form, Berlin's Jewish songs differ from his other ethnic novelties in one respect: Their sheet music covers, unlike those for his "wop" and "coon" songs, offer no hint as to the ethnic identity of the protagonists. The heroine of "Sadie Salome (Go Home)" is pictured as a voluptuous beauty, dark-haired but with no suggestion of what could be taken as stereotypically Jewish features (see Fig. 5, p. 45). Likewise, even though the young woman on the cover of "That Kazzatsky Dance" could be Jewish, her appearance is in no way exaggerated or even remotely offensive. And the other songs in this subgenre, all of them, skirt the issue of visual representation of their protagonists by having covers with abstract geometrical designs, unusual for this period.

Although Berlin intended these songs to be humorous, like his other ethnic novelties, and although they were taken that way by their audiences, some opposition to the stereotyping of Jews in vaudeville was emerging at the time, particularly among some rabbis who argued that "the stage representation is not a faithful one; is not true to life's types; ridicules the modern Hebrew and holds him up to the twinge of laughter." As a consequence of their activism,

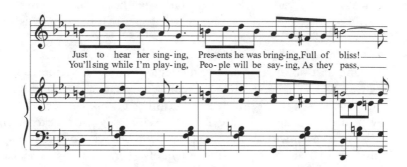

"in Cleveland Hebrew impersonators were hooted; in Cincinnati the question was agitated by men (who should have been calling on the ill) until the papers were full of it; in Denver this was repeated."[34]

The anonymous author of the article just quoted, who claims to be a Jew himself, insists that he has "witnessed more performances with Hebrews in them than any of the rabbis who will rush into print on the subject" and that "nowhere at no time, has an objectionable Hebrew impersonator been noted." Jewish comedians offer "innocent fun for people to laugh at," he argues, and "the heartiest mirth will be found to come from the Hebrews" in the audience. He thinks the problem may be that the Jew usually portrayed on the stage is old-fashioned, "the father of the American Hebrew," unchanged from when "Frank Bush first wore a black beard twenty-five years and more ago"; the protesting rabbis, on the other hand, are representative of "Jews with acquired wealth and social aspirations" who are inclined to "believe they are pedestaled above the average person of their race, while others have reached the point where they have forgotten or would like to forget that they are Jews."[35]

A few months later a certain Joseph R. Ginder noted with dismay that the major western vaudeville chain, the Orpheum Circuit, was no longer booking "Hebrew" acts.

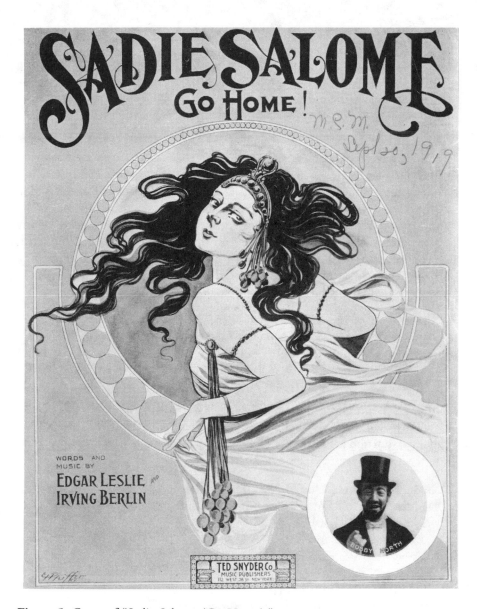

Figure 5. Cover of "Sadie Salome (Go Home)."

I find the Hebrew comedian is appreciated more than any other type, especially by the Jewish element, and I do not believe the public wishes to bar the funniest character on the stage. If an audience does not care for an act, it becomes apparent. I have never seen an audience in New York (where there are ten Hebrews to every one found in a western city), fail to show its appreciation of a Hebrew comedian. Some old fossil who never goes to the theatre writes a letter objecting to the Hebrew, and some one is foolish enough to pay attention.[36]

Some Jewish performers were reluctant to assume "Hebrew" roles in vaudeville or to write material for such skits or songs. Lew Fields and Joe Weber, for instance, portrayed black, Irish, and German characters but never Jewish ones, leaving these to specialists like Frank Bush, Joe West, and David Warfield. But even though, to the best of my knowledge, Berlin never performed a Jewish novelty song in public, he didn't hesitate to write such pieces, as I have shown. Although he never expressed himself publicly on the issue, his attitude must have been similar to that of Fanny Brice, who remarked about her Jewish monologues and songs:

I never did a Jewish song that would offend the race because it depended on the race for laughs. In anything Jewish I ever did, I wasn't standing apart, making fun of the race. I *was* the race, and what happened to me on the stage is what could happen to them. They identified with me, and then it was all right to get a laugh, because they were laughing at me as much as at themselves.[37]

Although Berlin wrote almost no Jewish novelty songs after 1914, with the notable exception of "Cohen Owes Me Ninety-Five Dollars," this was as much a function of his new focus on the legitimate stage (rather than vaudeville) as it was a change of heart.

Sadie Salome (Go Home) (1909)
Yiddle, On Your Fiddle, Play Some Ragtime (1909)
Yiddisha Eyes (1910)
That Kazzatsky Dance (1910)
Business Is Business (1911)
Yiddisha Nightingale (1911)
The Yiddisha Ball (1911) (unpublished lyric)
Becky's Got A Job In A Musical Show (1912)
Yiddisha Professor (1912)
In My Harem (1913)
Abie Sings An Irish Song (1913)
Jake! Jake! The Yiddisher Ball-Player (1913)
Yiddisha Wedding (1913) (unpublished lyric)
Rosenthal's Business Affairs (1914) (unpublished lyric; earlier version of "Cohen Owes Me Ninety-Seven Dollars")

Berlin's German and Irish Novelty Songs

Next to blacks, the Germans and the Irish had been favorite targets for comic stereotyping in the early days of variety entertainment, since the majority of new immigrants and hence a good portion of the audience for the popular theater were members of these two groups.

In every decade from the 1830s through the 1880s, emigrants leaving German-speaking lands accounted for at least a quarter of the foreign flow into the United States, and in the 1850s and 1860s they made up more than a third of the total immigrant population.[38] German-American characters began to be represented in popular culture almost immediately upon their arrival in such large numbers. "I Goes To Fight Mit Sigel," a song by F. Poole and Samuel Lover commemorating a German-American brigade that fought in the Civil War under the command of General Franz Sigel, was one of many German novelty songs performed on the minstrel stage.

> Ven I comes from der Deutsche Countree
> I vorks somedimes at baking;
> Den I keeps a lager beer saloon,
> Und den I goes shoe-making;
> But now I was a sojer been
> To save der Yankee Eagle,
> To schlauch dem tam secession volks,
> I goes to fight mit Sigel.

In the decades after the Civil War, German-Americans were a major presence in the Harrigan and Hart shows celebrating the ethnic mix of New York City, and variety performers like Gus Williams and then Joe Weber and Lew Fields made a specialty of "Dutch" (from Deutsch) characters, stereotyped as beer-drinking and sauerkraut-eating, somewhat slow and insensitive, but basically honest, earnest, hard-working, and patriotic folk. The music of "Dutch" novelty songs was usually stereotypical as well, with rhythms invoking either a slow waltz (ländler) or a march; robust, square, diatonic melodies were accompanied by oom-pah or oom-pah-pah figurations suggesting the sound of a *biergarten* band.

The pattern of Irish immigration into the United States was similar to that of the Germans. Between 1820 and 1860 the Irish accounted for a third or more of the total new population, a figure that dropped off to 15 percent in the last decades of the century, then down to virtually zero. Settling as densely in urban areas, particularly New York City, as the Jews would later do, and bringing with them an ancient animosity toward the English that carried over to the "Anglo" population of America, the Irish were caricatured more ruthlessly on the comic stage than any other immigrant group, and no variety entertainment was complete without one or more stage representations of a hard-drinking, fist-slinging, blarney-tongued "Paddy." But by the turn of the century the Irish had gained a certain grudging acceptance from America's "older" population, carving niches for themselves first as manual laborers and then as policemen, school teachers, domestics, firemen, and politicians.

By the time Berlin's family arrived in New York's Lower East Side, most of the Germans and the Irish in the ethnic neighborhoods of lower Manhattan were first- or second-generation. As they began to be assimilated into mainstream American life, they were also beginning to move to better neighborhoods in Harlem or Brooklyn as "newly arrived Italians crowded into the old Irish neighborhoods west of the Bowery. Russian and Polish Jews flocked to the former German district to the east."[39] When Berlin began writing songs for vaudeville, the Germans and the Irish no longer dominated the city's immigrant population and its popular stage, and he wrote only a handful of novelty songs with protagonists of these ethnicities.

Berlin published only three German novelty songs, all written in 1910 in collaboration with Ted Snyder. None broke new ground for the genre. All three are waltzes in moderate tempo, with lyrics in "Dutch" dialect depicting protagonists who are essentially good-natured and good-hearted, if a bit dense and bumbling. Berlin himself sang the earliest of these, "Oh How That German Could Love," on his first commercial recording,[40] in the performance style favored by vaudeville singers who wanted to give apparent authenticity to their delivery of ethnic novelty songs. Berlin's semispoken delivery, against a backing orchestra that sounds like a German wind band, only approximates the pitches and rhythms of the notated music, focusing attention on a lyric delivered with a much more pronounced accent than is suggested in the sheet music:

> Once I got stuck on a sweet little German,
> And oh what a German was she:
> The best what was walking, well what's the use talking,
> Was just made to order for me. [*printed text*]

> *Vunce I got stuck on a sveet little German,*
> *And oh vot a German vas she;*
> *The best vat vas valkin', vell vat's de use talkin',*
> *Vas joost made to order for me. [as Berlin sings it]*

Interpolated exclamations and patter phrases not found in the printed lyric, delivered in an equally thick accent, intensify the "Dutch" nature of Berlin's performance.

"Bring Back My Lena To Me," written for the famous "Dutch" comedian Sam Bernard, laments the loss of the protagonist's "sweet little neat Lena Kraus"; what he misses most is her "sweet sauerkraut that would swim in your mouth, like the fishes that swim in the brook." Lena Krauss-meyer, with "hair red as fire," tries to entice her beau onto the dance floor in "Herman Let's Dance That Beautiful Waltz."

> I heard that a coon who heard Mendelssohn's tune,
> Kissed the first man she saw, if it's true;
> That very same feeling I feel on me stealing
> And Herman I'm looking at you.
> So close both your eyes make believe you ain't wise,
> Only pucker your lips into place
> Think of five hundred meld or a sweet Anna Held,
> While I kiss the hole in your face.[41]

Although the printed lyric has little or no trace of a German accent, the singer was expected to supply this herself.

"It Can't Be Did!," a fourth "Dutch" novelty song, this one with both lyrics and music by Berlin, was copyrighted but never published. Julius clumsily steps on his partner's dress while they are dancing, where-upon she leaves the dance floor to prevent her dress from being pulled off: "If I let my dresses free, I'll have to show my dignity, You see it can't be did."

Although these four pieces may seem to offer less demeaning portrayals of their protagonists than do several of Berlin's Italian novelty songs,[42] the issue is not so much his own attitudes toward Germans and Italians as the received stereotypical stage portrayal of the two groups.

Oh How That German Could Love (1909)
It Can't Be Did! (copyrighted but unpublished, 1910)
Herman Let's Dance That Beautiful Waltz (1910)
Bring Back My Lena To Me (1910)

There were still Irish families in Berlin's childhood neighborhood, Irish gangs on the streets, and his school teachers were probably Irish. Despite this, and even though several of his early ballads ("I Wish That You Was My Gal, Mollie" and "Molly-O! Oh, Molly!") have Irish protagonists, only two of Berlin's songs might be classified as Irish novelty pieces, and neither is a clear-cut example of the genre. The ethnicity of the youthful protagonist of "No One Could Do It Like My Father!" isn't specified, but the narration of some of his father's exploits—he drinks, joins the police force, and at election times casts ballots under various Irish names—suggests that his family is Irish. "In My Harem" allows the singer to select either Pat Malone or Abie Cohen as the protagonist who finds himself with "wives for breakfast, wives for dinner, wives for supper time" while taking care of a harem for a Turk who goes off to war. Dialect is not written into the lyric but is to be supplied by the performer after he has chosen between

Pat and Abie; the music, with its drone-like open fifths in the bass, its minor key, and its quotation of James Thornton's "The Streets of Cairo," with its pseudo–Middle Eastern flavor, is intended to suggest the ethnicity of the absent Turk, not of Pat or Abie.

No One Could Do It Like My Father! (1909)
In My Harem (1913)

Berlin's "Native" Ethnic Novelty Songs

The ethnic novelty songs discussed to this point have protagonists representing immigrant or first-generation population groups. Other pieces of this genre draw their characters from two groups that have much longer histories in the United States but that nevertheless were as exotic and as alien to vaudeville's audiences as any more recent immigrants—African-Americans and rural Americans (or "rubes").

Novelty pieces with black protagonists were staple items on the popular stage throughout the nineteenth century and into the twentieth. The very foundation of the minstrel show, the most important genre of the popular musical stage throughout the middle third of the nineteenth century, they remained equally popular in vaudeville. Much the largest group of Berlin's ethnic songs, these songs are so numerous and varied as to warrant separate treatment in Chapter Two.

The term "rube" originated in the nineteenth-century circus and was immortalized in the popular song literature by Harry Birch and William Gooch in their song "Reuben and Cynthia," written in 1871 and subsequently revised by Charles Hoyt and Percy Gaunt for the hit musical comedy *A Trip to Chinatown* (1892).

Berlin didn't try his hand at a "rube" song until near the end of the period with which this book is concerned. The country folk represented in these songs are as stereotyped as any southern Italian or Polish Jew. Although they have been in America long enough for their national origin not to be an issue, they are clearly descendants of the stage "Yankees" of an earlier period and are thus of British ancestry. Poorly educated but shrewd, gullible yet resourceful, they are comically out of their element if they happen to wander into the modern urban world. In song lyrics and on the covers of sheet music covers, the men are pictured playing fiddles, wearing overalls and straw hats, and sporting chin whiskers; the women wear calico dresses and bonnets.

"Fiddler Joe from Kokomo," the protagonist of "Fiddle-Dee-Dee," Berlin's first song of this subgenre, "tuck[s] his violin beneath his whisker'd chin" and fiddles his way into and out of a series of comic situations. In "This Is The Life," Farmer Brown goes off to the city, where he discovers

Figure 6. Cover of "He's a Devil In His Own Home Town."

that even though he misses his cows and chickens, he prefers to "raise the dickens while cabareting, where the band is playing"; although he loves the trees and flowers on his farm, "I'd rather while away the hours picking daisies from a Musical Comedy." Not until "He's A Devil In His Own Home Town" did Berlin's depiction of a "hayseed" character, in this case Uncle Jerry, who owns "two thousand acres of the very, very best land in the whole United States," reach the keen focus of his earlier portraits of Italian, Jewish, and German characters.

> He spends a five cent piece, thinks nothing of it,
> His pants all creased, red vest above it, and
> When it comes to women, Oh! Oh! Oh! Oh!
> He's a devil, he's a devil,
> Telling stories in a groc'ry store,
> On the level, on the level,
> Has 'em rolling on the floor,
> Down at the fair with all the other heckers
> He received first prize for playing checkers,
> And he cheated, can you beat it!
> He's a devil in his own home town.

Even though Berlin had little contact with or knowledge of the music of rural Americans, the song's jaunty dotted rhythms and determinedly diatonic tune, supported by equally unadventuresome chords, are an attempt to suggest this repertory.

Although Berlin was turning away from the ethnic novelty song, he wrote several similar "rube" songs, including "I'm Going Back To The Farm" (1915), "Si's Been Drinking Cider" (1915), and "He's Getting Too Darn Big For A One-Horse Town" (1916), over the next few years.

Fiddle-Dee-Dee I (1912)
Fiddle-Dee-Dee II (1912)
Hiram's Band (1913)
Down On Uncle Jerry's Farm (1913, unpublished)
This Is The Life I (1914)
He's A Devil In His Own Home Town (1914)
This Is The Life II (1914)

In summary, Berlin's earliest ethnic novelty songs tend to be derivative of similar pieces by other songwriters, in both music and text, and their portrayals of Italian, Jewish, German, and Irish protagonists offer stereotypical images of these groups, in the tradition of the genre. His later songs of this type are often less broadly comical and are less dependent on assumed ethnic characteristics. Like many other Tin Pan Alley writers, Berlin published fewer ethnic novelty songs as the years went by.

Two related factors were behind these changes. Opposition within several ethnic communities to comic stereotyping on the stage and in literature, as noted earlier in connection with "Hebrew" comedians and singers, was bringing pressure on writers and performers to modify these portrayals and to stop writing and performing such pieces. At the same time, growing nativist sentiment against the influx of so many millions of people of allegedly "inferior racial stock" into the country led to more restrictive immigration policies and laws and to more and more overt racism on the part of politicians, organizations, and institutions.[43] By 1915, these trends were becoming pronounced enough to inhibit the public display or celebration of divergent ethnic identity, and the "open ethnicity" of the late nineteenth century was giving way to strategies of assimilation. Ethnic novelty songs, a mainstay of vaudeville for decades, became less viable in this new climate.

Berlin's songs of this genre gradually moved away from overt ethnic stereotyping, although it's not clear if this was a matter of personal conviction or of pragmatism in the face of the changing mood of the country. Some of his last pieces of this type show evidence of having been "cleaned up" to make them less potentially offensive before they reached the public. For instance, an early lyric sketch of the chorus to "Jake! Jake! The Yiddisher Ball-Player" ends with the line "Ike, Ike, Ike, Ike, you're a regular Kike," but by the time the song was published, Ike had become Jake and the word "kike" had disappeared;[44] even though "Hey, Wop!" was a hit when performed in vaudeville in 1913 and was recorded twice, Berlin decided against publishing it.

Berlin's Urban Novelty (or Suggestive) Songs

Some three dozen of Berlin's early novelty songs share the following features: They offer a view of life in the contemporary city as exciting and glamorous, unlike many songs of the period that contrast urban life unfavorably with rural;[45] their protagonists behave in ways contrary to America's public morality and sensibility; and these protagonists are not European immigrants, blacks, or "rubes" but rather "mainstream" Americans. Characters in these songs engage in and obviously enjoy drinking, smoking, flagrant flirtation, the acquisition of costly and ostentatious personal possessions, premarital sex, even adultery. These pieces were often referred to, usually by their critics, as "suggestive" songs; I propose the alternate label of "urban novelty songs" because of their setting, because they were written for the vaudeville stage, and because they are similar to other novelty songs in structure and substance.

To deal first with the moral issue raised by these pieces: Nineteenth-century ballads, as will be discussed in more detail in Chapter Four, often deliver the hegemonic message that certain standards of private and public behavior, as defined by Christian dogma filtered through bourgeois social practice during the Victorian era, are desirable. The protagonists of these pieces who adhere to these standards are portrayed as leading happy and fulfilled lives, although circumstances may sometimes delay the gratification and rewards resulting from their exemplary behavior. To give this message more punch, the occasional protagonist who strays from acceptable moral standards is punished. Although not all early Tin Pan Alley ballads can be classified as Victorian, they all nevertheless tend to promote the same moral code. To cite a famous example, the heroine of "A Bird In A Gilded Cage" (1900, by Arthur J. Lamb and Harry Von Tilzer) cynically marries an older man for his money, then becomes a social outcast, and dies; the song's chorus moralizes, to the strains of a waltz recalling the "ballroom filled with fashion's throng" where she had once been "the fairest of all the sights":

'Tis sad when you think of her wasted life,
For youth cannot mate with age,
And her beauty was sold for an old man's gold,
She's a bird in a gilded cage.

The explicit or implicit protagonists of such ballads are white, Protestant, and British-descended. By contrast, unpunished deviant behavior takes place only among protagonists of ethnic novelty songs, in which Irishmen and Germans drink to excess, blacks are violent and lead loose family lives, Italian men are lazy and promiscuous, and Jews are overly concerned with money and social status. Dan McGinty, who injures himself by falling into a hole while drunk, is thrown into jail for assault, finds that his wife has left him when he comes home after serving his sentence, and finally commits suicide by jumping into a river, is Irish, after all ("Down Went McGinty," by Joseph Flynn, 1889), and the sordid drama of spousal abuse and desertion laid out in "Bill Bailey, Won't You Please Come Home?" (Hughie Cannon, 1902) takes place in a black family.

But the young married couple who take turns staying out all night with other partners in Berlin's "I Didn't Go Home At All" are named Jack and May, and nothing about their language or behavior suggests that they belong to any marginalized ethnic group. The husband who sees his wife and children off for a vacation, then gets together with old friend Molly—"I love my wife, but oh! you kid, my wife's gone away"—and later with his cook in "My Wife's Gone To The Country (Hurrah! Hurrah!)," is a Mr. Brown. The manicurist who willingly accepts the advances of a "son of some millionaire" (and then takes money in return for her favors) is named Betsy Brown. Sally Brown, in "When You're In Town," meets and marries a salesman, then one night finds "seven diff'rent notes, that seven diff'rent females wrote" in his coat pocket, each inviting him to "look me up" when he's in town. Charlie Brown marries Mary Jane, "makes a heap" as a salesman, then one night hears his wife talking in her sleep, inviting someone named Fred to "come right in" while Charlie is on the road. The young woman who tells her beau that "If You Don't Want My Peaches, You'd Better Stop Shaking My Tree" is named Mary Snow. All these people, and others like them in similar songs, who patronize bars, proposition and deceive one another, and often end up fornicating with partners other than their spouses, are "ordinary" Americans with names like Charlie, Mary, Andy, Carrie, Henry, Geraldine, William, Betsy, and Johnny—not Antonio or Ephraham or Julius—and they don't shave other people or shine shoes for a living but work in offices, have maids and cooks, own automobiles, and take vacations at the seashore or in the country.

Period recordings of these songs verify that the protagonists were understood to be "ordinary" Americans, that is, not immigrants or blacks. Billy Murray's performances of "Daddy, Come Home" (Victor 17519-A) and "Snookey Ookums" (Victor 17313-B), Ada Jones's recordings of "Call Me Up Some Rainy Afternoon" (Victor 16508-B) and "I'm Afraid, Pretty Maid, I'm Afraid" (Columbia A1164, with Walter Van Brunt), and the version of "My Wife's Gone To The Country (Hurrah! Hurrah!)" by Arthur Collins and Byron G. Harlan (Victor 5736) are all sung in "standard" American, with no trace of the dialect or accented English that performers of the day assumed when singing ethnic novelty pieces.

Though these "ordinary" people themselves represented a minority population in New York and other cities, at least numerically, they were set apart from Italians, Jews, blacks, and members of other ethnic groups by the fact that they were "older" Americans, descended from the stock responsible for establishing the United States as an independent nation and then forming and administering its laws, customs, habits, character, and institutions. But it would be wrong to label these pieces as "British ethnic novelty songs"; even though this group thought of other people in terms of their ethnic origin, they considered themselves to be simply "Americans." As a recent writer describes this mind-set:

> If you stopped any native-born son or daughter whose ancestors had immigrated from Ireland or Italy or Puerto Rico or Serbia, and you asked them what nationality they were, they did not say they were American. They said they were Irish, Italian, Puerto Rican, Serbian, Hungarian, Chinese, Japanese, Albanian, whatever the hell, but they never said they were American. Jews called themselves *Jewish* wherever their ancestors had come from. The only people who called themselves *Americans* were WASPs. You never heard a WASP say he was anything but American. Oh, yes, he might make reference every now and then to his illustrious mixed British-Scottish heritage, but he would never tell you he was British or Scottish because he simply wasn't; he was *American,* by God.[46]

Suggestive songs were frequently and bitterly attacked by self-appointed arbitrators of America's public morality. It's not always clear whether the criticism was prompted by the implication in such songs that "ordinary" Americans were capable of improper behavior or merely by the behavior itself, whoever the perpetrator. Berlin's "My Wife's Gone To The Country" was one of several pieces singled out by Alexander Blume for "laugh[ing] openly at the sacred institutions of marriage [and] frankly prais[ing] and encourag[ing] the faithlessness and deceit practiced by either friend, husband or wife."

> What has come over us anyhow? Decent women and girls with their men folks sit in theatres and applaud vociferously, amid their boisterous laughter, some singer who with well-studied indecency proceeds to gush forth songs of the

most vulgar and immoral character. There is, alas, sufficient tendency to ignore the responsibility that every decent man should feel incumbent upon him, without lending a hand to those who would shirk their bounden duty, by the proclamation of immoralities and subterfuges through these songs. If I had my way I would appoint a rigorous censorship upon all so-called "popular songs," and make it a criminal offense to publish such songs as I have mentioned.[47]

"The refrain of a song [sung by Al Jolson] described the love-making that followed," complained a contributor to *American Magazine* in 1910 after visiting a vaudeville theater. "The thing was frankly filthy, and was so accepted by the audience. There is in every audience a certain percent that may be counted on to greet evil suggestion with enthusiasm. On this occasion that percentage laughed uproariously and applauded wildly."

Vaudeville management did its best to head off criticism of this sort by posting backstage notices and writing clauses into performers' contract forbidding the use of material that might be morally offensive to anyone in the audience, as I have noted, and crusading journalists liked to pretend that suggestive songs were a passing fad. "The lewd lyric never was in favor with real song writers," wrote E. M. Wickes in 1916. "In the past there was always a publisher ready to bring [such a] song out, depending upon the performer's reputation to bring him a few rot-rimmed dollars. [But] the public has tired of having filth served up in the form of amusement."[48] Attempts to rid vaudeville of suggestive songs proved to be a losing battle; they continued to be among the most popular items for vaudeville audiences. Incidents such as the following were all too common, and ineffectual in the long run:

> Following the Monday matinee at Keith's [Boston] every act on the program with songs was informed that either one or more numbers used by them could not again be sung on that stage. The eliminated songs were all suggestive ones, and had proven during the afternoon show they were the best applause winners for each turn. The acts obeyed the orders without a protest. The action by the Keith management may be the commencement of a ban against suggestive lyrics, of which there have been a great number since ragtime songs became prevalent.[49]

It's not always immediately apparent what the fuss was about when one looks at the songs in question. Berlin's "Call Me Up Some Rainy Afternoon," for instance, seems to involve nothing more than an afternoon "spoon"; since the two protagonists are casual acquaintances, not a married couple, Nellie's flirtation with another man would hardly seem to qualify as a case of moral turpitude.

> Nellie Green met Harry Lee,
> At a masquerade the other night;
> He liked she, and she liked he,

Just a case of love at single sight;
He took Nellie home that eve,
Also took the number of her phone,
Just before he took his leave,
Nellie whispered in the cutest tone.
   "Call me up some rainy afternoon,
   I'll arrange for a quiet little spoon,
   Think of all the joy and bliss,
   We can hug and we can talk about the weather,
   We can have a quiet little talk,
   I will see that my mother takes a walk,
   Mum's the word when we meet,
   Be a mason, don't repeat,
   Angel eyes are you wise?
   Goodbye."

He looked wise, then looked for rain,
Sure enough it rained that Saturday;
"Give me three, four, five, six Main,
Nellie dear, prepare, I'm on my way."
When he rang the front door bell,
No one there responded to his call,
Soon he heard his pretty Nell,
Singing to some body in the hall.
   "Call me up some rainy afternoon . . .

However, as I suggest repeatedly in this book, one must go beyond the printed music in order to recover the meaning of popular songs for their audiences. Two factors made these songs more risqué in performance than their published form would suggest:

1. Certain code words and phrases were understood by audiences of the day, although their meaning has since been lost. One example suffices: Understanding that the verb "to walk" was a euphemism for sexual intercourse puts a quite different spin on many of these songs. In "I'm Afraid, Pretty Maid, I'm Afraid," for instance, a young woman meets an old sweetheart on a streetcar and suggests that they "get off the car and do some walking"; he responds that "his walking days are done" because his "wife's right hand weighs half a ton." The second verse of "Meet Me To-Night" is even more blatant:

Charlie met Miss Molly, they got feeling jolly,
Talked a while, then walked a mile,
Then had another talk;
They grew tired of talking, they grew tired of walking,
Then to make things lively, for a change they took a walk.
That morning when he left her at the door,

> She whisper'd, "If you'd like to walk some more.
> Meet me tonight, meet me tonight . . .

2. Performances of songs on the vaudeville stage, and sometimes on recordings as well, often included words, phrases, catch lines, and even entire verses and choruses not found in the published sheet music. This additional material, which in many cases was more explicit than the published lyrics, usually came from the songwriter himself, who was expected to furnish his publisher with extra verses and choruses and who often coached singers in preparation for their turns on the vaudeville stage or in the recording studio. Most of this material has been lost or was never committed to paper in the first place, but enough remains on period recordings and in archives to give a sense of its nature. Berlin's "Call Me Up Some Rainy Afternoon" serves to show how a song could become much more "indecent" in performance. A recording made by Ada Jones in 1910 (Victor 16058-B) contains a second chorus, not found in the published version of the piece, in which Harry overhears Nellie addressing "somebody [else] in the hall" when he comes to her house:

> "Call me up some rainy afternoon,
> Then again how's the evening for a spoon?
> Call around tomorrow night,
> We can then put out that fire in the furnace;
> My Mama will sure be out of town,
> She'll be entertained by Mr. Brown,
> My Papa won't be 'round, he will call on Mrs. Brown,
> Angel pet, don't forget, goodbye."

To belabor the obvious: In this version the song's moral transgressions escalate from Nellie's suggestion that she and Harry have an "afternoon spoon" to her invitation to another man to spend an evening "put[ting] out that fire in the furnace" and to the revelation that her parents are involved in wife-swapping with another couple. In the latter context, Nellie's "I will see that my mother takes a walk" takes on a quite different meaning.

Since "ordinary" Americans had rarely been the protagonists of novelty songs written for the popular stage, there were no ready-made stereotypical features of behavior or appearance for Berlin to use in these songs, nor does he construct a consistent set of such characteristics, beyond the fact that protagonists are often made to seem ridiculous for comic effect. In "Snooky Ookums," a "little fellow, four feet tall, weighing just a hundred, clothes and all" is married to "a great big lady, weight a hundred eighty"; the two spend their time "billing and cooing," calling one another such names as "sugey ugar bowl" and "jelly elly roll," until the neighbors scream at them to stop. Mabel Beecher fancies herself a potential opera star in "Tra-La, La, La!," but when she starts singing,

All the neighbors get together and cry:
"It's most unbearable, terrible!
Why do they let her suffer?"
Ev'rybody hollers,
"Tie a can-o to her soprano!"

Johnny takes Geraldine out for the evening in "If That's Your Idea Of A Wonderful Time"; after he spends only a dime in a cabaret, for two cigars and two sodas, and then suggests going to a picture show where a friend of his can sneak them in for free, she asks to be taken home.

On the whole, however, the protagonists of these songs behave just like other urban folk: They enjoy eating and drinking, they go out to hear music and to dance, they flirt and deceive one another, they sometimes make fools of themselves, they try to better themselves financially and socially. It would probably be too much to suggest that Berlin was consciously motivated by a democratic spirit in writing songs in which "ordinary" Americans behave in ways similar to those of other ethnic groups, at least as they are portrayed on the vaudeville stage. If any conscious or subconscious ideology underlies these pieces, it's more likely a desire by the socially and politically marginalized community of which Berlin was a part to suggest that America's dominant population was prone to loose moral behavior itself, even as it publicly tried to associate such behavior with the "lower" classes only.

Gender equality, albeit of a somewhat crude sort, is a subtheme of many of these songs, as a woman who has been cheated, deceived, or taken advantage of turns the tables on the offending male. Jack stays out all night in the first verse of "I Didn't Go Home At All"; in the third verse it's May, his wife, who comes home at "sixty minutes past next morn." In "Someone's Waiting For Me (We'll Wait, Wait, Wait)" two wayward husbands arrange to meet Molly and May in a "swell cafe," where the four of them down "Manhattan cocktails and highballs galore" until the two wives, tired of waiting at home, happen to come into that very cafe and put an abrupt end to the tryst. The night after William C. Brown pairs up with "a queen in another machine" while "aviating" around the rathskellers, his wife retaliates by staying out until a quarter past four herself, explaining when she returns home that she was "saved" by an uncle who was out aviating around himself ("I Was Aviating Around"). The chorus of "Don't Leave Your Wife Alone" is a warning to husbands who might think of "lead[ing] a double life":

Don't leave your wife alone, waiting for you at home,
When you go out nights, I'll tell you what,
Maybe she's waiting home, and maybe she's not.
While you're out with Flo or May, hunting a new cafe,

She may go out with a feller, and not drink sarsaparilla,
So don't leave your wife alone.

"I'm Going On A Long Vacation" even introduces the element of class: Nellie Brown's boss tries to use his position of authority to force her to go with him on a trip, but the office boy threatens to tell the boss's wife about the plan and in the end himself goes away with Nellie for some "recreation."

Berlin's ethnic novelty songs make use of music associated in actual practice or in the public mind with the group in question. But just as there was no stereotypical stage image of the "ordinary" American on which Berlin could draw, neither was there a particular style or genre of music associated with this group. The music of suggestive songs is most easily described in negative terms: There are no minor keys or augmented seconds, no syncopated rhythms, no ländler-like waltzes, no echoes of Neapolitan serenades or Italian opera. The songs are mostly in duple meter, melodic lines are diatonic, harmonies rarely stray from tonic, subdominant, and dominant triads, chromaticism is limited to occasional secondary dominants and chromatic passing or neighboring chords, and modulation is rare. Symmetrical four-bar phrases that are in turn grouped into larger regular patterns are more common in these songs than in certain other genres. Taken together, these features result in a somewhat neutral, old-fashioned style that sometimes seems oddly inappropriate for the song's urban setting and the contemporary thrust of the lyrics, as in the following excerpts from "When You're In Town" and "Call Again."

Most of Berlin's songs of this type were written between 1909 and 1911, when he was a staff lyricist for the Ted Snyder Company. Their number dwindled after 1911 not because Berlin was deterred by adverse criticism of their lyrics but because he was turning away from songs for the vaudeville stage to other kinds of pieces, aimed at other audiences: the rhythmic-vernacular ballad, more evocative of the contemporary urban scene in its assimilation of syncopated dance music, and show songs for the legitimate stage. Even though such later songs as "You'd Be Surprised" (1919) might seem to be in the spirit of the suggestive song, they are written in a style that grew out of the rhythmic ballad rather than the suggestive song.

I Didn't Go Home At All (1909)
My Wife's Gone To The Country (Hurrah! Hurrah! Hurrah!) (1909)
Oh, What I Know About You (1909)
Someone's Waiting For Me (We'll Wait, Wait, Wait) (1909)
Oh! Where Is My Wife To-Night? (1909)
She Was A Dear Little Girl (1909)
If I Thought You Wouldn't Tell (1909)
Call Me Up Some Rainy Afternoon (1910)
I'm A Happy Married Man (1910)

Try It On Your Piano (1910)
"Thank You, Kind Sir!" Said She (1910)
Is There Anything Else I Can Do For You? (1910)
Innocent Bessie Brown (1910)
I'm Going On A Long Vacation (1910)
When You're In Town (1911)
Don't Put Out The Light (1911)
Run Home And Tell Your Mother (1911)
One O'Clock In The Morning I Get Lonesome (1911)
Don't Take Your Beau To The Seashore (1911)
Meet Me To-Night (1911)
How Do You Do It, Mabel, On Twenty Dollars A Week? (1911)
Take A Little Tip From Father (1912)
I'm Afraid, Pretty Maid, I'm Afraid (1912)
Call Again (1912)
The Elevator Man Going Up, Going Up, Going Up, Going Up! (1912)
Keep Away From The Fellow Who Owns An Automobile (1912)
Don't Leave Your Wife Alone (1912)
Keep On Walking (1913)
I Was Aviating Around (1913)
Tra-La, La, La! (1913)
Daddy, Come Home (1913)
If You Don't Want My Peaches (You'd Better Stop Shaking My Tree)
    (1914)

Miscellaneous Novelty Songs

During the period 1912–1914, Berlin wrote a number of pieces classifiable only as novelty songs but that belong to neither of the subgenres of ethnic or suggestive pieces. Although some were performed in vaudeville and were published, only a few attracted much attention, and many others remained unfinished and/or unpublished. They are important not as instances of successful songs, either artistically or commercially, but as evidence that at this time Berlin was trying, not always successfully, to expand the expressive range of the Tin Pan Alley song.

A few are similar in structure and expression to the novelty songs discussed earlier, but with different types of protagonists. "A True Born Soldier Man" is an attempt at a comic portrait of a soldier who didn't get his fill of fighting during wartime, so he marries and now "stays at home and fights with his wife." As with other novelty songs, the lyric is in the third person, and the singer is given the role of narrating this tale to the audience. Several other pieces—"That Monkey Tune," "The Monkey Doodle Doo," and "The Ki-I-Youdleing Dog"—are Berlin's contributions to a passing fad on vaudeville for animal songs. In the first of these, Emma Carus, who according to the sheet music cover introduced the piece, is asked to narrate a tale of simian miscegenation, a romance between a monkey and a chimpanzee:

> Down in a sunny jungle town
> Where monkeys run around
> Lived a crazy little monkey who loved to sing;
> A chimpanzee in a cocoa-nutty tree
> Heard his nutty melody, she
> Fell in love with his singing,
> From the branches a-clinging,
> She'd pitch her voice in a monkey key,
> And yell with all her might.

And then, in the chorus, to sing in the voice of the female chimpanzee:

> Sing that monkey tune
> You monkey loon
> Don't dare to stop, hurry up, hurry up,
> I want to hear that strain so queer
> Because I'm crazy about that monkey tune.

In an attempt to find an appropriate "ethnic" sound for the song, Berlin wrote the verse in a "jungley" minor key and rhythm, and as usual the protagonists are pictured on the sheet music cover, curiously enough without the exaggeration of physical features typical of the cover art of novelty songs with human characters. Apparently the song was never recorded, so there is no record of the dialect assumed by Carus in her portrayal of a chimpanzee.

Many of these pieces try in one way or another to break through the boundaries of the novelty song as Berlin had received and practiced it. Some have the same structure as conventional novelty songs, but their scenarios are neither comical nor satirical. Jack Jones abandons his wife for an entire year in "Welcome Home"; when he returns home, his wife greets him, in the first-person chorus, with news that was hardly the stuff of comedy for working-class vaudeville audiences.

> I need some brand-new winter clothes,
> Welcome home, welcome home,
> To protect me when the winter snows blow.
> Here's some bills that you can pay,
> They've been due since 'way last May;
> Landlord comes for rent today,
> Welcome home.

Samuel Brown, a waiter in a fancy restaurant, likes the operatic music played by the house orchestra but neglects his duties, is fired, and is then "pounded" by the other staff (to the music of the Anvil Chorus) until he "just laid down and died." Now, the song concludes, "old Samuel's forgotten, all alone, all alone, he is sleeping in an alley." Again there are not many laughs here.[50]

Other songs are topical. "They're On Their Way To Mexico" is the first of what would become a long series of songs written by Berlin in support of American foreign policy and the country's armed forces: "Come on and cheer them, they've got a right to fight this battle because they've been invited to go and fight it." In "Stay Down Here Where You Belong" (1914), the devil urges his son to stay in hell rather than venturing up to Earth, where war has broken out in Europe.

Still others have lyrics in the first person throughout. The performer thus appears to be telling the audience about something that happened to him, rather than to some other person, as is usually the case in a novelty song. "At The Devil's Ball," for instance, begins:

> I had a dream, last night,
> That filled me full of fright:
> I dreamt that I was with the devil, below,
> In his great big fiery hall,
> Where the devil was giving a ball.

A more conventional beginning for the verse of a novelty song would have been "Jonesy had a dream last night, that filled him full of fright: he dreamt that he was with the devil below. . . ." This is not an insignificant change; it positions both the songwriter and the singer in a way not usual in a novelty song. In this song, obscure references in the lyric to certain individuals—"the cute Mrs. Devil, so pretty and fat, dress'd in a beautiful fireman's hat," for instance, and "the little fellow who first put the pain in champagne wine, he was pouring it out in a stein"—suggest that the song refers to some social event attended by Berlin himself, as may also be the case with "The Old Maids Ball."

The protagonist of "Come Back To Me, My Melody" is a songwriter who hears an orchestra play "a sweet refrain" that he recognizes as his own, even though "they changed it cleverly." Rushing up to the band leader, he shouts, "That music belongs to me!"

> Come back to me, my melody,
> Come back to where you ought to be,
> I want you, don't you understand?
> Locked up in my baby grand,
> Just where I can lay my hand on thee.
> Oh! I miss you so,
> More than you may know,
> Don't you know it's very wrong

To be where you don't belong?
Oh! please come back to me, my melody.

The topical issue underlying the song is that Berlin, like other songwriters and composers, objected to the increasingly widespread unauthorized use of his music in public places. Two years later he would be one of the founders of ASCAP (the American Society of Composers, Authors, and Publishers), which succeeded in bringing an end to such practices. And as will be discussed in Chapter Three, "The Haunted House" is a thinly veiled commentary on an even more personal matter, Berlin's growing dissatisfaction with his treatment by his publisher, the Ted Snyder Company.[52]

In these and other songs of this sort, the true protagonist is Berlin himself. Two related lyric sketches, "I've Written Another Melody" and "I've Written Another Song," are rueful self-portraits: A compulsive songwriter insists on waking his wife (or girlfriend) at night, or telephoning her if she's away, whenever he writes a new song. In another fragment of a lyric, the songwriter has a nightmare in which he's attacked by a crowd of people "for writing all the horrible songs I wrote." Other sketches are soliloquies: "Somewhere (But Where Is It?)" is a wistful longing for a better world in which "the sun always shines in the sky," there's "a Washington who wouldn't lie," and "you needn't deposit your eye, when you borrow a dollar or two." "Brains" is an ode to common sense, from the perspective of Berlin's own background: "You need no college education, if you've only got brains."

Berlin's classic songwriter-as-protagonist piece is "What Am I Gonna Do?" Expected to deliver a speech when the Friars Club honored him with a banquet on 19 October 1913, he wrote and performed a song instead, in which he admitted that "making what you'd call a speech is away beyond my reach" and that "the only way out of it" was "to write a rag," in which "all I can say is I thank you, thank you with all my heart."

Most of these singer-songwriter pieces, as we would call them today, are preserved only as lyric sketches;[51] none was copyrighted, published, or even performed, with the exception of "What Am I Gonna Do?" Berlin, who throughout his songwriting career was a master at giving audiences pieces they would and could respond to, was trying news ways of writing songs.

That Monkey Tune (1911)
A True Born Soldier Man (1912)
Come Back To Me, My Melody (1912)
At The Devil's Ball I (1912)
At The Devil's Ball II (1912)
At The Devil's Ball III (1913)
The Apple Tree And The Bumble Bee (1913)

The Ki-I-Youdleing Dog (1913)
The Old Maids Ball (1913)
The Pullman Porters On Parade (1913)
The Monkey Doodle Doo (1913)
The Tatooed Man (1913)
Somewhere (But Where Is It?) (1913)
They're On Their Way To Mexico (1914)
The Haunted House (1914)
If That's Your Idea Of A Wonderful Time (Take Me Home) (1914)
Stay Down Here Where You Belong (1914)

Conclusion

Berlin wrote many songs after 1914 that have been classified as novelty songs because of their comical or satirical nature. In fact, most of the pieces in the folio entitled "Novelty Songs," brought out in 1991 by the Irving Berlin Music Company, were written after 1914, including such standards as "Lazy" (1924), "Puttin' On The Ritz" (1928–29), "Mr. Monotony" (1947), and "You'd Be Surprised" (1919), mentioned earlier.[53] But these later pieces are different from his early novelty songs, in both spirit and style. Rather than being sharp-edged, irreverent, sometimes crude or bawdy—but often hilariously funny—portraits of the people who inhabited the New York City of Berlin's youth and early manhood, they are clever, sophisticated pieces by a master songwriter.

Simply put, by late 1914 he had virtually stopped writing songs for the largely working-class, multicultural audiences of the vaudeville house in favor of other audiences in other performance spaces. Berlin was leaving vaudeville, with its audiences and the types of songs they preferred, behind; soon enough, vaudeville itself would be gone.

Chapter Two

Berlin and Blackface

Some thirty of Irving Berlin's songs published through 1914 have black protagonists or black characters and were sometimes, although not always, performed in blackface.

Some of these pieces are "coon" songs, a subgenre of the ethnic novelty song discussed in Chapter One, but others are quite different in style and content, and the group is in fact hetereogeneous enough to make it a mistake to approach these pieces as if they all had a single meaning for Berlin and his audiences. Although conditioned to some extent by the ambivalent and shifting attitudes of New York City's immigrant and first-generation Jews toward African Americans, they are also rooted in an American tradition of songs about blacks that dates from before the time that Jews came to New York City in large numbers.

Blackface and the Jew

Vaudeville appropriated many aspects of the nineteenth-century minstrel show, including the stage representation of African Americans by white entertainers in blackface. In the first decades of the twentieth century, as vaudeville and Tin Pan Alley came to be increasingly dominated by Jewish performers, songwriters, and entrepreneurs, Jews "almost entirely [took] over blackface entertainment,"[1] just as the Irish had done throughout most of the nineteenth-century history of the minstrel show.[2]

Various interpretations of the relationship between blackface performance and Jewish entertainers have been put forward. It's been argued that blackface makeup functioned as a mask for Jewish performers and songwriters, as it had earlier for the Irish: "Black became a mask for Jewish expressiveness, with one woe speaking through the voice of another. Blacking their faces seems to have enabled the Jewish performers to reach a spontaneity and assertiveness in the declaration of their Jewish selves."[3] In the words of another writer, the Jewish singer in blackface "ventriloquiz[ed] the black, sing[ing] through his mouth . . . to speak from his own, authentically felt interior."[4] The mythical American South and the black Mammy, lamented in so many minstrel and "coon" songs by the black protagonists who had left them behind, became icons for the Middle or Eastern European homeland of the Jew and the Jewish mother.

In an even more complex psychological interpretations of this relationship, African Americans were taken to "stand for something besides themselves" when Jewish performers made apparent reference to them by blackening their faces. Although Jews were a newly arrived, marginalized pariah group in their adopted country, they embraced their new identity as Americans, and the Jewish performer in blackface "escape[d] his immigrant identity through blackface," achieving "heightened authenticity and American acceptance."

> Blackface may seem not to express Jewishness at all but to hide it. . . . Why should [a] member of one pariah group hide his identity under the mask of another? . . . I see transfer as well. Switching identity, the [blackface] singer acquires exchange value at the expense of blacks. Miscegenation was regression, in racialist theory, because the dark drove out the light. Blackface mimed that process in order to reverse it. Stereotypes located within both pariah groups were exteriorized as black, embraced as regenerative, and left (along with actual blacks) behind.[5]

Much of the extensive literature on this issue is concerned with the period of the late 1910s and the 1920s, when Al Jolson, Eddie Cantor, and other Jewish entertainers performed in blackface on stage and film against a backdrop of the great northern migration of blacks, an intensifying climate of nativism and racism, the resurrection of the Ku Klux Klan, and the virtual end to immigration from the Mediterranean lands and Central Europe. A decade earlier, however, when Irving Berlin wrote the songs with which this chapter is concerned, things were somewhat different. The black population of New York City was much smaller than it would soon be, and although there was some concern among New York City's immigrant peoples that African Americans might have unassimilable cultural and physical traits that would keep them out of the melting pot, there was also at times a sense of common cause—that blacks were part of "an alternative, polyglot world, in which the children of Jewish immigrants found new, cosmopolitan identities among Jews, other immigrants, children of old-stock Americans, and African Americans as well."[6]

Berlin and the "Coon" Song

Although the term "coon" song was sometimes used in the first decades of the twentieth century as a generic label for any song with a black protagonist, it was most often applied to pieces in the tradition of the ethnic novelty song, discussed in Chapter One, in which protagonists take on stereotypical characteristics and behavior to comic or satirical effect. The chorus, or sometimes even the entire song, is cast in the first person, lending an apparent authenticity to the piece; in performance the black protagonist appears to be speaking for himself or herself and, by implication, for African Americans in general, through the singer.

Although ostensibly comic in nature, "coon" songs, in their lyrics and on their sheet music covers, often offer grotesque and derisive portrayals of black people as "all-dancing, all-laughing, all-excited, chickened- out, [and] watermelon-gorged."[7] Their titles give some sense of this: "Dat's De Way To Spell Chicken" (Sidney Perrin and Bob Slater, 1902); "Rufus Rastus Johnson Brown, What You Goin' to Do When De Rent Comes 'Round?" (Andrew W. Sterling and Harry Von Tilzer, 1905); "Plant A Watermelon On My Grave And Let The Juice Soak Through" (Frank Dumont and R. P. Lilly, 1910); and "If Every Star Was A Little Pickaninny And There Was A Little Chicken In The Moon," sung by Bessie Wynn in vaudeville, according to *Variety* for 2 December 1911.

In a typical "coon" song, "Ephraham Johnson Don't Live Here No More" (Greene and Werner, 1907), the protagonist is "a coon as pious as could be" who mistakes the sound of a youngster blowing on a fishhorn for Gabriel's trumpet, jumps into bed, pulls a blanket over his head, pretends to snore, then shouts out when he hears a knock at his door:

> Ephraham Johnson don't live here no mo',
> He's done left this place more than a week ago;
> Eph's gone away and that's a fact,
> I don't think he's ever coming back.

In notated form, "coon" songs establish the black identity of their protagonists through various conventions of the popular stage: proper names commonly associated with African American characters (Alexander, Ephraham, Mose, Eliza); code words such as "honey" and "baby" as forms of address; lyrics purporting to reproduce the syntax and pronunciation of black speech; behavior associated in the public imagination with black Americans; and sometimes the visual representation of stereotypical black characters on the front cover. At the moment of performance, on the vaudeville stage or in the recording studio, singers tended to introduce even more exaggerated dialect than is found in the published lyrics. And the music of many of these songs invokes stylistic elements thought at the time, accurately or not, to derive from the music of African Americans.

Three "coon" songs by Berlin, all of them written in 1909 and 1910, appear to perpetuate one of the traditions of the genre by dealing with the sexual activity of their black protagonists. In the first of these, "Do Your Duty Doctor! (Oh, Oh, Oh, Oh, Doctor!)," cowritten with Ted Snyder, Liza Green summons a doctor to her house to cure her "love attack":

> Oh, Oh, Oh, Oh, Doctor, won't you kindly hear my plea?
> I know, you know doctor, exactly what is best for me.
> Hear me sigh, hear me cry; surely you ain't goin' to let me die,
> For if some love will make me gain,
> Do your duty doctor, cure my pain.

In "Alexander And His Clarinet," the musical instrument that gains Alexander Adams entrance into Eliza's house and that he "played and played like sin" once he was inside is a transparent sexual symbol, as is the aroma of Liza's stew, which draws William back to her house in "I Just Came Back To Say Good Bye." In another bow to the tradition of the "coon" song, the sheet music cover of "Do Your Duty Doctor" offers a grossly exaggerated portrait of the song's two black protagonists.

As I pointed out in Chapter One, however, the protagonists of Berlin's Italian and German ethnic novelty songs are also sometimes portrayed as being greatly concerned with sex, and sheet music covers of these songs sometimes exaggerate the supposedly characteristic physical features of these groups. What might appear to be defining features of Berlin's first three "coon" songs, then, are in fact common to ethnic novelty songs in general.

Other early songs by Berlin with black protagonists develop another theme that carried over from nineteenth-century minstrelsy into the "coon" song: the comic appropriation by blacks of cultural products associated with the privileged classes. As I've suggested elsewhere, "the resulting satire is double-edged: the [black] protagonist is mocked for his or her pretensions to elite culture, which is itself mocked for the benefit of the working-class audiences of the popular theatre through parody by an unlettered protagonist."[8]

The lyric of "Woodman, Woodman, Spare That Tree," written by Berlin for the black vaudeville star Bert Williams, quotes and parodies a standard piece of nineteenth-century American "genteel" literature, a poem by George P. Morris.[9] Some of Morris's text is retained in Berlin's song, most importantly the opening lines of the first verse. But the tree in Morris's

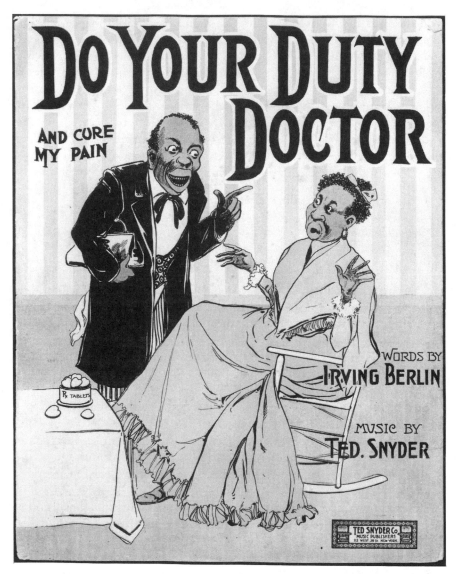

Figure 7. Cover of "Do Your Duty Doctor." (Lester L. Levy Collection of Sheet Music, Special Collections, Milton S. Eisenhower Library, The Johns Hopkins University)

poem was a noble "aged oak," a nostalgic symbol of happy childhood and lost innocence:

> Woodman, spare that tree, touch not a single bough!
> In youth it sheltered me, and I'll protect it now:
> 'Twas my forefather's hand that placed it near his cot;
> There, woodman, let it stand, thy axe shall harm it not.

In Berlin's song it has become a slippery elm, and the black protagonist begs the woodman to "cease, desist, refrain and stop, lay down that forest razor, man, chop not a single chop," not because of any sentimental attachment to the tree but because it's the "only tree that my wife can't climb"

and is thus a safe perch when his wife "starts after" him. The music has a related joke of its own: Both verse and chorus have unusually chromatic— "slippery"—motifs.

"Colored Romeo" links another classic piece of literature to a black protagonist, with comic and satirical intent. After Liza Snow "picked up a book called Romeo," she was determined to find a man who "sho' could love like a Romeo can." The joke carries through to the music, which features chromatic harmonies and propulsive melodic sequences, devices associated with more "cultured" musical styles, rather than the syncopated rhythmic patterns and diatonic tunes often found in "coon" songs.

— A man who sho' could love_____ — Like a Rom-e-o
— The aut-o struck a tree_____ — Then they did-n't go

can._____ She wan-dered out one night_____
far._____ Miss Liz-a from the ground_____

Dialect and code words identify the protagonists of "That Mesmerizing Mendelssohn Tune" as black:

> Honey, listen to that dreamy tune they're playin',
> Won't you tell me how on earth you keep from swayin'?
> Umm! Umm! Oh, that Mendelssohn Spring Song tune.

The "dreamy tune" in question, already identified in the lyric as Mendelssohn's well-known "chestnut," is then quoted in the first bars of the chorus.

The comical point of the song, the cultural gap between Mendelssohn's music and the song's black protagonists, was made even more explicit in performance on the vaudeville stage and in period recordings. In a recording made in early January 1910 by Arthur Collins and Byron C. Harlan (Columbia A801), for instance, the two singers assume much more pronounced "black" accents than are called for by the printed text— "Honey, lis'n to dat dreamy tune dey're playin'." In addition, they interpolate spoken dialogue before the second verse that resolves any possible doubt as to the race of the characters they're portraying:

> —Mmm, Mmm, Sam, I certainly am inspirated ovah dat meddlesome music.
> —What kinda music you say?
> —Meddlesome.
> —No, not "meddlesome."
> —Well, den, what is it?

Expressive and legato
Chorus

Love_____ me to that ev- er lov- in' Spring song mel - o -

dy, Please me, hon-ey, squeeze me to that Men-del-ssohn strain,——

—Why, Men-dels-sohn.
—What did I say?
—Why, you said "med-dle-some."
—Did I say dat? Why, how phantasmagorious! (both laugh)
—Liza!
—Yes, darlin'.
—Liza!
—What is it, love?
—Look me in de eye.
—What for?
—Nevah mind. Look me straight in de eye.
—Well, what for?
—'Cause I'se gwine to mesmerize you.
—Hyah, hyah, man! Don't you come around hyah wid dat fool mes-mes-mesmusm. Go on away! Go on away, I tell ya!

In several other songs, Berlin parodies familiar selections from the operatic repertory, a trick with antecedents in the nineteenth-century minstrel show, which often offered burlesque versions of arias and even entire operas.[10] Sam Johnson, the "op'ra mad" black protagonist of "That Opera Rag," hears a German band playing selections from *Rigoletto* and *Faust* while he's painting a house; he becomes so excited that he falls from his ladder, shouting to the tune of the "Toreador Song" from *Carmen* during his descent:

> Hear dat strain, Mister Verdi come to life again,
> Oh that operatic sweet refrain,
> Sho' would drive a crazy man insane,
> Just let me die and meet those brainy men,
> Who manufactured notes of opera grand.

The protagonist of "Opera Burlesque," an elaborate fourteen-page parody of the Sextette from Donizetti's *Lucia di Lammermoor,* is an "opera darkey" named Ephraham who haunts the Metropolitan Opera House to hear Caruso sing. "When he struck a high one, to the sky one," the lyric tells us, "Ephraham would begin to holler, 'That note alone is worth a dollar!' " Buying a score to *Lucia,* Ephraham recruits four other black men to sing through the sextet with him, but the sextet-minus-one soon gets out of hand. Ephraham tries to stop them ("You all are singing out of tune, where's my gun, where's my gun?"), but the others are so taken with the music—"It's as sweet as it can be, like pickin' cotton"—that they rush through to the end.

Like the "op'ra darkies" in these pieces, Berlin himself was fascinated with the operatic repertory and its performers. He frequently attended the Metropolitan Opera House where, like Ephraham and is brethren, he was an outsider because of his origins and his social status at this period in his life. In his "coon" songs cast as operatic parodies, blackface may have functioned as a mask for Berlin, enabling him to deal with his attraction to a musical genre in which he could not fully and openly participate.

> Do Your Duty Doctor! (Oh, Oh, Oh, Oh, Doctor) (1909)
> *Wild Cherries (1909)
> *Stop That Rag (Keep On Playing, Honey) (1909)
> I Just Came Back To Say Good Bye (1909)
> *That Mesmerizing Mendelssohn Tune (1909)
> *Grizzly Bear (1910)
> *That Opera Rag (1910)
> Alexander And His Clarinet (1910)
> Colored Romeo (1910)
> Woodman, Woodman, Spare That Tree (1911)
> Opera Burlesque (1912)
> *Ragtime Soldier Man (1912)
>   [songs marked with an asterisk are also ragtime songs]

Berlin's Songs About Black Musicians

The unnamed protagonist of Stephen Foster's "Susanna" (1848) announces in his first breath that "I come from Alabama with my Banjo on my knee," and Will S. Hays's "The Little Old Log Cabin In The Lane" (1871) speaks of a time when "de darkies used to gather round de door, when dey used to dance an' sing at night, [and] I played de ole banjo." These are but two of countless minstrel, plantation, cakewalk, "coon," and genteel parlor songs that take music making, in the form of supposedly carefree singing and dancing, to be a defining feature of African American culture.

Some of Berlin's early songs offer quite different images of black musicians and their music. "When Johnson's Quartette Harmonize," for instance, is an enthusiastic appreciation of the singing of a black male quartet. The verses describe the group and its singing:

> Johnson Jones from Tennessee,
> Father of sweet harmony,
> Organized a Quartette, goodness me!
> And they sang so wonderful,
> Kindly let me tell you, when
> It comes down to singing men,
> I've just got to say again.
> They're wonderful!

The chorus then invites one and all to share the enjoyment of this music:

> Come on and hear that harmony sweet,
> Come on and have a musical treat,
> From your head down to your feet,
> You'll be fairly hypnotized; . . .
> Ev'ry other chord
> Is a message from the Lord,
> When you hear old Johnson's Quartette harmonize.

Unlike the lyrics of most ethnic novelty songs, in which protagonists are first introduced in the third person in the verse and then speak for themselves in the first person, this text is in the first person throughout. The voice of the song is thus not that of Johnson Jones himself or that of his quartet but the voice of someone positioned as an observer. The "I" must be Berlin himself, telling us—through the performer(s) of his song—how much he enjoyed the singing of a black quartet and urging us to listen to this music ourselves. E. H. Pfeiffer's sheet music cover for this song would be appropriate for a demeaning "coon" song, with its depiction of blacks with thick lips and ridiculous hats, but Berlin's song has nothing to do with that genre, in content or in musical style.

Four black singers are making glorious music, music that has nothing to do with the older hegemonic image of supposedly happy black people singing and dancing to the accompaniment of banjos and fiddles. And Berlin's music for the song, with its striking chromaticism (including his first use of "blue" notes), attempts to suggest something of the harmonic richness of the black quartet style of the day.

Several other songs from this period that deal with black pianists are similarly free of stereotypical portrayals and hegemonic undertones and similarly praise the music in question. Although "When You Play That Piano, Bill!" borders on a "coon" song with its hints of sexual imagery, Eliza Johnson is referring to William Brown's piano playing, not his love-making, when she says, "When I hear you play that piano so sweet, my blood runs cold way down to my feet, you sure do bring forth music like I never heard before." "Ephraham Played Upon The Piano," an encomium to a black pianist who "didn't play by ear, he played by hand," is even more direct in its enthusiasm for his piano playing:

> Down below the Dixie line, in Alabam',
> Lived a lovin' piano player, Ephraham;
> 'Cause he never took a lesson, he had ev'rybody guessin',
> How he played with such a lovin' tone.
> Any old piano that he could annoy,
> Ephraham would call an instrument of joy;
> When it came to make a piano cry out in a fancy manner,
> Ephraham was in a class alone.

Ephraham played upon the piano,
Ephraham, he had a great left hand,
Ephraham in his fancy manner,
Made a upright sound like a "Baby Grand."

The music played by Ephraham clearly has nothing to do with the mythical banjos and fiddles of the Old Plantation, and in fact when Ephraham is asked in the second verse if he can play the fiddle, he answers, "Sister, I don't know, because I've never tried."

The racial identity of the unnamed "Piano Man," who "brings forth notes like no one can," may seem ambiguous today, particularly since the sheet music cover depicts a white pianist, but the language of the lyric makes it clear that the "lovin' piano man" is black, and a publisher's advertisement for the piece pronounces it to be "in a class by itself when it comes to a sure fire coon song." [11] Mose, in "He's A Rag Picker," is another Alabamian who "bangs upon the piano keys in search of raggy melodies" and "makes an ordinary ditty sound so pretty, like nobody can."

These songs are appreciative descriptions of the playing of black pianists, with no trace of caricature or condescension. Although there's little firm documentary evidence to suggest exactly which black pianists Berlin might have heard and then used as models for these songs, Edward Berlin has suggested that he almost certainly had contact with Scott Joplin in New York at just this time; if so, he may have heard him play.[12] He might have visited the Marshall Hotel on West Fifty-third Street, a favorite hangout for black musicians and not too far from his workplace at the Ted Snyder Company. Also, Eubie Blake reported that when he was playing at the Boathouse in Atlantic City between 1907 and 1915, Berlin "used to hang around asking me to play his songs, and I always did because they were very good. . . . He used to come by the place wearing his little derby hat and his yellow—I don't mean tan, I mean yellow—pointed shoes, and he'd say in his raggedy voice, 'Hey, Eubie, play my tune, play my tune!' "[13]

Ephraham and Mose turn up as characters in other songs by Berlin, always as musicians. As noted earlier, Ephraham is the piano-playing, Caruso-loving "opera darkey" of "Opera Burlesque" who conducts and accompanies his friends in the sextette from *Lucia*. Ephraham reappears as the "Leader man" of the band playing "At The Devil's Ball" and also as the "fiddler full of harmony" who writes a tune that "most everybody learned to love" in "The Funny Little Melody." Mose writes "a cute little beaut of a melody" that sets everyone dancing "like so many lunatics" in "The Humming Rag." In an unpublished lyric in the Irving Berlin Collection in the Library of Congress, "Musical Mose" is a "musical genius" and a "harmony inventor" who can "make a piano act just like a slave," and "Pickaninny Mose," a song sketched at this time but not published until

1921, describes how Mose's mother "croon[ed] her darky tunes" to him when he was a baby. Taken together, these songs and fragments suggest that Ephraham or Mose, or both, may have been projected protagonists for a more extended piece by Berlin, possibly his long-rumored ragtime opera. I've also suggested that Ephraham, who appears in so many songs of this period, may have been an alter ego for Berlin.[14] In this connection, Berlin chose to sing "Ephraham Played Upon The Piano" whenever he performed in public during this time—in the *Friars' Frolic of 1911,* during a week's engagement at Hammerstein's vaudeville house in September 1911, and when he sang in London in 1912.

I know of no contemporaneous songs by other writers in which the music of black performers is treated with such enthusiasm and professional respect and with such a complete absence of racial stereotyping and "comical" demeaning. And for that matter, Alexander's ragtime band isn't the object of humor or condescension, either. It is, quite simply, "the best band in the land."

> When You Play That Piano, Bill! (1910)
> Piano Man (1910)
> *Alexander's Ragtime Band (1911)
> Ephraham Played Upon The Piano (1911)
> *Ragtime Violin! (1911)
> When Johnson's Quartette Harmonize (1912)
> The Funny Little Melody (recorded, but never published, 1912)
> Musical Mose (unpublished lyric c. 1913)
> He's A Rag Picker (1914)
>   [songs marked with an asterisk are also ragtime songs]

Berlin's Ragtime Songs

Some twenty-odd pieces by Berlin are self-labeling ragtime songs, in that they use the term "ragtime" in their titles or texts. But during the so-called Ragtime Revival, initiated in 1950 with the publication of *They All Played Ragtime* by Rudi Blesh and Harriet Janis,[15] the term "ragtime" came to be reserved for a small corpus of pieces by Scott Joplin, James Scott, and a few other pianist-composers. These pieces of "classic piano ragtime" were defined as "musical composition[s] for the piano comprising three or four sections containing sixteen measures each of which combines a syncopated melody accompanied by an even, steady duple rhythm."[16] According to this definition, the term "ragtime song" was an oxymoron, and in fact all vocal pieces accepted at the time as part of the ragtime repertory were dismissed as "well-forgotten junk."

The real story of ragtime is not that of Tin Pan Alley and its million-dollar hits, of hacks and copyists, of song hucksters. . . . The commercial tunesmiths of Tin Pan Alley did their level best to ruin the music, to wring every last dollar from cheap and trumped-up imitations of a folk music, and to glut the market to the last extreme of surfeit. The popular nature of ragtime's acceptance, too, stamped it in the minds of serious music-lovers as mere ephemeral trash, and this a priori judgement still prevails.[17]

As the intellectual shackles of modernism began to rust and then fell away, a new generation of scholars began to question the practice of ignoring so much of the music accepted as ragtime by composers, performers, critics, and audiences in the first two decades of the twentieth century. In his revisionist history of ragtime, Edward A. Berlin observes that "piano ragtime accounted for only a small part, perhaps less than 10 percent, of what the music's contemporaries understood by the term 'Ragtime.' "[18] Expanding on this observation, he points out that:

The great ragtime successes were not piano pieces at all, but songs—such as *Alexander's Ragtime Band, Waiting for the Robert E. Lee, Hitchy-Koo,* and *Hello! Ma Baby.* When Rupert Hughes, Hiram K. Moderwell, and countless others wrote about ragtime, their concern was with *songs;* when pianist Mike Bernard performed in the Tammany Hall ragtime contest, he won it playing songs; when composer Charles Ives directed his keen and unbiased ears toward the popular music temper, he heard songs. Pianist Ben Harney, long reputed to be the "originator" or "first popularizer" of ragtime, acquired his reputation playing and *singing* ragtime, and his published compositions consist entirely of songs. Even Scott Joplin, the reigning prince of piano ragtime composition, discussed ragtime as a vocal music.[19]

Even if one accepts the notion that some of Irving Berlin's songs were part of the ragtime repertory, it's still no easy task to identify exactly which pieces these were. The question of what factors determined that a song was a piece of ragtime is a complicated and conflicted one, which I'll approach first by examining some of Berlin's pieces in question.

Some of Berlin's self-labeling ragtime songs have features in common with the classic piano ragtime repertory. An examination of "Wild Cherries (Coony, Spoony Rag)," for instance, reveals:

1. An apparent connection with African American culture. Ragtime was widely associated in the popular consciousness with blacks; as a writer of the day put it, "only songs having to do with the negro were looked upon as being ragtime numbers."[20] Many of the prominent ragtime pianist-composers, beginning with Scott Joplin, were black; the music of ragtime, even of pieces written by white composers, was thought to be grounded in styles and genres developed by blacks; protagonists in ragtime songs were usually black. The

chief characters in "Wild Cherries," for instance, are Jackson, a "looney, spoony coon" who leads a "big brass band," and his bride, Lucinda Morgan White, who responds ecstatically to the music of his band:

> I'm goin' crazy, that rag's a daisy,
> I just can't make my feet behave,
> Play that tune again, mighty soon again,
> Oh, you seven come eleven!
> Hon I'm goin' straight to heav'n.

2. The use of "secondary ragtime," a stylistic mannerism found in many piano rags, characterized by three-note repeated or sequenced melodic patterns in the right hand (and/or voice) contrasting with steady duple patterns in the left.[21]

3. An interior section, the chorus in this case, in the subdominant key. "Wild Cherries" was, in fact, a piano rag by Ted Snyder that was subsequently made into a song by Berlin and Snyder by the expedient of adding a text, dropping several strains, and inserting a vamp before the verse:

Snyder's piano rag (key: **C**)
     Intro[8]   A[16]B[16]A[16]   Trio (key: **F**) C[16]D[16]

Berlin-Snyder song (key: **C**)
     Intro[8]- vamp[2]   Verse: A[16]   Chorus (key: **F**) C[16]

"Oh That Beautiful Rag" was converted from a piano rag into a song in similar fashion:

Snyder's piano rag (key: **C**)

    Intro^4 A^{16}B^{16}A^{16} Trio (key: **F**) C^{32}D^{16}C^{32}

Berlin-Snyder song (key: **C**)

    Intro^4- vamp^2 Verse: A^{16} Chorus (key: **F**) C^{32}

And a third song, "Grizzly Bear," was originally "The Grizzly Bear Rag" by George Botsford:

Botsford's piano rag (key: **G**)

    Intro^4 A^{16}B^{16}A^{16} Trio (key: **C**) C^{16}B^{16}

Berlin-Botsford song (key: **E♭**)

    Intro^4- vamp^2 Verse: A^{16} Chorus (key: **A♭**) C^{16}

Several other early ragtime songs by Berlin, including "Ragtime Violin!" and "Everybody's Doing It Now," have the chorus in the subdominant, and still others have a chorus beginning with subdominant harmony, although the song doesn't modulate to that key.

4. Some measures of the right hand (and voice) fall into $3 + 3 + 2$ groupings, against a steady $2 + 2 + 2 + 2$ pattern in the left hand.

This pattern, which recurs in most of Berlin's ragtime songs, might be a simple example of the polyrhythmic patterns found in so much African and African American music, including piano rags, and a direct stylistic link with the piano rags of such black composers as James Scott.

> Underlying the surface variety of Scott's syncopation is the consistent, often unrelenting, use of a handful of basic rhythmic patterns. The most common of these by far is defined by a syncopated accent on the fourth sixteenth note of the measure, suggesting (assuming a subdivision of the 2/4 measure into eight sixteenth notes) the additive pattern $3 + 3 + 2$ against the even two beat pulse. It is not unusual to find this rhythmic pattern used as the basis for entire strains, not to say entire pieces [of his music]. . . . This rhythmic pattern was not unique to Scott. It is a staple of the African American folk tradition and is ultimately traceable to Caribbean and West African music.[22]

Even though this rhythmic pattern may have been appropriated from African American music, it permeates other early songs by Berlin as well, from the Jewish novelty song "Sadie Salome (Go Home)" to the ballad "Some Little Something About You" to the Italian novelty song "Sweet Italian Love."

One could argue, alternatively, that this ubiquitous rhythmic grouping of $3 + 3 + 2$ in Berlin's early songs is grounded in his method of setting a text. Berlin was once quoted as saying that "one thing I've done successfully few people know about—because they've never given the matter any consideration. I have vocalized the triplet, a favorite device for the instrumentalist, but avoided by the vocal writer. You'll find the triplet worded in almost everyone of my songs."[23] A curious claim on the face of it, since notated triplets are rare in his songs, the statement does in fact make sense when one bears in mind that Berlin created these pieces by ear, without reference to musical notation. His $3 + 3 + 2$ rhythmic groupings are always settings of patterns in his lyrics such as "Don't do that dance, I tell you Sadie" or "Ev'ryone talk-a how they make-a da love." But whereas an earlier songwriter might have used true triplets in setting these phrases,

Berlin set them in what could be thought of as syncopated triplets.

As noted, many of Berlin's early ragtime songs have black protagonists whose stereotypical language and behavior often approach those of the "coon" song. The female protagonist of "Grizzly Bear," for instance, is transported by the dance of the title into a state of comical near-hysteria:

> Hug up close to your baby,
> Hypnotize me like a wizard,
> Shake yo'self just like a blizzard,
> Snug up close to your lady,
> If they do that dance in heaven,
> Shoot me hon' tonight at seven . . .

In a recorded performance of the song,[24] the "coon shouter" Stella Mayhew interpolates a bit of spoken dialogue to sharpen the image of the protagonist she's portraying:

> Oh, dear, isn't it just too de-leet-ful,
> I could just dance all night, only my feet hurts me so.
> I think it's these doggone shoes,
>   —Oh, change em—
> I cain't, they was wished on me.
> Hoo, hoo, I'm about all in . . .

But not all ragtime songs of this period, by Berlin or other songwriters, have black protagonists. Sadie and Yiddle in Berlin's "Yiddle, On Your

Fiddle, Play Some Ragtime" are Jewish, and Abie Bloom, in Joe Young and Bert Grant's "Serenade Me Sadie With A Rag-time Song" (1912), wants his wife to sing ragtime songs for him rather than the operatic repertory she studied in Europe. "The Yiddisha Rag" by Joseph H. McLeon, Harry M. Piano, and W. Raymond Walker (1909) begins:

> Have you ever heard that clever Yiddisha rag, it's a daisy,
> It's so spoony, nothing cooney, still it will set you half crazy,
> It's so entrancing you have to smile,
> It keeps you dancing all of the while,
> That Yiddisha rag,
> Oh that Yiddisha rag.

Tony and Marie in Berlin's "Sweet Marie, Make-a Rag-a-Time Dance Wid Me" are Italian, as are the protagonists in "That Italian Rag" (1910) by Edgar Leslie and Al Piantadosi, "Viviano, My-a-rag-a-time-a-Queen" (1911) by Edith Middleton and Billy Smythe, and "Cavalier' Rustican' Rag" (1910) by Harry Williams and Egbert Van Alstyne.

If the protagonists of ragtime songs aren't black, they are Jewish or Italian or, more rarely, German or Irish, and the point of the song becomes the attempted appropriation of black music and dance by another of America's "alien" groups, to comic effect.[25] Ragtime remained the music of America's marginalized population. But this began to change in the second decade of the century.

The cover of "That Mysterious Rag," written by Berlin and Ted Snyder in late 1911, shows a fashionably dressed white couple, the woman playing a spinet while the man gazes into space searching for the mysterious music of the song's title. The written lyric has no trace of dialect or of ethnic syntax, and the American Quartet recorded the piece without accent or mannerism.[26]

> Did you hear it? were you near it?
> If you weren't then you've yet to fear it;
> Once you've met it, you'll regret it,
> Just because you never will forget it. . . .

The lyric continues in the first person throughout, addressed to the plural "you"—that is, the audience. The voice of the song is that of the song-writer, speaking through the singer, not that of a protagonist created by the songwriter and represented by the performer. There is no trace of syncopation beyond a single $3 + 3 + 2$ pattern in the chorus, no minor tonality, no other musical reference to one ethnic group or another. The most arresting moment, the cross-relation at the beginning of the verse, has no specific ethnic (or any other) connotation.

The protagonists of "At The Ragtime Ball" (1911) by Roger Lewis and Jimmie Monaco are also not black, clearly: They take a taxi to a ball, where they join a crowd of the "swellest folks in town" in "dress suits and silken gowns," and the sheet music cover pictures a society dance, the men in white ties and tails and the women in formal gowns.

None of Berlin's ragtime songs published after 1911 has an unequivocally black protagonist, none uses "black" dialect in the lyrics, and none makes pervasive use of rhythmic or structural patterns associated with classic piano ragtime. These pieces were sometimes sung in blackface, but this was a performer's decision, not demanded by the style or content of the song itself.[27] The second verse of "Ragtime Mocking Bird" demonstrates how far the lyrics of Berlin's ragtime songs have moved away from those of the earlier "coon" song:

> Honey dove, honey dove,
> Don't you love that feathered Tetrazzin?
> Ev'ry note in her throat,
> Is a boat chock'd full of peaches and cream;
> If your heart cares for art,
> Better part with that one dollar bill,
> Honey, why don't you buy that bird and keep me still?
> Say you will, say you will.

Note that "Honey," formerly a code word signaling a black protagonist, has been assimilated into Berlin's general textual style.

The content and spirit of "They've Got Me Doin' It Now," a ragtime song of 1913, stands in sharp contrast with the "coon" song "Do Your Duty Doctor!" of several years earlier. A woman visits a doctor in both pieces, but whereas the doctor and patient are black in the earlier song and are caricatured in music, text, and on the sheet music cover in broad strokes recalling the nineteenth-century image of the "coon" (see Figure 7), the music of the later song has no more than a hint of the syncopation associated with piano ragtime music, John Frew's cover shows a white doctor and a white patient dressed in the high fashion of the day, and the style and the content of Berlin's text make it unlikely that the two could be black:

> Doctor, cure me, won't you hurry up and temperature me?
> Of a quick recovery assure me,
> Tell me what's the matter, don't deceive me, relieve me;
> Capsule maker, oh, you friend of ev'ry undertaker,
> Won't you tell me why my shoulders keep going in the air?

By 1912, then, Berlin's ragtime songs no longer had unambiguously black protagonists; they had moved away from the spirit of the "coon" song and made only passing references to, or had assimilated into a more generic style, any music connected with blacks and their culture. As I discuss in Chapter Five, Berlin was shifting his focus from vaudeville to the legitimate stage at this time, in preparation for writing his first musical comedy. Whereas his earliest ragtime songs, those still invoking the images of the "coon" song, had been written for the working-class, largely immigrant/first-generation audiences of the vaudeville house, the later ones were aimed at people higher up the economic and social ladder, patrons of the legitimate theater.

In searching for an answer to the question of why the label "ragtime" was still applied to many of these later songs, one must keep in mind that the contemporary notion of what constituted ragtime music had nothing to do with structural, melodic, and rhythmic features observable *in the notated form* of a composition, as came to be the case during the Ragtime Revival and later, but depended on audience perception of a piece *at the moment of performance.* Ben Harney's instruction pamphlet on ragtime didn't offer compositions; it showed how popular and classical compositions could be "ragged" in performance,[28] and a slightly later writer observed that "now, everything that carries the jerky meter, or an irregular meter that possesses a pleasing lilt, is called ragtime," adding that "a clever pianist can 'rag' the most sacred song ever published."[29] As the

Figure 8. Cover of "They've Got Me Doin' It Now." (Lester L. Levy Collection of Sheet Music, Special Collections, Milton S. Eisenhower Library, The Johns Hopkins University)

songwriter and publisher Harry Von Tilzer put it, in *Variety* for 23 December 1912:

> "Ragtime" is not a type of song; it is a type of song-treatment; in fact it is the distinctive American treatment of song in general. It reflects the spirit of the American people, their extraordinary activity, restlessness, initiative, joyousness and capacity for work, and for play. . . . "Ragtime" pervades all styles and classes of American music, from the coon song to the parlor love-song and I think I am safe in saying that so long as America remains the land of the brave and the free and the busy, particularly the busy, so long shall we have "ragtime."

For a few years on either side of 1910, then, "ragtime" came to serve as a generic label for most popular music, just as "rock" was used in the 1960s and 1970s as an umbrella term for popular music of a remarkably wide stylistic range. Berlin was accepted and acclaimed as a writer of ragtime during this period because he was the author of the phenomenally successful "Alexander's Ragtime Band" and because he was the most commercially successful songwriter at a time when singing and playing in a fast, "ragged," and "jerky" fashion was the norm.

Berlin's ragtime songs, particularly these written after 1911, have little more than a label in common with the "classic" ragtime piano pieces of Scott Joplin, James Scott, and their peers, nor were they in competition with them in any way. The charge by writers of the Ragtime Revival that Tin Pan Alley songwriters "ruined" classic ragtime with their "trumped-up imitations of a folk music" is a fallacious one, impossible to sustain today.

For one thing, classic piano ragtime was written by musically literate pianist-composers with formal musical training, men and women who quite consciously intended to create a "cultured" product in which "artistic quality took precedence over the demands of the marketplace; a music that was composed with the integrity, seriousness, and skill that befits a classical art."[30] Some of Scott Joplin's contemporaries reported that he "let it be known that he preferred 'classical' music and wanted to be considered a serious artist";[31] the *American Musician and Art Journal* for December 1911 says that "Joplin doesn't like the light music of the day; he is delighted with Beethoven and Bach, and his compositions, though syncopated, smack of the higher cult."[32] John Stark, Joplin's most important publisher, used the covers of Joplin's rags for such pronouncements as "[The Maple Leaf Rag] is played by the cultured of all nations and is welcomed in the drawing rooms and boudoirs of good taste" and "[classic rags] are used in the drawing rooms and parlors of culture." The editors of the recent complete edition of James Scott's music speak of his rags as "a new serious composed music," characterized by an "unusual mixture of refinement and syncopated rhythm . . . [placing them in] a middle ground between the commercialized culture of ragtime songs, sung in Joplin saloons, and the fine art of concert hall music." They further suggest that Booker T. Washington "would have approved of the lofty ambitions of this endeavor, of [Scott's] refusal to compose in racial stereotypes, of his carefully crafted harmonic progressions, and of his advocacy of musical literacy."[33]

This classic piano ragtime repertory, disseminated through the medium of precisely notated sheet music, was performed and recorded by professional musicians or played socially by skilled amateur pianists. Even though some of its roots lay in oral music, it was not "folk" music itself, by any definition of that conflicted term. Like the classical repertory, and unlike either folk music or popular song, it was intended to be played just as it was notated, even by its composers. A son of Joplin's publisher remembers that "[he] was a rather mediocre pianist [who] composed 'on paper' rather than 'at the piano.' . . . This became a real problem when Scott had to play one of his own compositions and found that he had to rehearse it carefully before he could play it convincingly."[34]

Ragtime songs, like other products of Tin Pan Alley, belong to a different genre, one with its own musical and cultural roots, its own performance traditions, and its own audiences. Mass-disseminated popular song of the early twentieth century was a product of America's radically multicultural cities. Its songwriters, most of whom were themselves members of socially marginalized ethnic populations, combined stylistic and expressive elements from various components of this polyglot society in their attempts to represent it.

Berlin's ragtime songs, with the possible exception of a few early ones, were never intended to represent black people or their culture. The performers and audiences for whom these pieces were written were not those who played or listened to classic piano ragtime, and the popularity of these songs neither helped nor hindered the performance and sales of piano rags by black (and white) pianist-composers. And far from destroying American "folk" song, it can be argued that this is what they became themselves. As Isaac Goldberg puts it:

[Popular song] manages, stammeringly yet at times inimitably, to speak the yearnings, the sorrows and the joys of a new, emergent folk, different from any other folk in the world; and it is most gratefully accepted by that folk in the one true way that song may be accepted: it is sung. Tin Pan Alley, in brief, has cradled a new folk song, a song of the city, synthetic in facture, as short-lived as a breath, yet not for these reasons any the less authentic.[35]

To sum up, a few of Berlin's earliest ragtime songs, fashioned from piano rags by other composers or written collaboratively with other songwriters, have some of the stylistic features of "classic" piano ragtime, with lyrics invoking the legacy of the "coon" song. But Berlin himself never wrote a piano rag, and only traces of the rhythmic and melodic elements associated with piano rags can be found in the ragtime songs for which he wrote music as well as lyrics. He was a ragtime composer in the same sense that Bob Dylan, Paul Simon, and Ray Charles wrote rock music.

Wild Cherries (Coony, Spoony Rag) (1909)
Stop That Rag (Keep On Playing, Honey) (1909)
Yiddle, On Your Fiddle, Play Some Ragtime (1909)
That Mesmerizing Mendelssohn Tune (1909)
Sweet Marie, Make-a Rag-a-Time Dance Wid Me (1910)
When You Play That Piano, Bill! (1910)
Draggy Rag (1910)
Grizzly Bear (1910)
That Opera Rag (1910)
Oh, That Beautiful Rag (1910)
That Dying Rag (1911)
Alexander's Ragtime Band (1911)
The Whistling Rag (1911)
That Mysterious Rag (1911)
Ragtime Violin! (1911)
Everybody's Doing It Now (1912)
Ragtime Mocking Bird (1912)
Alexander's Bag-Pipe Band (1912)
The Ragtime Jockey Man (1912)
Ragtime Soldier Man (1912)
They've Got Me Doin' It Now (1913)
The International Rag (1913)
They've Got Me Doin' It Now (Medley) (1913)
That Humming Rag (1913)

Berlin's "Back-to-Dixie" Songs

Throughout this book I've argued for the necessity of identifying the protagonist, or the voice, of a popular song if one wishes to understand the meaning of the piece. At first glance, the lyric of Berlin's "When The Midnight Choo-Choo Leaves For Alabam'," which quickly became one of his greatest commercial successes following its publication in 1912, seems to contain few clues to the identity of the song's unnamed, first-person protagonist.

> I've had a mighty busy day, I've had to pack my things away,
> Now I'm goin' to give the landlord back his key; the very key
> That opened up my dreary flat, where many weary nights I sat,
> Thinking of the folks down home who think of me;
> You can bet you'll find me singing happily.
> When the midnight choo-choo leaves for Alabam',
> I'll be right there, I've got my fare.
> When I see that rusty-haired conductor man,
> I'll grab him by the collar and I'll holler "Alabam'! Alabam'!":
> That's where you stop your train, that brings me back again,
> Down home where I'll remain, where my honey-lamb am.
> I will be right there with bells, when that old conductor yells,
> "All aboard! All aboard! All aboard for Alabam'!"
>
> The minute that I reach the place, I'm goin' to feed my face,
> 'Cause I haven't had a good meal since the day I went away.
> I'm goin' to kiss my Pa and Ma a dozen times for ev'ry star,
> Shining over Alabama's new mown hay;
> I'll be glad enough to throw myself away.
> When the midnight choo-choo . . .

A number of details in the lyric would have identified the protagonist as black to audiences in 1912, however. There are elisions common to songs with black characters ("goin'," " 'cause," "Alabam' ") and code words such as "honey-lamb." A white person would hardly use the term "choo-choo" for a train or grab a conductor by the collar and "holler" at him. The protagonist's insistence that he has enough money for his fare seems unnecessary, unless something, his skin color for instance, might raise a question on this point. The train's midnight departure time suggests that fares are cheaper then than on trains leaving at more convenient hours. The protagonist is returning "down home" to Alabama at a moment in America's history when the population flow from South to North was virtually all black, as the children of former slaves began to seek economic opportunities in northern cities while white Southerners, still traumatized by the Civil War, rarely chose to live among the still-hated Yankees.

Audiences in 1912 would also have heard references in the music itself to earlier songs with black protagonists. The melodic beginnings of both verse and chorus avoid the fourth degree, suggesting the gapped scale of so many nineteenth-century minstrel and plantation songs, and the short-long-short rhythmic pattern at the beginning of the verse echoes the so-called cakewalk figure used to such effect in "Alexander's Ragtime Band."

Short-long "Scottish snaps" flavor both verse and chorus, and a phrase in mid-chorus makes use of the $3+3+2$ rhythmic pattern.

Period recordings of the song verify and exaggerate the black identity of the protagonist. In addition to assuming exaggerated "negro" accents when they recorded the song in 1912, Arthur Collins and Byron Harlan inserted the following spoken dialogue before the final reprise of the chorus, punctuated by giggles and chuckles of the sort expected from a stage black:

> [train whistle, approaching]
> —Here come de express.
> [train whistle, receding]
> —An' dar she goes.
> —Well, well, we'll catch de next one, anyway.

—If she don't catch us.
—Well, we'll take a chance.
—I don' wanna take a chance, I wanna take a train.[36]

The intended meaning of a popular song can often be clarified by locating it in the context of similar pieces—that is, by establishing its genre or subgenre. "Midnight Choo-Choo" is one of a cluster of "back-to-Dixie" songs published at just this time, all with similar scenarios and common textual and musical features; others include:

- "I Want To Be In Dixie" (Berlin and Ted Snyder, 1912)
- "All Aboard For Alabam' " (George Mann and Walter Esberger, 1912)
- "All Aboard For Dixie Land" (Jack Yellen and George L. Cobb, 1913)
- "I'm Going Back To Carolina" (Billy Downs and Ernie Erdman, 1913)
- "I'm Going Back To Carolina (Here Comes My Train, Ding Ding, Toot Toot, Farewell, So Long" (Billy Davis and Ernie Erdman, 1913)
- "Down Upon The Old Swanee" (William J. McKenna, 1913)
- "Oh, Mister Railroad Man, Won't You Take Me Back To Alabam' " (Stanley Murphy and Henry Marshall, 1914)
- "Back To Dixie Land" (Jack Yellen, 1914)
- "I'm Going Back To Alabam' " (Brown and Williams, 1914)
- "I Guess I'll Soon Be Back In Dixieland (Hear The Whistle, Hear The Bell" (Jack Rogers, 1915)

Each of these songs has a male protagonist who was born in the South and is returning there by train. Each intends to stay in the South, where he "belongs." Some songs have even more obvious clues to the black identity of the central character: the use of unmistakable dialect in the lyrics (Mann/Esberger: "I'se got my grip, goin' to take a trip, where I'm goin' I'se glad to go"); proper names associated with blacks in popular culture (Liza, Mandy, Rastus); code words and exclamations, such as "Mammy," "honey," and "Oh Lordy"; racially defining occupations: (Murphy/Marshall: "And when the snow is falling in the northern clime, I'll be picking cotton in the bright sunshine"); and, in at least one case (Mann/Esberger), the depiction of a black on the sheet music cover. Musical references to minstrel, plantation, cakewalk, and "coon" songs abound, including simple syncopated patterns, pentatonic scales, and melodic quotation from well-known earlier songs with black protagonists. Both Brown/Williams and Downs/Erdman quote Dan Emmett's "Dixie's Land," for instance.

Not all songs of this period in which the protagonist is traveling to the South are of this type. Despite superficial similarities between the lyric of "Steaming Back To Dixieland" (1913) and the songs just discussed, the former piece belongs to a quite different (and equally popular) subgenre of the period, the rustic/nostalgic ballad, to be discussed in Chapter Four. The language of Jean Havez's lyric implies a white protagonist:

> When you go steaming through Dixie,
> Through that beautiful land,
> If you should see my sweetheart Sue,
> Just tell her I'll be with her when the roses bloom.
> Say my heart is fond and true, so true,
> Just say I'm coming home to make her happy again,
> I'm coming back to claim her hand.

And Ted Barron's music is in the style of an old-fashioned march ballad, making no reference to musical materials associated with minstrel, "coon," or ragtime songs.

Some back-to-Dixie songs vary slightly from the scenario I have described, while still delivering its message. The (black) protagonist may be returning to the South by steamboat or paddle wheel rather than by train, as in "Down Upon The Old Swanee" (1913) by William J. McKenna, or he may be only planning a return to the South ("One thing is certain, I'm surely flirtin', with those southbound trains," from "Are You From Dixie" [1915] by Jack Yellen and George L. Cobb). Sometimes the impetus for such a trip comes from the South itself:

> I had a letter from my Mammy down in sunny Tennessee,
> And tho' it may sound queer to folks up here,
> 'Deed it sound might good to me . . .
> Ain't you comin' back to Dixieland where the sweet magnolias grow?
> Don't you ever yearn just to return to the land of Old Black Joe?
> All the little pickaninnies seem to miss you so . . .
>
> "Ain't You Coming Back To Dixieland" (1917)
> by Raymond Egan and Richard A. Whiting

Still others are concerned with rationalizing the protagonist's return to the South by romanticizing the life of black people there:

> When it's cotton pickin' time down in Alabam'
> The folks out there are all gay
> For work with them is like play . . .
> When work is done the fun is just begun,
> Lordy but those darkies sure can hum.
>
> "When It's Cotton Pickin' Time In Alabam'"
> (1915) by Harry Tobias

Sometimes the back-to-Dixie message of a song is apparent only from the context in which it's performed. There seems to be nothing in the lyric of "Don't You Wish You Were Back Home Again?" (1913) by Charles K.

Harris to suggest a black protagonist ("Don't you wish, dear old pal, you were back home again, Where fair hearts, they are yearning for you?"), and the South is never mentioned. Yet when the song was performed in blackface by Joseph Gillespie in George Evans's "Honey Boy Minstrels," as pictured on the sheet music cover, it would have been clear that the person yearning to return to a more congenial place is intended to be black and that the place in question must be below the Mason-Dixon line.

Songs depicting black people happily headed South or planning to do so or rhapsodizing over the good life supposedly enjoyed by blacks in the South constituted a not inconsiderable part of the popular repertory in 1912 and the next several years. But why did songs of this sort appear in such numbers at just this time?

One explanation could be that since songwriters tend to imitate one another, the success of Berlin's "Midnight Choo-Choo" prompted a flood of similar pieces. But there is more to it than that. Each of these back-to-Dixie songs emphasizes that its purported black protagonist is not merely returning to the South but that he wants to go there, belongs there, and plans to stay there. This was hardly a new theme; songs about blacks returning to the South had been common fare on the minstrel stage throughout most of the nineteenth century. One need look no further than Stephen Foster's prototypical "Old Folks At Home" (1851), with its "darkey" whose "heart grows weary, far from de old folks at home," or Dan Emmett's "Dixie's Land" (1860), which begins with the line "I wish I was in de land ob cotton, old times dar am not forgotten," or any one of hundreds of subsequent songs reiterating the same sentiment.

> To live and die in Georgia, dat's good enough for me,
> I'll hoe the corn and cotton, and oh so happy be.
> I'll hunt the coon and possum, and dance and sing and play,
> And when I once get back there, I'll never come away.
>
> "Trabling Back To Georgia" (1874) by Arthur R. French
> and Charles D. Blake

The message of all these songs is that blacks belong in the South and are happy there, and if circumstances take them elsewhere they want to go back home. But the reasons given in the lyric for the black protagonist's leaving the South, and the songwriter's motivation in insisting that he wants to return, changed over time.

Before the Civil War, blackface minstrel performers of such songs represented blacks who were in the North as contraband—escaped slaves. According to the minstrel show's proslavery ideology, they were property that should be returned to the rightful owner. In one verse of Emmett's "Dixie's Land," to cite the most famous song of this type, this scenario, always implicit for performers and audiences of the day, was made explicit:

To Canada old John was bound, all by de rail-road underground,
Look away, look away, look away, Dixie Land.
He's got no clothes, he's got no tin, he wishes he was back again,
Look away, look away, look away, Dixie Land.[37]

Even after Lincoln's Emancipation Proclamation, minstrel songs continued to offer the same scenario, as in Septimus Winner's "Ellie Rhee; or, Carry Me Back to Tennessee" (1865):

Oh why did I from day to day, keep wishing to be free,
And from my massa run away, and leave my Ellie Rhee,
Then carry me back to Tennessee, back where I long to be.
They said that I would soon be free, and happy all de day,
But if dey take me back again, I'll never run away.

Nor did the tenor of such songs change after the war's end, when blacks were theoretically free to leave their former owners and the South:

When I was free, I left that land, where the days are bright and fair,
Where Missus spoke to me so kind, when I was bow'd with care;
I left that home no friends to find, my heart was fill'd with pain,
Oh! take me to that good old home, to see it once again.

"I Want To See The Old Home" (1873) by Frank Dumont
and James E. Stewart

Postwar songs of this sort were written and published almost entirely in the North and sung in minstrel shows performed mostly in the North and the West, a reflection of the postwar economy and of the political climate of the day. Although the message of back-to-Dixie songs remained the same, the implication now was that blacks simply weren't wanted in the North, at least by the people who wrote, produced, and attended minstrel shows.

In the 1890s and 1900s, as songs for the popular stage were increasingly written by and for a new urban population dominated by immigrant and first-generation Americans from the Mediterranean countries and from Central Europe, people who had been no part of the country's mid-nineteenth-century struggles and agonies, almost no new back-to-Dixie songs were written. Their resurgence around 1912 seems to have been occasioned by a new set of political factors.

In the presidential election of 1912, Theodore Roosevelt, running as a third-party candidate, was popular among New York City's Jews because of his "progressive rhetoric and philo-Semitism"[38] and because he was less supportive of the country's growing nativist backlash against the recently arrived immigrant population than were the other two candidates, Woodrow Wilson and William Howard Taft. An important subtext of this election, particularly in northern cities, was the intensifying competition between immigrants and northward-migrating African Americans for unskilled jobs. If blacks stayed in the South, there would be more jobs for immigrants and for their families and friends still in Europe who were waiting for the chance to come over; if blacks came North in large enough numbers, the demand for new immigrant labor would be lessened, playing into the hands of those who wanted to restrict or end the flow of "inferior racial stock" from the Mediterranean region and from Central Europe into the United States. It could hardly be a coincidence that Tin Pan Alley and vaudeville, with so many immigrants and first-generation people among the leading songwriters, producers, and performers, turned out a rash of back-to-Dixie songs at just this time.

Taken as a group, these pieces were hegemonic in making it appear commonsensical that blacks should stay in or return to the South. But even if a specific back-to-Dixie song were written to encode a political message—a plea for the protection of Italian, Jewish, and Irish jobs—another songwriter might well write a similar piece merely in emulation, without intending the same content. Popular song is a notoriously inefficient medium for the communication of specific messages; even if Berlin did intend for "Midnight Choo-Choo" to make a political statement, which is not at all certain, popular music's tradition of flexible modes of performance and perception would have made it uncertain that this message would be communicated in any given rendition. And eventually, in such performances as that by Fred Astaire and Judy Garland in the film *Easter Parade* (1948) and on recent recordings by Max Morath [39] and Benjamin Sears, [40] "Midnight Choo-Choo" lost not only all trace of its original hegemonic message, if it ever had one, but even its black protagonist.

I Want To Be In Dixie (1912)
When The Midnight Choo-Choo Leaves For Alabam' (1912)
When It's Night Time In Dixie Land (1914)

In Conclusion

Berlin's early songs with black protagonists or black characters vary in style and content and offer no single image of African Americans and their place in American society. Some of the earlier ones approach the spirit of the "coon" song, with their stereotypical, supposedly comic but near-demeaning portrayals of black people. Others are appreciative, admiring portraits of black musicians and their music. The protagonists of some of the first of Berlin's two dozen ragtime songs are blacks engaged in dancing or otherwise enjoying themselves or are members of other marginalized ethnic groups attempting to emulate black music and dance; the later ragtime songs make no reference to black people. Three songs belong to a subgenre that gave hegemonic support to the notion that black people belong in the South and should stay there.

Berlin's attitude toward black people and their culture was anything but monolithic, judging from these songs. The only generalization possible is that there is chronological change in these pieces: Protagonists who are unmistakably black largely disappear in the later songs, to be replaced by characters with no clear ethnic identity, and stylistic elements drawn from or suggesting black music become more integrated into an increasingly generic musical language.

Berlin was fashioning his own melting pot.

Postscript

A fascination with blackface performance continued as a minor thread throughout most of Berlin's career as a writer for the musical stage. The finale of the second act of his first musical comedy, *Watch Your Step* (1914), is a "ragtime" parody of a succession of operatic standards in the styles of popular dances of the day: *Aida* and *Rigoletto* as rags, *La Boheme* as a hesitation waltz, *Faust* as a maxixe, *Carmen* as a tango, and *Pagliacci* as a one-step. The third edition of his Music Box Revue (1923–24) contained an "operatic version" of the hit song "Yes! We Have No Bananas" (Frank Silver and Irving Cohn, 1923), in which performers in blackface parody the song in the style of well-known arias from *Il Trovatore, Rigoletto, The Tales of Hoffman, Lucia di Lammermoor, Aida,* and finally the "Hallelujah Chorus" from Handel's *Messiah.*[41]

The minstrel show in particular intrigued Berlin. In his own words, in the lyric of "I'd Rather See A Minstrel Show," written for the *Ziegfeld Follies of 1919:*

> I'd rather see a minstrel show,
> Than any other show I know,
> Oh! those comical folks
> With their riddles and jokes
> Here is the riddle I love the best
> "Why does a chicken go?"
> You know the rest
> I'd pawn my overcoat and vest
> To see a minstrel show.

Most of his revues and musical comedies, from *Yip, Yip, Yaphank* (1918) and *The Cocoanuts* (1925) all the way up to *This Is The Army* (1942), have minstrel songs or production numbers, performed in blackface. In 1928 he wrote the book (with James Gleason) and some music for a musical comedy titled "Mr. Bones," set in a traveling minstrel show. Although the musical was never produced, the script became the screenplay of *Mammy,* a movie of 1930 starring Al Jolson.[42]

There is no contradiction between this activity and my earlier concluding remarks. By 1912 Berlin had lost whatever interest he might have had in writing songs purporting to depict black people. But what continued to fascinate him was the notion of the minstrel show as a dramatic form in which performers speak from behind the mask of blackface.

Chapter Three

Alexander and His Band

"Alexander's Ragtime Band" wasn't Irving Berlin's first commercial hit; a dozen or more of his songs had chalked up substantial sheet music sales before it was published early in 1911. It wasn't his first song to attract international attention; Bert Feldman had brought out eight of his songs in London, in *Feldman's Sixpenny Editions,* before adding "Alexander" to the series. It isn't his best-selling song of all time—"White Christmas" enjoys that distinction—or even his best song, in the opinion of most critics. But it did attract more public and media attention than any other song of its decade, it quickly became an icon for the ragtime era, and its popularity has persisted to the present.

Given the amount of attention paid to "Alexander" from 1911 on, it's hardly surprising that several controversies have sprung up around it and that some aspects of the song and its history have been misrepresented. A review of these difficulties will serve as an introduction to a more general discussion of the song and its history, which will serve to develop further some of the issues raised in Chapter Two concerning Berlin's songs with blackface protagonists.

The Ragtime Connection

A recent biographer of Berlin claims that the text of "Alexander" is "the kind of old-fashioned 'coon' lyric that came easily to him,"[1] but in fact the protagonist's excited invitation to his "honey" to come along and listen to the "best band in the land" is nothing of the sort. The gesture of the

102

piece, a first-person exhortation to anyone and everyone within earshot to come and listen to a band, has no precedent in earlier "coon" songs or in any other songs of the Tin Pan Alley era, or even in the "come-all-ye" command of British balladry to heed the words of the bard. Berlin himself was convinced that the song "started the heels and shoulders of all America and a good section of Europe to rocking" largely because of this direct, exuberant, first-person outcry.

> [Its] opening words, emphasized by immediate repetition—"Come on and hear! Come on and hear!"—were an *invitation* to "come," to join in, and "hear" the singer and his song. And that idea of *inviting* every receptive auditor within shouting distance became a part of the happy ruction—an idea pounded in again and again throughout the song in various ways—was the secret of the song's tremendous success.[2]

His first biographer agrees that the song was unusual and effective because of its "exultant" nature, so unlike many of Berlin's "lugubrious melodies" that betray a heritage of "generations of wailing cantors."[3]

Although there's no exact precedent in Berlin's earlier songs for this "come-and-hear-the-band" gesture, he came close to it in "That Kazzatsky Dance," a Jewish novelty song, copyrighted and published in December 1910, in which the female protagonist enthuses to her friend Abie, "Can't you hear very clear, they're playing that Kazzatsky dance, Cohen with his hand leads the band, ain't it grand." But once the gesture had worked so well with "Alexander," Berlin used it again and again, in such later songs as "A Little Bit Of Everything," "Follow The Crowd," and particularly "Lead Me To That Beautiful Band":

> Dear, lend an ear to the finest music in the land,
> You'd better hurry and take a hand;
> I want to linger beside that grandstand band, and
> Hon', better run, just because I hear them tuning up.
> Just hear that slide trombone a-blowin' for me,
> Just hear those sweet cornets all goin' for me,
> Hear the piccoloer pick a melody,
> See the clarionetter clarionetting me,
> Hear that cello moan . . .
> Lead me, lead me to that beautiful band.

The urgency of this lyric is captured wonderfully in Stella Mayhew's performance on Edison Blue Amberol 2173, recorded in April 1912.

Much of the literature on "Alexander" deals with its relationship, or more often its alleged nonrelationship, to ragtime. Alexander Woollcott rhapsodized that the song made the "first full use of the new rhythm which had begun to take form in the honkey-tonks where pianists were dislocating old melodies to make them keep step with the swaying hips and shoulders of the spontaneous darky dancers,"[4] but most later writers have insisted that the song has little or nothing to do with ragtime music. According to Sigmund Spaeth, "it is now an old story that *Alexander's Ragtime Band*' not only had nothing to do with the development of ragtime, but is actually a song with hardly a trace of ragtime in it."[5] Alec Wilder says, "I have heard enough ragtime to wonder why [it] was so titled,"[6] and in the curious but clumsy language of Laurence Bergreen, "the 'ragtime' melody Berlin devised . . . was actually a march: a safe choice, for a march suggested ragtime without incurring the liability of being ragtime. His melody employed only a brief jumpy phrase of being ragtime."[7]

"Alexander" does have features of ragtime, however. At the most general level, it "has to do with the Negro," as contemporary writers insist was one measure of ragtime:[8] Its obviously black protagonists make it a "coon" song, a label that was sometimes put on the song in advertising copy and in the press. Beyond that, it has structural elements in common with ragtime. The claim that it was the first popular song with a chorus in a key different from that of the verse is simply wrong, and pointless in any event, since a shift of key for the chorus never became an important feature of subsequent Tin Pan Alley songs. As noted in Chapter Two, three earlier songs by Berlin himself, "Wild Cherries," "Grizzly Bear," and "Oh, That Beautiful Rag," have choruses in the subdominant. All three were written and published as piano rags before being reworked into songs, and this is exactly the point: Instrumental ragtime pieces, like marches of the period, usually move to the subdominant for the trio, which became the chorus if the piece was converted into a song. By fitting "Alexander" with a chorus in the subdominant, Berlin was making a musical connection with ragtime. The often-noted fact that "Alexander's" chorus is thirty-two bars in length, rather than sixteen as in most songs of the period, can be explained in the same way: While most strains in piano rags are sixteen measures long, they are intended to be repeated, with a second ending; so thirty-two-bar AA' segments are a feature of piano rags, as well as marches, waltzes, and other dances.

Also, despite assertions to the contrary, Berlin's music for "Alexander" does make repeated, if simplistic, references to rhythmic patterns associated with ragtime. The chief motif of the verse, repeated a number of times, places an accent on a weak beat in the right hand (and voice), and the chorus just as insistently features a short-long-short pattern suggesting the "cakewalk" figure common to proto-ragtime pieces of the 1880s and 1890s and persisting in the early rags of James Scott and his peers before yielding to more sophisticated syncopations.[9] There is, of course, a difference between the "cakewalk" rhythm in Scott's "The Fascinator"

and the rhythm permeating the chorus of "Alexander."

Come on and hear,———Come on and hear——— Al- ex- an-der's rag-time

band,——— Come on and hear,——— Come on and hear,———

But the listener hears both as short-long-short patterns, and in fact the two are not always clearly distinguished from one another in performance.

Dismissals of "Alexander" from the canon of ragtime music have been based on latter-day notions of what constitutes a piece of ragtime. Edward

Berlin has argued forcefully that the Ragtime Revival's insistence on making the term "ragtime" synonymous with "piano ragtime" has no historical justification, since in the first years of the twentieth century many popular songs and pieces for instrumental ensembles, particularly marching or concert bands, were considered to be ragtime also.[10] If one wishes to understand why "Alexander" was judged to be a piece of ragtime in 1911, one shouldn't compare it only to the piano rags of Scott Joplin and James Scott but also to other ragtime songs of the day and to syncopated pieces played by the bands of John Philip Sousa and Arthur Pryor.

When Alec Wilder, after finding "no elements of ragtime" in "Alexander," modifies this pronouncement by adding "unless the word 'ragtime' simply specified the most swinging and exciting of the new American music,"[11] he comes close to the real issue—that in 1911 a piece of popular music wasn't judged by how it looked on paper, in musical notation, but how it sounded in performance. To understand why period audiences thought that "Alexander" and other songs by Berlin were ragtime pieces, one must listen to the "swinging and exciting" performances by such performers as Stella Mayhew and Blossom Seeley, preserved on period recordings, our only aural access today to the way in which "ragtime" performers, particularly female "coon shouters," projected these songs. As *Variety* explains in a review of a performance by Seeley at the Brighton Theatre in its issue for 24 June 1911, ragtime performance was as much a matter of spirit, attitude, and even stage deportment as of rhythmic patterns: "There is a wild craze on in New York for the 'rag' style of singing and dancing, at which no one has yet shown who can handle this better than she. When Blossom starts those hands agoing, and begins to toddle, you just have to hold tight for fear of getting up and toddling right along with her."

The instrumental accompaniments to period recordings of ragtime songs provide another aural link to what was perceived to be ragtime then. Several phrases of the last chorus of Billy Murray's recording of "Alexander" (Edison Blue Amberol 2048), for instance, are taken by the accompanying orchestra, which sounds like a scaled-down Sousa band playing a ragtime or cakewalk piece, complete with piccolo obbligato and trombone phrase-ending runs; the band accompanying Stella Mayhew in "Grizzly Bear" (Edison Wax Amberol 479) plays an entire chorus of that song in the same style.

In the end, arguments over whether or not "Alexander" draws on specific elements of ragtime or looks like a piece of ragtime on the page, are pointless. It *was* a piece of ragtime music, and as such it helped define the genre for its audiences.

Who Really Wrote "Alexander"?

Questions were raised concerning the authorship of the song almost as soon as it became a hit. As Berlin himself tells it, "two years or so ago, when 'Alexander's Rag-time Band' was a big hit, some one started the report among the publishers that I had paid a negro ten dollars for it and then published it under my own name." The real author might have been the black pianist Lukie Johnson, it was whispered, but even though Johnson himself insisted that he had nothing to do with "Alexander" or any other song by Berlin and no other likely candidate was identified, the rumors refused to die, and Berlin was finally moved to respond:

> When they told me about it, I asked them to tell me from whom I had bought my other successes—twenty-five or thirty of them. And I wanted to know, if a negro could write "Alexander," why couldn't I? Then I told them if they could produce the negro and he had another hit like "Alexander" in his system, I would choke it out of him and give him twenty thousand dollars in the bargain. If the other fellow deserves the credit, why doesn't he go get it? [12]

The controversy flared up again several decades later, this time with Scott Joplin as the purported composer. Joplin's widow was quoted as saying that "after Scott had finished writing [*Treemonisha*], and while he was showing it around, hoping to get it published, someone stole the theme, and made it into a popular song. The number was quite a hit, too, but that didn't do Scott any good." The piece in question was supposedly "Alexander's Ragtime Band." [13] At about the same time, Rudi Blesh and Harriet Janis interviewed a descendent of John Stark, Joplin's most important publisher, who remembered that "the publication of *Alexander's Ragtime Band* brought Joplin to tears because it was his [own] composition." [14] Stark's grandson later elaborated on this story: "Joplin took some music to Irving Berlin, and Berlin kept it for some time. Joplin went back and Berlin said he couldn't use it. When *Alexander's Ragtime Band* came out, Joplin said, 'that's my tune.'" [15] Sam Patterson, Joplin's friend and colleague, reported essentially the same story to Blesh and Janis, adding that Scott identified his "Mayflower Rag" (an unrecovered work) and "A Real Slow Drag" from the opera *Treemonisha* as pieces from which Berlin supposedly stole material.

Attributing these claims to "Joplin's declining mental health," Blesh and Janis downplayed the matter in their book. [16] More recently, Edward Berlin has uncovered circumstantial evidence that Joplin and Berlin almost certainly had contact with one another during the period in question. Although admitting that "there is no information on specific meetings between Irving Berlin and Scott Joplin," he suggests that "they *must* have known each other and that Berlin had the opportunity to hear the score [of *Treemonisha*] prior to its publication," through "the association of both with Henry Waterson and others in the Waterson circle."[17] Waterson was co-owner of Crown Music, a distributor of Joplin's rags and his *School of Ragtime* in 1908–1909. He also owned an interest in Seminary Music, which published eight piano pieces by Joplin in these same years, and was manager and treasurer of the Ted Snyder Company, which Berlin joined as staff lyricist in 1909. All three publishing companies—Crown, Seminary, and Snyder—shared offices at 112 West 38th Street. "Given Joplin's relationship with the Waterson companies," says Edward Berlin, "he might well have brought them the score for examination, thus giving Irving Berlin the opportunity to hear it." He finds some similarity between several measures of Joplin "A Real Slow Drag" and the verse of Berlin's "Alexander" but hastens to add that "the resemblance is not extensive and could not, legally or otherwise, be called a theft." He summarizes:

> We can be pretty sure that Joplin made the charge of musical theft, that the opportunity for it to occur existed, and that there were rumors that Berlin had stolen his song from a black man. However much this convergence of evidence may fuel our speculations, it does not prove the charge.[18]

There's evidence in the lyrics of several of his songs that Irving Berlin heard and admired the playing of black pianists around 1910, as discussed in Chapter Two. Given Joplin's presence in New York at this time, and given the fact that one of Berlin's functions at the Ted Snyder Company was to be on the lookout for publishable music by other composers, Edward Berlin's hypothesis that the young songwriter could have heard Joplin's music in the one of the company's offices, played by a staff musician (since he couldn't read music) or by Joplin himself, is quite plausible. Even if this did happen, however, and even if a phrase or a melodic fragment of one of Joplin's pieces did find its way into "Alexander," it still doesn't follow that Berlin "stole" the song from Joplin. "The theme could simply have lodged itself in Berlin's memory, to be drawn out inadvertently a few months later," as Edward Berlin suggests,[19] and even if Berlin did consciously appropriate a bit of Joplin's music into "Alexander," the song didn't become a hit because of this. I've suggested elsewhere that Berlin had unprecedented success in writing song after song that listeners wanted to hear again and again because

> [he] knew all the music his audience knew, and his songs make use of the common melodic, harmonic and rhythmic patterns of this music and frequently offer direct quotations from one familiar piece or another. The same thing could be said of other Tin Pan Alley songwriters, true enough. But Berlin, more effectively than any of his peers, drew on the collective knowledge and memory

of his audience to fashion dramatic situations and musical phrases similar to those found in songs they already knew, [but] shaped in slightly unexpected ways. His best songs were almost—but not quite—already known to his listeners when heard for the first time. They were old stories with new twists.[20]

Berlin, like other early Tin Pan Alley songwriters, deliberately and routinely used rhythmic, melodic, and harmonic patterns similar to those found in other pieces, as well as direct quotation of lyrics and music from other songwriters, for associative or expressive effect. Ian Whitcomb describes Berlin as "a concoctor, almost an inventor. He wasn't stealing anything from anybody,"[21] and Berlin himself said that songwriters were always attempting to "connect the old phrases in a new way, so that they will sound like a new tune."[22]

If Berlin did quote a fragment of *Treemonisha* in "Alexander's Ragtime Band," it puts Joplin in the company of Georges Bizet, whose opera *Carmen* is quoted in Berlin's "That Opera Rag," of F. Paolo Tosti, whose song "Good Bye" is quoted in "Keep Away From The Fellow Who Owns An Automobile," of Gaetano Donizetti, whose *Lucia di Lammermoor* is quoted in "Opera Burlesque," of Reginald DeKoven, whose "Oh Promise Me" is quoted in "He Promised Me," of Felix Mendelssohn, whose "Spring Song" is quoted in "That Mesmerizing Mendelssohn Tune," of Harry Von Tilzer, whose "Down Where The Wurzburger Flows" is quoted in "I Was Aviating Around"—not to mention Stephen Foster, whose "Old Folks At Home" is quoted in "Alexander's Ragtime Band," and Irving Berlin himself, whose "Alexander's Ragtime Band" is quoted in "Hiram's Band" and many other later songs by Berlin.

As a coda to this discussion, I'd like to toss out the suggestion that, in a most curious way, it could be argued that someone other than Irving Berlin *did* write "Alexander's Ragtime Band" and some of his other songs.

As I've pointed out elsewhere,[23] the lyrics of a number of Berlin's early songs that have black musicians as protagonists could be self-portraits, in that their descriptions of the musical background, piano playing, and songwriting of these protagonists could apply equally to Berlin himself. In "Ephraham Played Upon The Piano," for instance, "any kind of music he could understand, still he didn't play by ear, he played by hand"; and since Ephraham (like Berlin) had no formal musical training, "he had ev'rybody guessin', how he played with such a lovin' tone." The unnamed protagonist of "Piano Man"

> Sits on his stool like a king on the throne,
> And plays and plays with ease,
> Why, the melody just nestles in his finger tips
> And oozes out in the keys.

In "He's A Rag Picker," the protagonist Mose "bangs upon the piano keys, in search of raggy melodies" and "makes an ordinary ditty sound so pretty, like nobody can"; and in "That Humming Rag," Mose writes a tune that everyone is "simply daffy over" and that sets them humming and "act[ing] like so many lunatics"—just as happened with "Alexander's Ragtime Band."

Several decades later, after the emergence of blues and jazz, some white musicians were drawn so strongly to African American music and were so convinced that only blacks could perform it in an "authentic" fashion that they wished, or even imagined, that they were black themselves. The jazz clarinetist Mezz Mezzrow, born Milton Mesirow in Chicago in 1899, stands as the classic instance of this syndrome. His first contact with blacks and their music came in his teens, when he was serving a sentence in the Pontiac Reformatory for car theft. "It was in Pontiac that I dug that Jim Crow man in person," he writes in his autobiography. "During these months I got me a solid dose of the colored man's gift for keeping the life and the spirit in him while he tells of his troubles in music. I heard the blues for the first time, sung in low moanful chants morning, noon and night." As a result of this exposure, he says,

> By the time I reached home, I knew that I was going to spend all my time from then on sticking close to Negroes. They were my kind of people. And I was going to learn their music and play it for the rest of my days. I was going to be a musician, a Negro musician, hipping the world about the blues the way only Negroes can. I didn't know how the hell I was going to do it, but I was straight on what I had to do.[24]

Mezzrow accordingly became a jazz musician, befriended black players and performed with them, lived in Harlem, and at times passed himself off as black.

Berlin did none of these things, of course, but he did develop an honest and deep appreciation for black musicians and their music, and in some of his early songs he created black protagonists with whom he identified so closely that these men became his alter egos. At some level, the Alexanders and Ephrahams and Moses in Berlin's songs of this period are extensions of the songwriter's own ego.

Public identification of Berlin the songwriter with the protagonist of his "Alexander" ran high. The *Telegraph*, for instance, ran a feature story on 8 October 1911, under the headline "Wherein You Meet Irving Berlin, the Leader of 'Alexander's Ragtime Band.'" And even though at first glance the sheet music cover of the song seems to picture a white band, a closer look reveals that the group seems to be racially integrated. The faces of three musicians—the violinist third from right, another one (the shape of whose head suggests negroid features) just under the conductor's left arm, and, most interesting, the "leader man" himself—are hatched, making their

Figure 9. Cover of "Alexander's Ragtime Band."

skin appear darker than that of the other members of the band. Alexander also resembles Berlin in physique and hair style, as can be seen from contemporary photographs of the songwriter. It may be that none of this had anything to do with Berlin, since it's not clear that he had input into the design of the covers of his songs. Nevertheless, someone took pains to see to it that Alexander was pictured as black and that he resembled Berlin.

In the last chorus of a recording of Berlin's "He's A Rag Picker" made by the Peerless Quartet in 1914 (Victor 17655), the song's protagonist, Mose, who has been described in the third person in the lyric, suddenly makes a first-person appearance: He's heard playing the piano in ragtime style, then engaging one of the other singers in dialogue.

> —What you gonna do now, Mose?
> —Why I'se gonna loosen up on these ivories, boy. Now watch these . . . [don't] take yo eye off it, you hear . . . (laughter and chuckles)
> —Can you play "Alexander's Ragtime Band?"
> —Why sure, I'm de man what wrote it! (chuckle)

Berlin may well have coached the singers and supplied the extra material for this recording, including Mose's spoken lines, taken by Arthur Collins, a member of the quartet.[25] Although Berlin was later angered by rumors that a "little black boy" had written "Alexander's Ragtime Band," in this recording a black character, Mose, is allowed to lay claim to the song's authorship. This makes sense only if Berlin regarded Mose as an extension of himself.

Which Came First, the Song or the Rag?

Another controversy has to do with whether "Alexander" originated as a song or as a composition for piano.

The facts seem straightforward. A copyright entry card in the Library of Congress reads:

> ALEXANDER'S RAGTIME BAND; words and music by Irving Berlin. Registered in the name of Ted Snyder Co., under E 252990 following publication March 18, 1911.

The song was published with the famous cover by John Frew showing Alexander and his men performing in a bandstand. Almost half a year later, after the song had begun to enjoy phenomenal success on the stage, in vaudeville, and as an item of sheet music, another copyright was issued to another piece:

> ALEXANDER'S RAGTIME BAND; march and two step, by Irving Berlin; piano. Registered in the name of Ted Snyder Co., under E 265784 following publication September 6, 1911.

Figure 10. Cover of piano version of "Alexander's Ragtime Band."

This piano version, with a cover by E. H. Pfeiffer picturing Pan playing on an archaic double pipe, has a third strain not found in the song itself, a quodlibet combining "Dixie" in the right hand with "Old Folks At Home" in the left.

The claim that the piano piece was written first is apparently based on a passage in the first biography of Berlin, published in 1925 by his friend Alexander Woollcott:

> "Alexander" differed, too, in having been fashioned as an instrumental melody with no words to guide it. As such it had gathered dust on the shelf, wordless and ignored, until one day when he himself needed a new song in a hurry. He had just been elected to the Friars' Club and the first Friars' Frolic was destined for production at the New Amsterdam. He wanted something new to justify his appearance in the bill and so he patched together some words that would serve to carry this neglected tune of which he himself was secretly fond.[26]

Later writers have taken this passage as evidence that the piano rag was written before the song. Ian Whitcomb, for instance, imagines in typically lively and fanciful fashion:

> Early one morning, in one of the Snyder cubicles, [Berlin] knocked out a lively march with a bugle-call motif in the main strain (the trio) plus a snatch of "Swanee River." It had all the other parts and modulations like any decent march or rag classic form. . . . A leftover from the march (which has the same form as classic ragtime) gave the verse a novel twist to the ear: it modulated at the end into the subdominant key, thus setting the chorus onto a fresh path. No popular song had done this before.[27]

And Laurence Bergreen fantasizes that "so intent was Berlin on showing off his newfound expertise as a composer that he chose the risky course of offering the song as an instrumental, though he did endow it with an evocative title, 'Alexander's Ragtime Band.' . . . With its mixed ancestry, the instrumental failed to find an appreciative audience."[28]

This interpretation of the genesis of "Alexander" assumes that Woollcott's phrase "instrumental melody with no words to guide it" is a reference to the later-published piano version of the piece. But a "melody," even one without words, is not at all the same thing as an extended piano composition. As Berlin once explained, the first stage in writing a song could be, at least for him, finding a tune: "I get an idea, either a title or a phrase or a melody, and hum it out into something definite."[29] A number of contemporary sources support Woollcott's report that "Alexander" began life as a *melody*—but not as a piano composition. Rennold Wolf wrote in 1913:

> The greater portion of the *song* was written in ten minutes, and in the offices of the music publishing firm, Watterson, Berlin and Snyder, while five or six

pianos and as many vocalists were making bedlam with songs of the day. Berlin was not impressed by it when the *melody* first came to him. In fact, after playing it over a few times on the piano, he did not take the trouble to note the *melody* on paper. (emphases mine) [30]

Berlin himself was quoted several years later as saying that the piece was "simon-pure inspiration. I had long admired certain of its progressions, but the *melody* came to me right out of the air. I wrote the whole thing in eighteen minutes, surrounded on all sides by roaring pianos and roaring vaudeville actors." [31]

Berlin had never published a piece for piano when "Alexander's Ragtime Band" was copyrighted as a song, nor are any piano pieces listed in the several handwritten inventories, now housed in the Irving Berlin Collection in the Library of Congress, of his unpublished compositions from 1910–1913. Two later songs by Berlin were made into more extended piano pieces, some months after their initial publication, by the addition of new introductions and third strains. "That Mysterious Rag," published as a song in August 1911, was reworked into a "Characteristic Intermezzo" for piano by William Schultz, and "The International Rag," from August 1913, was later converted into a "March and Two-Step." This pattern is similar to what happened with "Alexander's Ragtime Band": in order to tap a different market, a successful song was made into a piano piece. There's no evidence that in 1910 Berlin was interested in, or for that matter capable of, writing a complete piano rag; his first published instrumental piece was the fox-trot "Morning Exercise," copyrighted on 8 October 1914.

Internal evidence supports the argument that the piano piece was an expanded version of the song rather than the other way around. The structure of the piano version of "Alexander" is peculiar, to say the least.

Alexander's Ragtime Band: March and Two-Step: (key: **G**)
    Intro^4 A^{16} Trio (key: **C**) B^{16}B^{16}C^{16}B^{16}B^{16}

A is the verse of "Alexander," B is the chorus, and C is a strain not found in the song. The first two strains (A and B) of most marches and rags are in the tonic key, with the third strain (C) usually in the subdominant; more than half of the piece is thus in the tonic, with the third section (C) affording tonal and melodic contrast. But here a mere twenty measures in the key of the tonic, consisting of the introduction and first strain, are overwhelmed by eighty bars in the subdominant. The obvious explanation for this misshapen tonal structure is that the song, with a verse in the tonic and a chorus in the subdominant, was written first:

Alexander's Ragtime Band: (key: **C**)

      Intro^4 Verse: A^{16} Chorus (key: **F**) B^{16}B^{16}

When a third strain (C) in the subdominant was added to make it into a longer piano piece, it was inserted after the chorus (B), which was already in this key.

Michael Freedland takes the myth of the instrumental genesis of "Alexander" a step further by imagining that it was first performed in an instrumental arrangement by the pit orchestra of a show.

> The lyricless *Alexander's Ragtime Band* had its first public performance by the orchestra on the opening night of the Follies Bergere's *International Revue*. But it appeared that the audience was much more interested in the décor, the girls, the champagne and the menu than they were in the music. . . . Lasky saw the way it was being treated with a splendid indifference—and ordered it out of the show.[32]

Bergreen embroiders this imaginary episode into "the orchestra flailed away at Berlin's instrumental, but the song made little impression."[33]

After this fiasco, Freedland continues, "Berlin tried to forget 'Alexander' and filed the song away" until the Ted Snyder Company was reorganized with Berlin as a partner, thus putting him in a position to "decide for himself which of his numbers he was going to have published." When invited to join the Friars Club and take part in their annual Frolic, he "took 'Alexander' out of mothballs and wrote a set of words to go with it."[34]

This account of the early history of "Alexander," repeated uncritically by later writers, is filled with factual mistakes and outright fabrications, and it plays loose and free with chronology. To give some sense of the problems with Freedland's narration: "Alexander" was not a "lyricless" piece when it was supposedly played by a pit orchestra, since the show in question—which, by the way, was not titled *International Revue*—opened on 27 April 1911, six weeks after "Alexander's Ragtime Band" had been copyrighted and published as a song, complete with text. Nor did Berlin write the "words to go with it" when he supposedly "took it out of the mothballs" for the Friars' Frolic, which had its first performance on 28 May; the lyrics were written before the song's publication in mid-March. Also, the Ted Snyder Company wasn't reorganized into Waterson, Berlin and Snyder until December 1911, by which time countless performances of "Alexander" in several shows and on the vaudeville stage, and sheet music sales of the song running into the hundreds of thousands, had dictated such a move.

There is a far more important issue involved here than a wish to call attention to shabby journalism posing as biography: most of the early history of "Alexander" is known to us only from this sort of offhand and undisciplined research and writing. A song so important to the history of American popular music deserves better.

Alexander's Early History

According to Rennold Wolf, the melody of "Alexander" came to Berlin sometime in the summer or fall of 1910, but "he did not take the trouble to note the melody on paper."

> He might never have completed the song had it not been for a trip to Palm Beach, Florida, which months later he arranged to take with Jean Schwartz and Jack M. Welch. Just before train time he went to his offices to look over his manuscripts, in order to leave the best of them for publication during his absence. Among his papers he found a memorandum referring to "Alexander," and after considerable reflection he recalled its strains. Largely for the lack of anything better with which to kill time, he sat at the piano and completed the song.[35]

Although I haven't been able to pinpoint the date of the trip to Florida that prompted Berlin to complete his song, it had to be before March 1911, when "Alexander" was sent off to Washington to be copyrighted.

A banner across the top of the cover of "Alexander" announces that the song was "Intruduced by Emma Carus"; the spelling error wasn't corrected for many years, after millions of copies had been sold. Carus was an established star as an actress, comedienne, dancer, and singer, both on the legitimate stage and in vaudeville, noted particularly for her "coon shouting" in a voice often described as a "female baritone." Born in Berlin on 18 March 1879, she claimed to have "learned the negro dialect from a colored man, known only to posterity as 'Frog Eyes.' This dusky person also taught me to do the todolo dancing step and cakewalk."[36]

Berlin and his publisher must have had good reason to believe that Carus was the first to perform "Alexander" in public, a claim found also in the promotional material for one of the earliest recordings of the song[37] and in every biography of Berlin. But no one has suggested when and where this first performance took place.

On Monday, 17 April 1911, Carus, billed as "The Whoop-Em-Up Singing Star" and "The Big Noise in Comedy," began a week's engagement as the headline performer in the Big Easter Vaudeville Carnival at Chicago's American Music Hall. The *Chicago Tribune* for 16 April says that this is "her first appearance in vaudeville in two years," and although this claim may have been somewhat of an exaggeration, it was her first vaudeville turn in at least a year. She had costarred with Eddie Foy in *Up and Down Broadway*, a Lew Fields production that opened at New York's Casino

Theatre on 18 July 1910, ran there through the summer, then toured through the fall and winter before finally closing in Albany in mid-February. A search of the weekly performers' routes in *Variety* and *Billboard* has turned up no bookings for Carus between the closing of *Up and Down Broadway* and her mid-April engagement in Chicago, which was therefore the first possible occasion on which she could have sung "Alexander."

A writer for the *Chicago News* reported on 19 April that Carus was "splendidly dressed and fitted out with a fine repertoire of songs ranging from ballads to ragtime," and a notice in the *Chicago Tribune* for 23 April, announcing that she would be held over at the American for a second week, added that her present act contained only "New Songs." The Chicago correspondent for *Variety* wrote on 22 April that Carus had indeed been the "big noise" of the bill and was "the same old Emma with new songs." *Billboard*'s review, on 26 April, noted that "Miss Carus was next to closing and sang five songs, with two of them going big and the others fair."

Cutting her second week in Chicago short, she accepted an engagement at Hammerstein's in New York. A review in *Variety* for 26 April reported that

> Emma Carus hove into sight at 10:40, considered early at Hammerstein's these days, but the audience was already a bit weary and many started to leave. The singer got a little fun from the walking out, but it didn't hold anyone in. Emma sang five songs, two too many. It would have been better for everyone concerned if she had bowed away after the "rag" number.

After an engagement at the Temple Theatre in Detroit, on 9–16 May, Carus was back in the New York area. The *Morning Telegraph* for 20 May reported:

> Emma Carus will return to vaudeville next week at the New Brighton Theatre after two years in the legitimate as co-star with Eddie Foy. She has a monologue written by Vincent Bryan and five new songs which are characteristically of the Carus kind. Several of them were written by Irving Berlin. The song with which she is expected to "get them" is "When I'm in Town I'm Lonesome."[38]

But another song by Berlin proved to be the hit of the bill, as noted in a prophetic review in the *Sun* for 25 May:

> [She] sings new songs, which are the best she has ever had, and which have been written especially for her. It is in her songs that Miss Carus is most impressive, and she has five new ones that are quite worthy of the headliner. "Alexander" has all the swing and metrical precision of "Kelly," which Miss Carus brought to the country with her from England three years ago. In a few days "Alexander" will be whistled on the streets and played in the cafés. It is the

most meritorious addition to the list of popular songs introduced this season. The vivacious comedienne soon had her audience singing the choruses with her, and those who did not sing whistled.[39]

Carus offered her five new songs in later engagements at Hammerstein's Roof, the Fifth Avenue Theatre, the Criterion Theatre in Asbury Park, the Chase Theatre in Washington, and elsewhere. By late August, "Alexander" had been taken up by so many other performers that she decided to give it a rest, replacing it with "Oh You Beautiful Doll" by Seymour Brown and Nat Ayer, which the *Morning Telegraph* for 29 August found to be "a quite pleasing successor to 'Alexander's Ragtime Band.'" In October she left vaudeville again for the legitimate stage, joining rehearsals for John Cort's *Jingaboo*, then leaving that never-opened show to take the lead role in Lew Fields's *The Wife Hunters*, in which her big number was a "coon" song entitled "Mammy Jinny."

Although none of the notices of Carus's Chicago engagement of mid-April specifies that she sang "Alexander," it's clear that she prepared five new songs for her return to vaudeville and performed them in each of her bookings that spring and summer, beginning in Chicago. "Alexander" was identified as one of the five in subsequent reviews. In view of suggestions that "Alexander" was a failure early in its history, it's worth noting that virtually every review singles it out, either by title or indirectly as the "rag" piece in the set, as being received enthusiastically by her audiences.

As a cast member of *Up and Down Broadway* himself, singing "Sweet Italian Love" and "Oh, That Beautiful Rag" with Ted Snyder, Berlin had been in daily contact with Carus over a period of some months in the summer and early fall of 1910. Even earlier, he had written two songs for her to be interpolated into another Lew Fields production, *The Jolly Bachelors*, although she never sang them in the show, having left the cast before the opening on 10 January 1910. And an unidentified clipping from a Buffalo newspaper on the occasion of Berlin's marriage in that city to Dorothy Goetz early in 1912, preserved in a scrapbook in the Irving Berlin Collection in the Library of Congress, reports that "[he] is the discovery of Emma Carus, the well-known musical comedy star, who, with a party of friends, heard him sing at one of New York's East Side entertainments. It was the interest and influence of Miss Carus that gave [him] his first start and his gratitude is one of the pleasing traits of his character." Whether or not all of this is true, the picture that emerges is that Berlin wrote several songs for Carus, probably as a result of their contact in *Up and Down Broadway* and earlier, that she agreed to perform these songs on her return to vaudeville, that "Alexander" was one of them,[40] and that Carus sang it on her first turn in vaudeville after the show closed.

Carus deserves full credit for introducing "Alexander," but much of the subsequent early history of the song was tied up with several musical shows, to be examined in turn.

The Folies Bergere

Sometime in 1910, Henry Harris and Jesse Lasky decided to open a restaurant-theater on the French model as a luxurious place of entertainment for New York City's Tired Business Man. The Folies Bergere, as they named the place, was located on 46th Street just off Broadway. The restaurant, in the front of the house, had 286 seats at tables, all facing the stage; the boxes were also equipped with tables for food and drink, while the orchestra and gallery had regular theater seats. Total seating capacity was 700.

The *Morning Telegraph* reported that "in the history of New York theatre-going there perhaps has never been an event that equalled the opening of the new Folies Bergere, [which] is at once a cafe, a music hall, a theatre, a restaurant, a club."[41] Admission tickets for opening night, 27 April 1911, were sold at auction a week earlier, bringing in $14,242, a handsome sum for the day. The restaurant opened for dining and drinking at 6:00 P.M., with two orchestras and an Italian singer entertaining early comers. The stage entertainment began at 8:15 with *Hell*, a burlesque (or travesty) by Rennold Wolf with music by Maurice Levi, followed by a ballet, *Temptation*, featuring forty dancers choreographed by Alfredo Curti of Paris; the three-part show finished with a second burlesque, *Gaby*, with music by Paul Lincke of Berlin, satirizing the well-publicized affair between the entertainer Gaby Deslys and the king of Portugal. After a brief break, a cabaret show with half a dozen vaudeville acts ran from 11:15 until 1 o'clock in the morning.

It was on this opening night, according to Freedland and Bergreen, that the show's pit orchestra "flailed away" at an instrumental version of "Alexander" with such disastrous results that the song was dropped from the show and "shelved" for a while. In order to rid Berlin's biography of this myth, it is necessary to examine in some detail his complicated involvement with this complicated show.

On 15 April, two full weeks before opening night, "the entire organization, including phalanxes of chorus girls, affluent prima donnas, lugubrious comedians, a large orchestra, various managers, and relatives, friends and chauffeurs of managers" went off to Atlantic City for rehearsals and a trial run at the Apollo Theatre.[42] Berlin, who had written two songs for *Gaby* in collaboration with Ted Snyder and Alfred Bryan ("Down To The Folies Bergere" and "Spanish Love") and another one alone ("I Beg Your Pardon, Dear Old Broadway"), came along to coach the singers in these pieces.

A first run-through of *Hell*, in which Berlin was not involved, lasted for four hours, an impossible length for the opening third of the bill. As a result, as *Variety* reported on 22 April, *"[Hell]* will be cut considerably before opening in New York" and "there was no end to the changes made by the chorus and female principals." A production number entitled "The Messenger Boy" was an obvious weak link. Maurice Levi, the show's composer, wasn't on hand to patch things up, and in a panic Rennold Wolf and the lyricist, Channing Pollock, went to Berlin's suite in Young's Hotel, where Berlin quickly came up with a tune that seemed promising as a replacement number. The lyrics proved to be more of a problem.

> All night, until dawn was breaking, [Berlin] sat on the [piano] stool, playing the same melody over and over and over again, while two fagged and dejected lyric writers struggled and heaved to fit it with words. . . . One cigarette replaced another as he pegged away; a pitcher of beer, stationed at one end of the keyboard, was replenished frequently; and there he sat trying patiently to suggest, to two minds that were completely worn out by long rehearsals and overwork, a lyric that would fit his melody.[43]

As the *Morning Telegraph* for 28 April describes the fruit of this night-long session, "in another number, composed by Irving Berlin, and entitled 'Don't Keep the Taxi Waiting, Dear,' a dozen messenger boys delivered notes in the audience, notes to which facetious answers were afterwards read from the stage." Although the piece remained in the show for its entire run, it was never copyrighted or published, and all that remains is a fragment of the lyric.

> Dearie, please keep the taxi waiting;
> Dearie, don't be so hesitating—
> There'll be just you and me.
> And if your wife comes buzzin',
> Tell her that I'm your cousin—
> Please keep it waiting, dear, for me.[44]

Berlin approached Lasky at some point with the suggestion that his recently published "Alexander" be included in the show, but "the management refused to accept [it]."[45] Nothing in Wolf's account suggests that the song was actually tried out, and there's no trace of it in playbills for the opening night or in any of the notices or reviews of the show.

A member of the cast did attempt to introduce "Alexander" into *Hell* on his own initiative, however.

> It was the habit at the time to interpolate songs by composers other than those working on the show. Irving Berlin was brought in. He played his latest opus and on a Wednesday matinee in Atlantic City the song was introduced for the first time on any stage. Without permission the star, Otis Harlan, added the song during a pantomime he performed with Taylor Holmes. The sketch was a burlesque of a prize fight between two society gentlemen. Harlan sang the song

a capella and brought down the house. Unfortunately the management didn't appreciate the song and it was never again sung in the show. The song was "Alexander's Ragtime Band." [46]

To sum up Berlin's contributions to the opening night of the Folies Bergere, he was commissioned to write three songs for the final burlesque, *Gaby*, and at the last minute he wrote the music for a replacement production number in the opening burlesque, *Hell*. "Alexander's Ragtime Band" was interpolated into *Hell* one night during the show's trial run in Atlantic City but did not survive to the New York opening.

As a final note, "Alexander" did make it to the Folies Bergere eventually, although not as a number in *Hell*. After shutting down for three weeks in July because of poor attendance and the summer heat, the show reopened on 31 July with its three parts in a different order—the ballet first, *Gaby* second, *Hell* as the closing number. *Variety's* review on 5 August reports that "Alexander" was a prominent part of the new evening-ending cabaret show, entitled "Hello Paris."

> Two of the acts use "Alexander," and the big finishing number is a "Grizzly" dance. One girl played "Alexander" on the violin. The other act sang it. "Alexander" is a hot old rag, but it is apt to never grow old, for the reason that no two sing or play it the same. Irving Berlin is some little ragger, and when he wrote "Alexander," Irving built himself a monument at the same time.

The Folies Bergere closed down after little more than a year. As *Variety* observed on 27 September 1912, "[although] the restaurant portion of the enterprise has yielded a profit, the scheme has proven itself impractical owing to the limited capacity of the house." Rennold Wolf, after reporting that the Folies Bergere lost about $400,000 before it closed, offers the opinion that "no feature of the gigantic failure was so tragic as the lack of judgement that resulted in the declination of 'Alexander's Ragtime Band.' The Folies Bergère might have had the exclusive rights of this song for nothing, but it was turned aside, only a few weeks later to sweep the country." [47]

The Friars' Frolic of 1911

In the fall of 1910 Berlin was invited to join the Friars Club, an organization of actors, musicians, writers, entrepreneurs, and other professionals of the theatrical and literary world. An annual Friars' Frolic had been mounted since 1908, with club members performing; since the group's meeting place at 107 West 45th Street, the "Monastery," was proving to be inadequate, it was decided to make the show for 1911 the biggest ever and to take it on the road to raise money for the Friars' Building Fund.

The *Friars' Frolic of 1911*, advertised in the *New York Times* as "A Gigantic Entertainment with a Host of Original Novelties & Unique Features by a Sensational Cast of Players" and in the *Chicago Tribune* as "$1,000,000 worth of Vaudeville," brought together a veritable who's who of the day's male entertainers (it was a male-only club): George M. Cohan and his father, Jerry; the female impersonator Julian Eltinge; the comedian and dancer William Collier; the comedians Richard Carle, Raymond Hitchcock, Emmett Corrigan, and Harry Kelly; the minstrel performer and entrepreneur Lew Dockstader; the songwriters Jean Schwartz and Ernest Ball; the singer Andrew Mack; Sam Harris; R. A. Burnside; Jean Havez; and dozens of others. As a special feature, Joe Weber and Lew Fields revived their "Dutch" act for the first time in many years.

The three-and-a-half-hour entertainment, opening at the New Amsterdam Theatre in New York on Sunday, 28 May, began with "an old time minstrel show" in four segments, each with a different interlocutor and end men, followed by "The Pullman Porter Ball," a minstrel sketch written by George M. Cohan and starring Julian Eltinge in one of his famous "wench" roles. The second half of the show was an extended olio, beginning with "The Friars' Piano Bugs," a parody of Jesse Lasky's Pianophiends act, which according to the next day's *New York Times* "required seven pianos and nine composers and songwriters [who] played and sang their own compositions." Next, according to the souvenir program, came "Two Hot Potatoes," a comic sketch with George M. Cohan and William Collier; a burlesque of the fourth act of Shakespeare's *Julius Caesar*; a monologue by George (Honey Boy) Evans; a "Prophetic Sketch" by Walter Hackett titled "The Moving Picture King"; and a concluding comic sketch, "The Great Suggestion," written by Bertram Marburgh and Bennet Musson. Numbers were apparently added and dropped from one performance to another; the special appearance of Weber and Fields, for instance, wasn't listed on the program and took place only on opening night, and none of the reviews mentions the *Julius Caesar* burlesque.

The twenty-two-year-old Irving Berlin more than held his own in this company. According to *Variety* for 3 June, "in the minstrel first part Mr. Berlin delivered 'Ephraim' to several encores, with the united voices of the blackface troupe behind him,"[48] and his contribution to "Piano Bugs" was equally well received:

> Jean Schwartz (at a baby grand), Ernest R. Ball, George Lodge, George Botsford, Tom Kelly, Les Copeland, Harry Williams, Ted Barron and Irving Berlin were the upright pianists. This "act" held enough material for a full evening of songful joy. Messrs. Berlin, Williams and Ball supplied two songs, Williams and Berlin making a "two-act" of themselves, with Irving Berlin attending to the singing mostly, while Harry Williams did an acrobatic dance to close that disclosed he's not as stout as he looks. With the music and the songs, the skit was a huge success.

Although "Alexander's Ragtime Band" isn't mentioned here by title, Percy Hammond's review in the *Chicago Tribune* for 5 June verifies that it was one of the two pieces performed by Berlin and Williams:

> Another incident of the entertainment was the accumulation of nine composers of popular music and nine pianos upon the stage at one time, the result being considerable furore. Mr. Harry Williams, whose principal opus is "I'm Afraid to Go Home in the Dark," assisted a bright brunette young person to sing "Alexander's Rag Time Band," and they sang it so effectively that encores were as the sands of the sea.

After this one performance in New York, the cast boarded the chartered train that would be their home for the next ten days, taking them on the following itinerary:

May 29   Atlantic City, Apollo Theatre
May 30   Philadelphia, Chestnut Street Opera House (matinee)
May 30   Baltimore, Academy of Music
May 31   Pittsburgh, Nixon Theatre
June 1   Cleveland, Euclid Avenue Opera House
June 2   Cincinnati, Music Hall
June 3   St. Louis, Olympic Theatre
June 4   Chicago, The Auditorium
June 5   Detroit, Detroit Opera House
June 6   Buffalo, Star Theatre (matinee)
June 6   Rochester, Lyceum Theatre
June 7   Boston, Boston Theatre
June 8   New York, New Amsterdam Theatre

The show played to large and enthusiastic audiences everywhere. The Chicago performance alone took in some $10,000, and *Variety* reported on 17 June that the tour "netted the club $60,000, and assured it of the new club house so badly needed." On 21 October 1915, a cornerstone was laid at 106–110 West 48th Street for the Friars' new clubhouse.

Thus, between 28 May and 8 June "Alexander" was given high-visibility performances by the composer himself in thirteen of America's major cities.

The Merry Whirl

In the first decades of the century, burlesque houses weren't yet the strip-tease palaces they were to become later. Their productions in fact featured entertainment quite similar to that offered on the vaudeville stage: mixtures of singing, dancing, comic routines, and, most important, burlesque versions of currently popular dramatic and musical works. Burlesque did tend to emphasize chorus girls in scanty costumes and suggestive comic material, and the level of talent tended to be somewhat below that found on the legitimate stage and in vaudeville. Under the management of Cliff Gordon and Bobby North, the Columbia Theatre, the Broadway house of the Eastern Burlesque Wheel, set out to offer a "higher" class of entertainment. For the New York summer season of 1911, the two men decided to run a revised version of a show called *The Merry Whirl*, which had been playing on the road for some months.

The new production, which opened at the Columbia on 12 June, was "as classy as burlesque ever held—classier even," according to *Variety* for 17 June. The large, elaborately costumed cast included "sixteen chorus girls, eight 'ponies' and four 'show' girls, also six chorus men to give them strength." Of the principals, Mildred Klaine came in for particular praise as "a classy miss who can dance, sings well, handles herself decorously, and comes under the classification of an actress, [which] makes itself felt." The reviewer found the show a "meritorious" one, as "becomes a high ranking burlesque organization going much higher than it did a couple of years ago," although he took exception to such details as the overly intimate fondling of a human dressmaking dummy by one of the male principals. There was no mistaking the high point of the show, wrote the reviewer:

> The big song hit of the evening was "Alexander's Rag Time Band," sung by [James C.] Morton and [Frank F.] Moore, with the chorus in for a "Grizzly Bear" dance. The "Rag Time Band," arriving near the finale of the first part, was so strong nothing could follow it. Another somewhat similar number in the second part "Paris Push" (from "The Deacon and the Lady") seemed mild in comparison. Had the places of the two numbers been changed, the "Rag Time Band" song would have done much to hold up the latter end of the performance.

The *Morning Telegraph*'s account of the show, on 13 June, stressed that "the musical numbers are a distinct feature. The most of them are of the ragtime variety, or border on it." In particular, "in two or three of the musical numbers [sung by Morton and Moore], notably 'Alexander's Ragtime Band,' the audience yesterday afternoon stopped the show with its applause."

"Alexander" was in *The Merry Whirl* in the first place largely through the efforts of Berlin's friend Max Winslow, now an employee of the Ted Snyder Company.

> Max asked Ted Snyder to call with him on Aaron Hoffman, who was in charge of the production, and try to induce Mr. Hoffman to give the song a chance in the show. When the couple reached the stage door a boy got Winslow's name wrong, and Mr. Hoffman sent out word that he was too busy. The next morning on the subway Max met Aaron and told him of the "turn down." Hoffman explained, and asked Max to come around that afternoon. The song went into

the show, and the verdict of the first night crowd at the Columbia was that "Alexander" made "The Merry Whirl" that season.[49]

In an otherwise slow season for the New York stage, made worse by a spell of uncommonly hot weather, *The Merry Whirl* went from strength to strength, in large part because of Morton and Moore's performance of "Alexander." Business was so good that on 18 June the management ran an ad in the *Morning Telegraph* trumpeting the show as "The Sensation That Has Made Broadway Jealous" and advising that tickets for this new "Stunning, Startling, Surprising, Stupendous, Soothing Show" were on sale four weeks in advance. *Variety* reported on 8 July that receipts for the show had reached $5,000 the previous week and added on 29 July:

> "The Merry Whirl" caused a lot of talk in show circles last week, through the business it pulled into the Columbia. Three nights were complete sellouts, with matinees on "good days" running over $300. The total was $7,000. It has decided the Gordon & North firm, and the management of the theatre, to keep the show at the house, until the "Trocaderos" come in Aug. 17. "The Whirl" may even stay there for the five days of the Aug. 5 week, leaving the Columbia Friday to open at the 125th Street Music Hall, Saturday.

The first week of August was more profitable yet, with receipts of $7,400. The announcement in *Variety* on 12 August that the show would end its New York run and "proceed over the regular Eastern Wheel route assigned to it" was made "much to the regret of the house and the management."

The departure of *The Merry Whirl* from the Columbia didn't prevent patrons of New York's burlesque houses from seeing and hearing "Alexander." The show moved to Hurtig and Seamon's Music Hall for a week before leaving town, and its successor at the Columbia, Charles C. Waldron's *Trocaderos*, which had opened in Albany the week before, also depended heavily on Berlin's song.

> "Alexander's Rag Time Band" was moved up from the second to the first act. The question remains what is to follow that. All the numbers after seem tame. "The Whirl" gave "Alexander" twice daily at the same house, but along comes Finney and his company literally tearing the house apart with it. The number was roughened up some in the dancing, but it was permissable, for it brought laughs, more permissable in fact than to have those chorus girls continually harping on that side to side swing that they always did in any number where dance steps could be used. Minnie Burke and Geo. Brennen led the "Band" number.[50]

Almost simultaneously, *The Whirl of Mirth*, a show with a title obviously chosen to lure the unwary theater patron into expecting to see and hear *The Merry Whirl*, opened at the Casino Theater in Brooklyn with two separate acts in the olio portion offering versions of "Alexander."

"Alexander" in Vaudeville

While the *Friars' Frolic* and *The Merry Whirl* brought "Alexander" to the attention of the theater-going public, performances in vaudeville gave Berlin's song the even more extensive exposure that translated into phenomenal sales of sheet music. It's difficult to track the performance history of any given song in vaudeville; playbills and advertisements give names of performers but not their repertory, and reviews and other notices in newspapers and weeklies such as *Variety* and *Billboard* rarely mention individual songs. While what follows is far from a complete account of "Alexander" in vaudeville, the fact that even this much information can be pieced together attests to the special nature of the song and its extraordinary reception.

As detailed earlier, Emma Carus introduced "Alexander" to Chicago and to the world at the American Music Hall on 17 April. Less than a week later, on 22 April, the *Morning Telegraph* carried a half-page advertisement of Neil McKinley's forthcoming appearance at the Bronx Theatre featuring several "syncopated melodies," including "Some of These Days" and "Carolina Rag."[51] The *Telegraph*'s review of McKinley's performance, carried on 26 April, reported that he had sung three ragtime songs, of which "The Leader of the Band" was singled out for particular mention. Reviewers had to depend on their ears for the titles of unfamiliar songs, and it seems likely that the piece in question was Berlin's "Alexander."

By early May, even before it was featured in *The Merry Whirl*, Berlin's new song was being picked up by "two or three people in vaudeville" in addition to Carus and McKinley.[52] According to the songwriter Ray Walker, this phase of "Alexander"'s history began at a Madison Avenue cafe offering vaudeville-style entertainment for its patrons.

> Eddie Miller and Helen Vincent were appearing at the Garden Cafe, in New York City, and were the first to sing the song in public. . . . I heard "Alexander's Ragtime Band" in Ted Snyder's office and thought it would be a good number for the Garden. I asked Max Winslow, manager of the firm, to buy zobos (toy musical instruments) for the song, to be used at the Garden, but he refused as he said the song wasn't worth it, and the toys would cost $5. Paul Salvin, owner of the Garden, put out the money for the zobos [himself] and the song was used the next night there. It was a sensation. Winslow . . . heard what a hit it was so [he] went to the Columbia Theatre and brought the manager of the show there over to the Garden to hear the song--next week it was in the burlesque show at the Columbia. The rest is history.[53]

Adele Oswald began singing "Alexander" in May and June, including it in her act at the Brighton Beach Music Hall.

> Miss Oswald has an engaging personality, wears her stage frocks becomingly, and has a soprano voice of good range and quality. She sang four numbers

Monday night, "Twilight," "Alexander's Ragtime Band," "Come Back, My Antonio," and "I'm Lonesome when Alone," changing dresses for each song. Her
biggest hit was made with the "Alexander" and "Lonesome" songs. . . . Barring
a slight nervousness and her inability to make her hats behave when bows were
in order, she got along swimmingly, and was voted a capital entertainer by the
audience.[54]

By the end of June the floodgates had opened, and throughout the summer and fall of 1911 "Alexander" dominated vaudeville in a way that no
song had before or would again, in performance by vocalists and instru-
mentalists of every level of talent. Among these were Lillian Graham and
Edith Conrad, two young women with no previous theatrical experience
who were booked into Hammerstein's in July. The two had been in the
news, although not as entertainers; they had been jailed for shooting a
businessman, W.E.B. Stokes, who had allegedly made improper advances
to them. *Variety*'s review of their act, appearing on 22 July, is worth quot-
ing at some length for the glimpse it gives into the workings of vaudeville.

> While Max Winslow, of the Ted Snyder Music company was rehearsing the
> Misses Graham and Conrad in "Alexander's Rag Time Band," Willie Hammer-
> stein standing by, remarked, "Why don't you go on with them and strengthen
> it up?" "Not for a million dollars," replied Max. "Oh, go on," said Willie,
> "They won't shoot you." And that's the whole story about the sharpshooting
> girls. The audience wants to see them because they have been well advertised.
> They pinked a young man of about sixty-five in the legs. They say he was a
> fresh old guy anyway, while the old guy says the girls were out for a little easy
> change. But the audiences won't believe the old guy's statement, after seeing
> the Misses Graham and Conrad. They don't look anything like that kind of a
> girl at all. It is their appearance, pretty and refined, which passed them over so
> well at the two shows Monday. Neither of the girls will claim to have had any
> stage experience of moment. Miss Conrad has the most confidence. Miss Gra-
> ham seems shy and retiring. She played the piano, while Miss Conrad sang. But
> Miss Graham was so nervous she never knew the key she was playing in, nor
> the key Miss Conrad was on. The matinee audience recognized this right away,
> and applauded the young women in the middle of the song to reassure them.

Variety's review on 5 August of an act by O'Donnell and Framey describes how "Alexander" was made into a production number, even in
vaudeville: "This sister act has been handed the 'Alexander Rag' outfit that
is being passed around by the publishers of the song. It consists of a set of
band uniforms and some zobos. The zobos and uniforms are worn by men,
and they march around the audience with the two girls in the lead. The
same thing is being done in nearly all the restaurants, where singers are
part of the program."
By summer's end *Variety* was calling "Alexander" the "musical sensation
of the decade,"[55] and the review on 2 September of Adele Oswald's perfor-

mance of the song at the Majestic Theatre in Chicago claimed that "Alexander" had become "as familiar to the Majestic going public as 'Dixie' is to the southerner"--this only four months after Emma Carus had introduced it. And the song's presence was felt even when it wasn't being performed; Kathleen Clifford finished up a scene in Gus Edwards's *High Flyers* at the Fifth Avenue vaudeville house with a ragtime song, which *Variety* said on 29 July was "pretty weak after some of the 'Alexander Band' numbers on this and other bills."

One climax in "Alexander's" early history came in September when Berlin sang it himself in vaudeville. A notice in *Variety* for 2 September said that the young songwriter, "who is understood to have refused a guaranteed income of $40,000 yearly for the sole rights to publish his compositions, something now held by Ted Snyder & Co., [will open] in vaudeville at the Hammerstein's, Sept. 11." In a departure from the usual practice whereby "composer-vaudevillians" (or singer-songwriters, as we would call them today) "had a grand piano as a necessary adjunct to their turns," Berlin was accompanied by the theater orchestra. According to reviews, his set included "Alexander," "That Mysterious Rag," "Ephraham Played Upon The Piano," "That Kazzatsky Dance," an Italian dialect song titled "Marie, Marie" (possibly "Sweet Marie, Make-a Rag-a-Time Dance Wid Me"), and the otherwise unknown "Don't Wait Until Your Father Comes Home." "Berlin has a dandy style in delivering a song," noted the reviewer for *Variety*. "A pleasing personality assures him of success."

In a crescendo that reached a climax in the fall, vaudeville acts of ever-expanding diversity and level of talent offered the song in response to the public's apparently insatiable appetite for it. For instance:

- *Variety* for 2 September records a performance by "three boys" calling themselves the Lyric Trio. The reviewer observes that, judging from their other two numbers, it was a good thing that they included "Alexander" on their turn, since the song "will bring its own encores, whether used as a song or instrumental piece. The Lyric Trio caught a couple [of encores] with it, rather a low percentage nowadays for that number."
- "It was a big night for the 'Ragtime Band' at the Colonial Theatre," according to *Variety* for 23 September. "Merrill and Otto danced to its strains, the Musical Cuttys put it over with great effect with their brass instruments while Burt Green was unable to resist playing it in different keys on the piano. The audience seemed to never tire of it."
- The same week, an act calling itself Nace Murray and Girls was booked at the Thalia in Chicago. "Every song has been well fitted and equally well costumed," reported *Variety*." Opening with a 'Tommy Atkins' number (led by Murray) the [five] girls go into 'Alexander's Band.' "

- *The Cleveland Press* reported on 27 September that five of the acts booked into Keith's Hippodrome that week had performed "Alexander" at the final rehearsal on Monday afternoon. Mr. Daniels, the theater manager, insisted that four of the acts "cut that band song out" and instructed the theater orchestra to play the song just once during the show. "But one [other] act got past the manager. It was the Majestic Trio [which] didn't need the orchestra. There was another meeting Tuesday, and all in reference to that band song."
- The Big City Four featured Berlin's song at the Colonial the following week, says *Variety* for 30 September. "With the quartet singing 'Alexander's Ragtime Band' and 'Mysterious Rag' at the finish and 'Land of Harmony' for an encore, 'The Rosary' piece wasn't missed," the last comment being a reference to Ethelbert Nevin's perenially popular song.
- The same issue of *Variety* reported that at Hammerstein's, the "Hebrew comedians" Joe Morris and Charles Allen offered "Irish songs and parodies. The 'Alexander' parody contains little sense."
- A banjo ensemble, The Sandreos, "started well, playing a popular medley mixing a little classical music in between the popular songs. There is some trick playing done with the aid of the piano, both playing the two instruments at the same time." And, concludes this review in *Variety* for 7 October, "of course, they finished with 'Alexander's Band.'"
- "[Evelyn] Ware has an excellent song arrangement, but nature overlooked her for a voice," quibbled *Variety* on 18 October, in reviewing that singer's vaudeville turn. "If your voice doesn't show an operatic quality, don't let a little thing like that stand between you and the stage. Just pick out several songs and be sure 'Alexander's Ragtime Band' is in the lot, and then lay in a wardrobe that would make the coronation display of gowns assume one deep shade of envious green." The reviewer suggests that Ware "needs much coaching, and should get some one to teach her the 'raggedy' steps for the 'Alexander' number."
- On 9 November, "Alexander" was performed on a vaudeville/cabaret program offered by the all-black Clef Club orchestra, under the direction of James Reese Europe.[56]

"Other songs by others come in and are liked, but the present season Irving Berlin has had nearly to himself," observed *Variety* on 23 December in a year-end assessment of "Berlin, the Hit Maker." The article suggests that Berlin "paralyzed the popular music retail business for over four months with 'Alexander's Ragtime Band.' All the publishers complained because 'Alexander' was the only seller. They held back numbers waiting for the 'Alexander' sales to drop off." In the fall another song by Berlin, "That Mysterious Rag," began to replace "Alexander" in the major variety and burlesque houses, "through the fact that 'Alexander' was used in such a large number of shows on the road they did not care to repeat it in their troupe."

Recordings

More commercial recordings were made of "Alexander" than of any other early song by Berlin. The first one, recorded for Columbia by Arthur Collins and Byron G. Harlan on 7 June, was released in September 1911. Victor's monthly record supplement noted that " 'Alexander's Ragtime Band' is a colored organization which will make any audience sit up and take notice"[57] in announcing its version of "Alexander", which remained in the Victor catalog for more than a decade, until 1922. Collins and Harlan also recorded the song for Indestructible Cylinder (3251), U.S. Everlasting Cylinder (399), Edison Amberol (720), and Zon-o-Phon (5766). The most successful solo vocal performance, brought out as both two- and four-minute cylinders in the Edison Blue Amberol series, was by Billy Murray.

As on the vaudeville stage, recordings of "Alexander" featured a wide range of performers. In addition to the solo and duo vocal versions just mentioned, "Alexander" turned up as the last number of a "Song Medley" (Victor 31848), with the Victor Mixed Chorus singing the choruses (only) of six songs published by the Ted Snyder Company. There were performances by the Victor Military Band (Victor 17006) and Prince's Band (Columbia 1126). Other Edison Blue Amberol cylinders included an "Alexander's Ragtime Band Medley" by the banjoist Fred Van Eps, who combined Berlin's "Ragtime Violin!" and "Grizzly Bear" with "Alexander," and a solo piano version by Melville Ellis in which "Alexander" was "intermixed with strains of the 'Magic Fire Music' from Richard Wagner's 'Die Walkure.' "[58]

These and other period discs and cylinders represented only the beginning of "Alexander"'s recorded history. From the 1920s until the present day, hundreds of recordings of the song appeared on 78 RPM discs, 33⅓ LPs, tape cassettes, and now CDs, by performers ranging from Al Jolson and Eddie Cantor to Bing Crosby, the Andrews Sisters, Noel Coward, Ethel Merman, Bessie Smith, Red Nichols, Benny Goodman, Bunk Johnson, Johnnie Ray, and Lawrence Welk.[59]

To condense all this information on "Alexander" into a brief outline history:

- Summer or fall, 1910. Berlin comes up with the tune of "Alexander" but puts it aside without fitting it with lyrics.
- Winter, 1910–1911. Just before a trip to Florida, he completes the song by adding lyrics to the tune, intending the piece for Emma Carus, with whom he had had extended professional contact, most recently as a fellow cast member in the show *Up and Down Broadway*.
- 18 March 1911. The song "Alexander's Ragtime Band" is copyrighted and published.
- 17 April. Emma Carus sings it for the first time anywhere at the American Music Hall in Chicago.
- 24 April. Neil McKinley introduces it to New York vaudeville at the Bronx Theatre.
- 27 April. The new Folies Bergere restaurant-theater opens in New York. The first part of the show, *Hell*, does *not* contain the song, in any form, although Berlin had offered it to the producers and it had been interpolated by a member of the cast into the production one night in a tryout performance in Atlantic City.
- April–May. Emma Carus continues to sing "Alexander" in various cities, and other performers, including Eddie Miller and Helen Vincent and Adele Oswald, also take it up in vaudeville.
- 28 May. Berlin sings it himself in the opening performance of the *Friars' Frolic of 1911* at the New Amsterdam Theatre. Over the next ten days, the show plays in twelve other cities.
- 12 June. "Alexander" is the big hit of the opening night of *The Merry Whirl* at the Columbia Theatre. The show runs through mid-August, then goes on tour.
- June–December. The song is taken up by countless vaudeville entertainers and interpolated into other shows, including *Trocaderos* and *The Whirl of Mirth*.
- 11–18 September. Berlin features "Alexander" in his six-song set during a week's engagement at Hammerstein's vaudeville house.
- 6 September. A piano version of "Alexander" is copyrighted and published.

Alexander and Irving and Ted

The Ted Snyder Company did little to promote "Alexander" in the months following its publication, not even after it had been enthusiastically received in vaudeville, in the thirteen-city tour of The *Friars' Frolic*, and in *The Merry Whirl*. As *Variety* noted on 23 December, "it was kept on the Snyder Co.'s shelves for four months," and even when an unnamed vaudeville performer wanted to use the song as part of his or her turn at Hammerstein's, "the Snyder firm did not feel positive about the quality, and withdrew the song from them, substituting another." A full-page ad by the Snyder company in *Variety* for 22 April lists six of its recently published songs, but "Alexander" is not one of them; even as late as 15 July, six weeks after Berlin had sung the piece with such success in the *Friars' Frolic* and more than a month after it had begun attracting crowds to *The Merry Whirl*, another full-page ad in *Variety* lists five of the Snyder Company's recently published "Healthy Hits," including Berlin's "When I'm Alone I'm Lonesone," "When You're In Town," "When You Kiss An Italian Gal," and "Dreams, Just Dreams," but "Alexander" is still conspicuous by its absence.

It was not until mid-August that the Snyder Company acknowledged the song and its success. A full-page ad in *Variety* for 19 August calls it "The Song Sensation of the Century" and claims that "managers, critics and the public want it. Any act can make good with it. The double version is a knockout. The instrumental lends class to any dumb or dancing act; in fact, it is the only song on the market to-day that makes 'making good' child's play." The Snyder ad appearing in *Variety* on 23 September was more effusive yet: "Acts are taking bows to the tune of it. I wonder why? Managers are asking acts to use it. I wonder why? **The whole world has fallen in love with it. THAT'S WHY."**

Despite the publisher's early reluctance to promote the song, *Variety* reported on 23 December that "by Nov. 15 over 1,000,000 copies of 'Alexander' had been sold. It was one of the greatest 'natural hits' in the history of popular music."

Henry Waterson had put up the capital to establish the Ted Snyder Company in July 1908, with Snyder as the featured composer. Berlin was hired as a staff lyricist the following year, and Berlin and Snyder collaborated on several dozen songs, many of which enjoyed some measure of success. Songs with both lyrics and music by Berlin were soon published as well, and several of these—"Call Me Up Some Rainy Afternoon," "Stop, Stop, Stop (Come Over And Love Me Some More)," "Dat's-A My Gal," and "When You're In Town"—were among the most successful pieces brought out by the company, judging by performances and sales. It was Berlin, not Snyder, who was asked to perform in the *Friars' Frolic of 1911*, singing his own songs. All of this suggests that Snyder was responsible for the company's foot-dragging on "Alexander," possibly because he felt that it wasn't a good song, but perhaps because he was jealous of his younger colleague who was so suddenly outstripping him professionally. It's interesting to note in this connection that after the success of "Alexander," the company put its full resources behind "That Mysterious Rag," cowritten by Snyder and Berlin, in an attempt to make it a successor to "Alexander" on the vaudeville stage.

Retribution was quick to follow. A terse announcement in *Variety* for 4

January 1912 reads: "The Ted Snyder Co. goes out of business at once and will be succeeded by the Watterson-Berlin-Snyder company, a new $100,000 corporation. This means the taking into the firm of Irving Berlin, who has been the star writer for the Snyder Music Publishing Co." Even under the new setup, Berlin was apparently still not satisfied that he was getting his due or his fair share of the proceeds. The lyric of his song "The Haunted House," copyrighted and published on 27 May 1914, is a transparent commentary on the publishing company (the haunted house) and the tall, slender Snyder (the "boney skeleton").

> I often have been told,
> That there's a bag of gold,
> In the house that's haunted,
> I'm poor, but I don't want it.
> The doors are open wide,
> But noone steps inside,
> Noone needs the money, because
> That house is
>   Haunted, haunted,
>   Lanky, hanky, panky skeletons go sneakin' around;
>   You see that boney, croney, I mean that boney skeleton
>   Hiding behind that statue,
>   Look out, he's looking at you!
>   Listen! Listen!
>   Tell me, can't you hear him whistleing
>   That Mysterious Rag, so noted,
>   He wrote it,
>   In that rickety, haunted house.

Late in 1914, Berlin established his own company to publish his show songs, beginning with those from *Watch Your Step*, and eventually he gained full control over his own "bag of gold" by publishing all of his songs.

In Conclusion

The myth surrounding the early history of "Alexander's Ragtime Band" was built on the sort of "hook" favored by journalistic writers: A piece of music that nobody wanted at first and was shelved for a while, even by its author, later and quite inexplicably became one of the greatest hit songs of all time.

There's much in this myth that should have aroused suspicion, not least that it's an atypical case history for a popular song. The actual events, to the contrary, make sense in the context of how the world of popular music functions. After Berlin had finished the song by adding lyrics to a tune that had come to him earlier, Emma Carus agreed to perform the piece in vaudeville. Berlin gave her credit for introducing it before the fact, on the cover of the sheet music, and the song went unperformed for a month after publication, awaiting Carus's first vaudeville engagement after a year or more on the legitimate stage.

"Alexander" was well received in Carus's first and subsequent performances and was taken up almost immediately by other vaudeville performers. Its rejection by the producers of *Hell* was more a judgment about the nature of the song than about its quality; it was too American in style and content for the Folies Bergere, which emphasized the pseudo-European character of the establishment and the entertainment offered there. The song was a sensation in its first two appearances on stage: Berlin chose it for the high-profile *Friars' Frolic*, and audiences responded by demanding encores as numerous as "sands of the sea"; and all reports agree not only that it was the best moment in *The Merry Whirl* but that it was largely responsible for the unexpected summer-long run of the show in New York.

In sum: Although circumstances delayed the first performance of "Alexander" until some weeks after it was published, and although it wasn't promoted for several months by its publisher, it was a hit with audiences from the moment of its first performances. No doubt about it: "Alexander's Ragtime Band" was quickly accepted as "the best song in the land."

Coda

Well after this chapter had been completed and published in a slightly different form in *American Music*, Linda Emmet, Berlin's youngest daughter, told me of a letter in the files of the Irving Berlin Music Company, written by her father to Ward Morehouse on 19 June 1947, that dealt in part with the early history of "Alexander." Robert Kimball kindly located it and made a photocopy for me. Rather than using the letter only to correct a few minor details in what I had found out myself, I decided to print in their entirety those parts of it that refer to "Alexander," to allow Berlin to tell the story in his own voice.

> I checked with Jesse Lasky and here are the facts regarding the ALEXANDER'S RAGTIME BAND story in connection with the Folies Bergere: Henry B. Harris doesn't enter into this at all. He and Jesse Lasky built what is now the Fulton Theatre, and, incidentally, it was the first theatre cabaret in America. They had engaged Ethel Levey to come over from England for this show. Jesse Lasky asked me to write a song for her. I wrote a song called I BEG YOUR PARDON DEAR OLD BROADWAY. Levey had been away from America for many years, and this was a special number to fit that situation. (By the way, it was a very bad song and never got anywhere, although Levey sang it beautifully.) I came to a rehearsal to hear Levey sing I BEG YOUR PARDON DEAR

The whole world moves to Berlin's music.

Figure 11. Cartoon by Herb Roth for a Friars' Club dinner in honor of Irving Berlin, Hotel Astor, October 19, 1913.

OLD BROADWAY. Jesse told me they needed a spot-in-one for Levey and asked if I had a song that might be suitable. I said I had a new song and sang ALEXANDER'S RAGTIME BAND for him. He said, "This is a good song, but certainly not for Ethel Levey who's a contralto and needs a song that can be sung much slower." So ALEXANDER'S BAND was not sung by Levey but instead was whistled by Otis Harland, the comedian of the show, for one performance. It was taken out of the show after the opening night [in Atlantic City] of Folies Bergere. Later, it was sung for the first time by Emma Carus in Chicago. This is particularly interesting because after the Folies Bergere flopped and Ethel Levey had returned to England, the song became a tremendous success and ALEXANDER'S RAGTIME BAND finally got to Levey in London. She sang it there and caused a sensation with it, singing it very slowly. Several years later, she played a return engagement at the Palace Theatre and sang ALEXANDER in her act. I remember how upset I was at her rendition of it. The audience, of course, did not agree with me. She was a riot. Lasky just told me over the telephone that he likes to refer to himself as the man who turned down ALEXANDER'S RAGTIME BAND. He added that had he been smart enough to choose it for Ethel Levey, the Folies Bergere might have been a big success. I doubt it very much. That's Jesse being sweet. Personally, I believe Lasky and Harris were way ahead of the times when they built the first cabaret theatre in America.*

*Used by permission of the Estate of Irving Berlin, and with grateful acknowledgment to the Morgan Guaranty Trust Company of New York, executors of the estate.

Chapter Four

Berlin and the Ballad

Many of the most enduring songs of Berlin's middle and later years are ballads, as a mere listing of a few of their titles—"Always," "Remember," "How Deep Is The Ocean (How High Is The Sky)," "Blue Skies," "It Only Happens When I Dance With You," and "All Alone," for starters— is enough to remind one. But writing pieces of this sort wasn't a matter of "doin' what comes naturally" for Berlin. Relatively few of his early songs were ballads, and only a handful of these enjoyed much commercial or critical success, even after his novelty and ragtime songs had catapulted him into a position as the leading songwriter of the day.

In what follows I'll attempt to account for his relatively late start in writing successful songs of this genre and trace the genesis of the unique style of ballad that became so characteristic of his later years.

Berlin's First Ballads

Berlin's first published song, "Marie From Sunny Italy," was a ballad of sorts. Written in collaboration with Mike Nicholson while the two were working together at the Pelham Cafe in Chinatown, its reception may be judged from the fact that a payment voucher to Berlin from the publisher, Joseph W. Stern, for June and July 1908 records that Berlin earned twenty-seven cents in royalties for that period, and a similar voucher for a slightly later period is in the amount of thirty-seven cents.[1]

The sheet music cover by Etherington shows a couple in a Venetian gondola, the man serenading the woman to the accompaniment of a mandolin. These hints that the protagonists are Italian are supported by the facts that "Marie" is a stock name for an Italian protagonist in ethnic novelty songs and that the minor key of the verse and the rocking rhythm of the accompaniment suggest some sort of Italian song, possibly a barcarolle, although the meter is 2/4 rather than 6/8. The text is a first-person expression of romantic sentiment addressed in "poetical" language to a second party.

> Oh, Marie, 'neath the window I'm waiting,
> Oh, Marie, please don't be so aggravating,
> Can't you see my heart just yearns for you, dear,
> With fond affection,
> And love that's true, dear?

Musically, there are references to the melodic and accompanimental patterns of Italian opera, added sixths in the melody, an asymmetric (twenty-eight-bar) chorus, and touches of chromatic writing.

The song combines characteristics of several different genres of the period without being a convincing example of any one of them; while Berlin's conflation of elements from two or more different types of songs later in his career was often a deliberate and successful attempt to breathe fresh air into one or another of these, here it seems more a matter of compositional inexperience. His second published song, "Queenie," cowritten in 1908 with Maurice Abraham, likewise exhibits some characteristics of the ballad and is no less conflicted. Traces of dialect in the lyric suggest that the protagonists are black, which would make it a "coon" song, and the chorus has a few simple syncopated patterns. But the music contains chromatic and dissonant touches not usually found in "coon" songs, and the lyric's romantic sentiments and clumsy attempts at "poetical" diction seem likewise inappropriate for a song of that type:

> The moon above am shining, love, I'm out here waiting,
> Don't be so shy, I can't see why, you're hesitating;
>
> Impatiently I wait for thee here in the moonlight,
> Don't be afraid, my dusky maid, this is a spoonlight.

"The Best Of Friends Must Part," Berlin's first attempt at writing both words and music of a song, abandons "poetical" content and language in favor of vernacular expression.

> What's that you say? No work today?
> Done lost your job? Where is your pay?
> Been shooting dice? That's very nice . . .
> That stuff don't go, You'd better blow,
> Can't buy a meal with that lovin' you know.

The genre of the song is unclear; perhaps "confused" would be a more apt term. Although the first-person lyric, dealing with personal emotions and addressed to a second party, suggests some sort of ballad, the song's diction and content are alien to the genre. Nor would the piece, with its confused and bitter lyric, seem to be appropriate for the vaudeville stage.

> A friend in need, is a friend indeed,
> That's just the kind of friend I've been to you,
> When poverty smiled down on thee,
> I hung around and stuck like glue,
> It's a long, long lane that has no turn,
> You can never tell your finish when you start,
> But when you find you can't make both ends meet,
> Then the best of friends must part.

The verse has some hints of syncopation; the chorus doesn't. An odd climactic phrase on a single note, quoted on the next page, is unlike any passage found in other songs of the day, by Berlin or anyone else.

The clumsiness of these three pieces can be explained as much or more by the circumstances of Berlin's cultural background as by his inexperience as a songwriter. To understand this point, one must look more closely at the history and the nature of the ballad.

"Marie From Sunny Italy" (1907)
"Queenie" (1908)
"The Best Of Friends Must Part" (1908)

The High-Class Ballad in Victorian America

When Berlin began writing songs, "ballad" was the label for a piece with a first-person lyric expressing a romantic, nostalgic, or moralistic sentiment. Although the term itself didn't come into general use for songs of this sort until early in the Tin Pan Alley era, the genre had an unbroken if complex history in America extending back to the first years of the nineteenth century.

Early in the nineteenth century, musical literacy among amateurs was confined largely to the elite classes, among whom it was considered one marker of social status. Successive decades brought a steady proliferation of this skill, in sheer numbers and across social strata, as basic instruction in music was introduced into the curricula of private schools for young women and then into public schools and was also taught, more informally, to participants in singing schools and town bands. This spread of musical literacy echoed changing social structures in the United States, as more people gained access to education and economic self-sufficiency, facilitating the pursuit of leisure and cultural activities.

Nothing dramatizes these changes more strikingly than the growing number, through the nineteenth century and into the twentieth, of American families owning pianos. There were two prerequisites to having a piano: the considerable capital necessary to purchase one and a family member, or at least visitors to the household, who could read music or had the prospect of learning to do so. According to Arthur Loesser, a historian of the piano in America,

> For the forty-five years after the close of the Civil War, we can chronicle a prodigious rise in the density of the piano distribution. In 1870 about one person out of about 1540 bought a new piano in the course of the year; by 1890 the rate had gone up to one out of 874; while in 1910 it reached one in 252—pianos having crowded themselves more than six times thicker in forty years. Or, every working day of 1870 eighty persons bought a new piano; in 1910 twelve hundred persons did so, fifteen times as many, whereas the population had multiplied itself by no more than two and one half in the meanwhile.[2]

This proliferation took place chiefly among the elite and bourgeois classes, and the majority of these pianos were bought for use by girls, for whom instruction in music was part of their "domestication"—their transformation, through education, into cultured and refined young women ready for and capable of their preordained roles as wives and mothers. A considerable body of keyboard music was written specifically for this constituency; even more often, the piano was used in the American home to accompany singing. As Loesser puts it:

> All the concerts added together, lofty and shallow, spectacular and dull, with all the opera performances thrown in, did not make up a tiny segment of America's musical life, or account for more than an infinitesimal fraction of the total use to which America's pianos were being put. Only a very restricted number of people, in the United States as elsewhere, conceived of music as a fine art or as an object of absorbed scrutiny. To most . . . it was an amusement eminently suited to the home circle and to private gatherings of friends. . . . Songs for a single voice, designed in a familiar rhythmic symmetry and in well-grooved harmonic successions, with piano accompaniment, made up the chief musical fare in families of middling situation of life.[3]

Some sense of this cultural environment, and the place of music in it, can be gleaned from an examination of publications designed specifically as aides to the process of domestication. A typical one of these, *Gathered Pearls: A Choice Selection of Poetry and Music*, describes itself as a "companion in the home," where its "most refining sentiments, most beautiful descriptions of domestic life, [and] most elevating thoughts" are sure to "awaken afresh the joys of home life and create that influence which is the mother of all true character." The volume contains "a vast treasury of all that is most captivating, most soul-stirring, most pathetic, most sublime, most lofty in thought."[4] Lest there be any question as to its intended users, a full-page frontispiece pictures a young woman, lost in reverie.

Another collection, *Beautiful Melodies*, contains "The World's Most Famous Lyrics of Love and Romance; Pathos and Sentiment; Home and Country" written by "the world's most eminent and popular composers, who shine resplendently in the firmament of dazzling genius." This anthology contains "something for every mood of mind and heart—for the joy that clamors for expression in melody, and the sorrow that is soothed by the mysterious influence of music." The editors have been "careful to introduce no songs of an objectionable character," and as a result the collection is "suitable for every family; without any reserve whatever it can be placed in the hands of the young without fear of evil suggestion or any injurious effect."[5]

Most of the songs found in these collections are "high-class" ballads, as they came to be called in the late nineteenth century. In the first edition of his seminal history of music in the United States, Gilbert Chase discusses this repertory as part of America's "genteel tradition," a term taken over from George Santayana and referring to "the cult of the fashionable, the worship of the conventional, the emulation of the elegant, the cultivation of the trite and artificial, the indulgence of sentimentality, and the predominance of superficiality."[6]

But more was at stake than the bad taste implied by the comments of Loesser and Chase. America's schools, where musical literacy was taught, as well as the publishing houses responsible for bringing out music for school and home use, were to varying degrees under the cultural influence of a group of "mostly middle-income, mostly Whig-Republican, literary men and women" who made up the intellectual core of America's emerging Victorian ideology. In their writings and lectures, they proposed to "humanize the emergent industrial-capitalist order by infusing it with a measure of social responsibility, strict personal morality, and respect for cultural standards," in part by promoting a value system whereby people were to "work hard, to postpone gratification, to repress themselves sexually, to 'improve' themselves, to be sober [and] conscientious."[7]

According to this ideology, the ideal "family romance" should follow a pattern of abstinence from premarital sexual relations, a monogamous marriage, and loving, supportive relationships among parents and their children. The lyrics of most high-class ballads are concerned with one or another stage of this romance: finding and courting one's ideal mate, for instance; triumph over any temporary setbacks or misunderstandings during this courtship; the development of a strong and stable marriage, with physical attraction and affection continuing into old age; the shaping of children of this union according to the same values. These themes are in fact so pervasive that if these songs were the only source of information

Figure 12. "The Maiden's Reverie," frontispiece for the anthology "Gathered Pearls."

about American domestic life in the nineteenth century, one would never suspect the existence in this society of premarital sex, adultery, desertion, divorce, or domestic abuse.

This emphasis on high moral content in songs aimed primarily at women was not motivated only by concern for their own spiritual and emotional well-being. Their husbands needed their emotional support and domestic help in order to be free to pursue their own business and pleasure; after all, half of the children these women bore and reared were male. A writer of the time put things in what seemed to be proper perspective:

> Woman's life is made up of little pleasures, of little tasks, of little cares, and little duties, but which, when added together, make a grand total of human happiness; she is not expected to do any arduous work; her province lies in gentleness, in cheerfulness, in contentment, in housewifery, in care and management of her children, in sweetening her home. . . . We must not lose sight of [woman's] most divine and sublime mission in life—womanhood and motherhood. The hand that rocks the cradle, the mother of the coming man, is too important a factor to be disregarded even in the slightest degree. . . . Great men of all times have traced their lofty ideals and talents, and indeed the whole of their success, to their mothers.[8]

"Child-bearing and rearing should be woman's chiefest study, as well as her crowning joy," the author continued, and chief among her concerns should be "the imparting of a healthy body, a cheerful spirit and a sound mental activity to the child." Since it was "now common belief among all intelligent people" that a mother "may, during the period of gestation, exercise great influence, by her own mental and physical action, either unwittingly or purposely in such a way as to determine the traits and tendencies of her offspring," women were urged to think only pure and elevated thoughts and to occupy themselves with only the "highest" forms of art through pregnancy. An example is offered: A teacher noted that one of her pupils was "remarkably bright, sensitive and talented," with a "fine poetic temperament accompanied by a keen appreciation of the beauties of nature," despite the fact that her two siblings were "dull, inert, and slow to learn." A conversation with the mother revealed that, during the pregnancy of the favored child, she had constantly read from a volume of Walter Scott's poems.[9]

Such attitudes toward women were deep-seated in American society even before the Victorian era. According to *The Young Man's Aid To Knowledge, Virtue, and Happiness* (1837), a "discreet young man" should look for the following ideal "qualifications for a good wife": 1. Good disposition; 2. Domestic virtues ("No young woman is fit to be married, till she has learned how to keep house."); 3. Good sense and intelligence; 4. Agreeable person and good health; 5. Neatness; 6. Sympathy toward his occupation;

and 7. Religion. Not only is "the intellect of the mother intimately connected with that of her children," who are at risk of being contaminated "if the mind of the mother is weak, or odd, or trifling, or vain, or one-sided, or in any way unhappily peculiar"; her husband might suffer as well. "Whatever is weak or eccentric in her . . . will find its way more or less into his own mind, and at length induce him to act in many instances with weakness and indiscretion."[10]

The high-class ballad of the nineteenth century was an affair of women in more ways than addressing hegemonic messages to them. It was performed by women both in the home circle and in public, more than any other sorts of music, and it was one of the few genres in which female composers were encouraged to work. Songs by the British songwriters Harriet Browne, Virginia Gabriel, Claribel (Charlotte Alington Barnard), and Dolores, and by the Americans Susan Parkhurst and the somewhat later Carrie Jacobs-Bond and Amy Beach make up a not inconsiderable part of the repertory of the high-class ballad. Male writers sometimes took female *noms de plume* for their songs of this sort; Septimus Winner published many of his ballads under the name of Alice Hawthorne, for instance.

It was not merely the subject matter of their lyrics that made these songs appropriate for the "improvement" of the minds and morals of America's young women; it was also their relationship, real or putative, to the classical repertory. Lawrence W. Levine has written about the "sacralization" of culture in the late nineteenth and the early twentieth centuries in the United States, a movement based on the assumption that the classical arts "make no compromises with the 'temporal' world; [they remain] spiritually pure and never become secondary to the performer or the audience; [they are] uncompromising in [their] devotion to cultural perfection."[11] Classical music was seen as not only technically superior to other styles and genres but more morally elevated as well. Accordingly, the repertory of the high-class ballad included some of the art songs of Franz Schubert and Robert Schumann, as well as simplified versions of the operatic music of Donizetti, Bellini, Verdi, and even Wagner. The bulk of it, however, was made up of songs by Henry Bishop, Samuel Lover, Henry Russell, Franz Abt, Friedrich Kücken, Ciro Pinsuti, Arthur Sullivan, Adam Giebel, and other European composers who wrote in a more popular style that still had clear stylistic ties to the music of the Great Masters.[12]

"Fly Forth, O Gentle Dove," with words by F. E. Weatherly and music by Ciro Pinsuti, a prolific Italian-born composer of operas, piano pieces, and songs who spent much of his professional life in London, typifies the nineteenth-century high-class ballad. The lyric is cast in "poetical" diction:

I sent a letter to my love,
Made bright with loving words and sweet,

I gave it to a tender dove
To carry to my darling's feet!
Fly forth, O gentle dove, I cried,
Spread westward, spread thy pinions fleet.
O'er hills and wood and meadows wide,
And bear my letter to my sweet!
And when beneath her bow'r thou art,
And seest her leaning from above,
Fly upward straight into her heart,
And nestle in the warmth thereof.
My love will love thee for my sake,
And give thee welcome, happy dove!
Then westward swift thy journey take,
And bear my letter to my love!

The song's celebration of romantic love, explicit enough in Weatherly's lyric, is elevated to a "higher" moral level through its music, which draws on techniques associated with the classical repertory: chromaticism, a brilliant but easily performed piano accompaniment featuring right-hand octaves, a vocal melodic range spanning a tenth, and melodic climaxes on high notes. Even its notational practice is in line with that of the classical repertory. Determination of details of performance was shifting from performer to composer as modernism took shape in the nineteenth century; ever more precise notation required the performer to follow the composer's intentions in every detail, rather than to be a creative collaborator in shaping the sounding version of a piece. Pinsuti's notation of this song specifies not only precise pitches, general tempo, and mood *(andante grazioso)* but also details of phrasing, changing dynamic levels, ritards and accelerations, and even expression *(con grazia, con animo, leggiero brillante)*.

When the song is performed, the audience hears a first-person text that first sketches the dramatic scenario and then speaks directly to the dove. If either the song itself or the songwriter was already well known to the listeners, the voice would be perceived as that of the author; if the performer was better known than the songwriter, or if she gave a convincing enough performance, the voice would be heard as hers. If the lyric of a song of this sort is addressed to a second person, as in F. N. Crouch's "Kathleen Mavourneen," the audience is placed in the position of overhearing a private communication addressed by the songwriter or the singer to another person.

Mavourneen, Mavourneen, my sad tears are falling,
To think that from Erin and thee I must part!
It may be for year, and it may be forever!
Then why art thou silent, thou voice of my heart?
It may be for years and it may be forever!
Then why art thou silent, Kathleen Mavourneen?

Edward Cone argues that in a performance of nineteenth-century art song, the singer is perceived as "the conscious composer of words and music alike."[13] In other words, she becomes identified with the protagonist. But even if listeners perceive the voice of a song to be that of a singer-protagonist, the content and the message were of course put into the piece in the first place by the songwriter. Ruth Solie has argued that Robert Schumann's song cycle *Frauenliebe und -leben,* although cast as a first-person expression of a woman's worshipful devotion to her husband, always sung by a woman, and often uncritically taken as an expression of female sentiment, wasn't "made by a woman" and isn't even "a man's portrait of a woman." It represents, rather, "the *impersonation* of a woman by the voices of male culture, a spurious autobiographical act," invoking "powerful mythic images of women, or marriage, and of domesticity," images that were "a necessary part of the social message it was the cycle's job to transmit."[14]

The same argument could be made for the nineteenth-century high-class ballad, since its emphasis on enduring romantic love can be seen as giving hegemonic support to the notion that women were intended to maintain a stable, comfortable, and supportive household, so as not to distract their husbands from their work and play and so as to indoctrinate their children into the type of "family romance" considered desirable in America's nascent capitalist society.

The Popular Ballad in America

The high-class ballad was chiefly a product of nineteenth-century European culture, although Americans composers wrote more and more songs of this type as the century neared an end. A second variety of ballad also originated in Europe but took such deep root in the United States that by the second half of the century the most widely sung pieces of this sort were the products of American songwriters.

Growing out of the late eighteenth-century fascination with "folk" culture as an antidote to what many intellectuals and artists of the day saw as the dehumanizing aspects of the dawning modern industrial era, the earliest pieces of this sort were arrangements for voice and keyboard of actual "folk" songs collected by literary figures and amateur folklorists. Haydn's arrangements of folksongs from the British Isles and Beethoven's collections of Irish, Welsh, and Scottish songs became the best-known specimens of the genre among scholars, but similar pieces written for the popular musical stage and the home circle enjoyed much wider and more lasting dissemination and reception.

James Hook's "Within a Mile of Edinburgh Town," for instance, became one of the most familiar songs in the United States after being printed in the first large American song anthology, the *American Musical Miscellany* (North-ampton, 1798), and the songs of Thomas Moore became more popular yet. A number of Moore's *Irish Melodies*, published in ten volumes between 1808 and 1834, "quickly entered the mainstream of music in America and stayed there throughout the nineteenth century," becoming "instrumental in shap-ing indigenous popular music in America."[15] Although their tunes were adapted from traditional Irish melodies, the texts were inventions of Moore himself, most of them having little or nothing to do with those originally sung to these tunes. Many of Moore's lyrics deal with Ireland's past glories, leg-ends, and heroes; the dominant mood of the *Irish Melodies*, however, whether in tunes about Ireland or songs expressing personal emotions, is an intense sense of melancholy and nostalgia.

> Has sorrow thy young days shaded,
> As clouds o'er the morning fleet?
> Too fast have those young days faded,
> That, even in sorrow were sweet.
> Does Time, with his cold wing wither
> Each feeling that once was dear?
> Then, child of misfortune, come hither,
> I'll weep with thee, tear for tear.
>
> "Has Sorrow Thy Young Days Shaded"

> 'Tis the last rose of summer, left blooming alone;
> All her lovely companions are faded and gone.
> No flow'r of her kindred, no rosebud is nigh,
> To reflect back her blushes, or give sigh for sigh.
>
> "The Last Rose of Summer"

As reworked traditional airs, the *Irish Melodies* are strophic in structure, often diatonic or pentatonic and frequently showing the octave leaps and inverted rhythmic patterns (the "Scottish snap") characteristic of some Celtic music. Moore's arrangers, John Stevenson for the first eight volumes and Henry Bishop for the other two, fitted these tunes with diatonic, tri-adic keyboard accompaniments, with chromaticism limited to an occasional secondary dominant, usually V of IV or V of V.

Widely sung in the home circle as part of the genteel repertory, Moore's songs were also performed on the stage by professional singers and enter-tainers, himself among them. The songs' wide dissemination in sheet music form, their simplicity compared to high-class ballads, and the fact that many of the tunes were already known from oral tradition meant that they could be published in text-only songsters as well, and some of them, with their new texts, filtered back into the oral tradition from whence they had come. As a result of their transmission in these three different modes—in musical notation, as printed texts, and orally—and because of their adaptability to a wide range of performance venues and situations, they became known to a much wider spectrum of the American population than did high-class ballads.[16]

The most important successors to Moore's *Irish Melodies*, in musical means, expressive content, and widespread popularity, were the plantation songs of Stephen Foster. Although not drawn directly from folk melodies, Foster's tunes, like Moore's, are pervasively diatonic, with frequent traces of pentatonicism. Melodic and rhythmic patterns often invoke traditional Celtic music; harmonies are restricted to tonic, subdominant, and dominant triads, relieved only by an occasional passing secondary dominant; and structures are strophic, although Foster adds a brief chorus to be sung after each strophe.[17] Lyrics are shot through with nostalgia—laments for lost childhood, lost family, lost friends, lost love, a lost way of life. Unlike Moore, who wrote in an almost self-conscious "poetical" style, Foster used vernacular English for his lyrics, simple in syntax, direct in expression, and limited in vocabulary.

> The forms I call'd my own have vanished one by one,
> The lov'd ones, the dear ones have all passed away.
> Their happy smiles have flown, their gentle voices gone.
>
> "Old Dog Tray"

> They hunt no more for the possum and the coon
> On the meadow, the hill and the shore,
> They sing no more by the glimmer of the moon,
> On the bench by the old cabin door.
> The day goes by like a shadow o'er the heart,
> With sorrow where all was delight.
>
> "My Old Kentucky Home"

> Where are the hearts once so happy and so free,
> The children so dear that I held upon my knee?
>
> "Old Black Joe"

> My days of youth have passed away
> And the shades of life are near,
> But I still remain to mourn the happy days
> When dear departed friends were here.
>
> "Why Have My Loved Ones Gone?"

In his discussion of nostalgia in nineteenth-century American song, William Austin contrasts this theme as manifested in "a broader current of European social, cultural, and political change" with its somewhat different meaning in the New World.

Coleridge and Wordsworth were among the first to generalize the use of the English word "homesick," while Heine and Baudelaire and others were exploring the metaphorical uses of the idea. "Homesickness" belongs to the vocabulary of the "avant-garde," along with "folk," "proletariat," "alienation," and "repression"—all terms foreign to Stephen Foster. For him and the tradition he knew, the dream of home was thought to be altogether wholesome.[18]

To most newcomers and visitors to the United States in the nineteenth century, the American people appeared to be extroverted, aggressive, and self-confident. Most of them, however, of every class and national origin (with the exception of Native Americans), had in common that they were all recently displaced persons; that is, within their own memory or that of their parents or grandparents, they or their near ancestors had left their homelands, extended families, and friends to take up residence in a far-off, alien land. Small wonder, then, that so many of them responded to the nostalgia-laden songs of Moore and Foster, even though the cause of this appeal may have lain deep in their subconscious.

The minstrel stage was an important venue, although not the only one, for Foster's plantation melodies. Eric Lott argues that a minstrel performer in blackface was not necessarily perceived by his audience as giving an "authentic" portrayal of a black person; there was, rather, a "tendency [for] minstrel products to air from behind the mask, as though live and direct from the white unconscious, just about anything that chanced to surface, . . . [for] after all the minstrel show featured displaced and condensed portrayals of the white audiences's concerns and desires."[19] He paraphrases Alexander Saxton:

> [N]ostalgic blackface songs spoke at once to restless migrants moving west, recently transplanted rural folk in cities, and rootless urban dwellers beginning to experience the anomie of modern metropolitan life. . . . This is also, perhaps, minstrelsy's strongest connection with Irish-American audiences and performers, whose displaced self-masking in minstrelsy involved, further, a lament for home and circumstances that deepened and extended the minstrel show's sentimentalism.[20]

One could argue similarly that Moore's *Irish Melodies* had also spoken from behind their own mask of Irish ethnicity to the concerns of a wider constituency. Be that as it may, the plantation song quickly dropped its black mask. Protagonists of later songs of this type by Foster and the countless other songwriters who emulated him are no longer unequivocally black, and several generations of white Americans who sang these pieces in their homes took them to be generic laments for lost love, youth, and home. In one of the most lastingly popular of these, Septimus Winner's "Listen to the Mocking Bird" (1855), the hints in the second verse that the protagonist might be black probably didn't even register with singers and audiences:

I'm dreaming now of Hally, sweet Hally, sweet Hally,
I'm dreaming now of Hally,
For the tho't of her is one that never dies;
She's sleeping now in the valley, the valley, the valley,
She's sleeping in the valley,
And the mocking bird is singing where she lies.
    Listen to the mocking bird, listen to the mocking bird,
    The mocking bird still singin o'er her grave,
    Listen to the mocking bird, listen to the mocking bird,
    Still singing where the weeping willows wave.

Ah! well I yet remember, remember, remember,
Ah! well I yet remember,
When we gather'd in the cotton side by side;
'Twas in the mild September, September, September,
'Twas in the mild September,
And the mocking bird was singing far and wide.
    Listen to the mocking bird . . .

Songs of this sort were written in great numbers by two generations of American (and British) songwriters. In order to distinguish them from the high-class ballad, I refer to them as "popular ballads," a label chosen because of these songs' stylistic similarities to certain bodies of vernacular music, and also because they were disseminated and taken up much more extensively among the country's complex social and economic layers than were the high-class ballads.

Both high-class and popular ballads were performed primarily in the home circle by amateurs, but both types, particularly the popular ballad, were also sung in public by professional musicians before paying audiences. Ballad singers were common fare in the country's theaters in the first half of the nineteenth century. Some, such as the Englishman Henry Russell, who sang in virtually every part of the United States between 1836 and 1844, and the Irishman Samuel Lover, who was in America between 1846 and 1848, were from the British Isles. Others were native sons; Lyman Heath, Bernard Covert, and Walter Kittredge, for instance, were from New England. In addition, the programs of singing families, in great vogue during the two decades before the Civil War, often included solo ballads sung by one or another member of the group or in quartet arrangements of such pieces. And with the standardization of the minstrel show into three parts around mid-century, popular ballads were often featured in the opening section and sometimes during the following "olio."

In the late nineteenth century, British music publishers began promoting public concerts in which ballads from their catalogue were performed.[21] The audience and the ambience of early vaudeville and variety had not been appropriate for either the high-class or the popular ballad, but as this form of theatrical entertainment spread from New York and other urban centers to hundreds of smaller cities and towns, and as theater managers began devising strategies to attract more diverse audiences, including members of the more "respectable" classes, to their theaters, the singing of popular ballads in vaudeville became more common:

> Ernest Ball is the latest song writer to attempt vaudeville. . . . Playing his own accompaniments, he sings one of his latest ballad hits and puts it over in fine style. A light number and the best liked of his repertoire, something like "Rose" followed. "Just for a Girl," pretty much done to death both on this side and in Europe, got over much better than the song warranted, and Mr. Ball was forced to sing an Irish song that he wrote for Chauncey Olcott. On early at Hammerstein's, the writer did very well indeed.[22]

Despite their different cultural origins, both high-class and the popular ballads were brought out in sheet music form by the same publishers. Both types appeared in the same song anthologies; both were preserved, often side by side, in the bound volumes of sheet music assembled in so many American homes; both were brought out in commercial recordings, on cylinder or disc, in performances by classically trained singers.

Ballads of both sorts sank deeply into the consciousness of a large part of the country's population. Together they make up a major portion of the contents of *Heart Songs* (1909), a retrospective anthology that enjoyed phenomenal sales of both the original printing and later reprints and revisions for some decades.[23] The Introduction to this collection testifies to the persistence of the ideology of the genteel tradition well into the twentieth century.

> [These songs] represent the history, the sentiment of the American people today, as well as of the various European races who, in this new world, have been moulded into a great and powerful nation. [It] is a valuable and striking gauge and indicator of the popular taste of the people now comprising the republic of the United States of America. Songs that have entertained thousands from childhood to the grave and have voiced the pleasure and pain, the love and longing, the despair and delight, the sorrow and resignation, and the consolation of the plain people—who found in these an utterance for emotions which they felt but could not express—came in by the thousands. The yellow sheets of music bear evidence of constant use; in times of war and peace, victory and defeat, good and evil fortune, these sweet strains have blended with the coarser thread of human life and offered to the joyful or saddened soul a suggestion of uplift, sympathy and hope.[24]

Berlin's First High-Class Ballads

When Berlin began writing songs, then, the two most important subgenres of the ballad were the high-class, with its romantic, "poetical" lyrics and its musical invocations of the art song, and the popular, with its nostalgic, vernacular texts and its more populist musical means. It should be apparent after this excursion that Berlin's first three ballads, described earlier in this chapter, don't fit into either subgenre in style or expression. This is hardly surprising, since as a member of an urban immigrant family living in an immigrant community he had no ties whatsoever to America's nineteenth-century "genteel" culture in which both types of ballad had flourished.

"Just Like The Rose" (1909), however, written in collaboration with Al Piantadosi, exhibits many textual and musical features of the high-class ballad. The conceit of Berlin's lyric is that a rose pines and dies when its love, a lily, is plucked and taken away; the song's first-person protagonist likens the sorrow he feels over the loss of his own love to that of the rose. Expressive dissonances, augmented chords, and the minor subdominant used for dramatic effect, coupled with the absence of a vamp before the verse, all suggest the musical style of the high-class ballad as opposed to that of the novelty song.

In a gesture aimed at classically trained performers, who could not be expected to transpose as readily as popular musicians, the publisher, Harry Von Tilzer, brought the song out in three different keys, for low, medium, and high voice. However, the vocal line and the piano accompaniment remain within the performance capabilities of an amateur musician. Songs exhibiting this mixture of elements from high-class and more popular songs were sometimes labeled semi-high-class ballads.

"Dreams, Just Dreams," written a bit later in collaboration with Ted Snyder, is described in advertising copy in *Variety* on 22 April 1911 as a "semi-high-class song hit." It has a fashionably melancholy lyric: Ever since "the love that I gave found a grave," mourns the first-person protagonist, he finds consolation only in his dreams, which can "turn gloom to a bright sunbeam." The music is sprinkled with augmented chords and minor subdominants, and, in expectation of performance by classically trained musicians, the voice range encompasses a tenth, with a climactic high note, and the piano accompaniment includes tremolo passages and left-hand leaps. The cover is appropriately chaste, depicting a sylvan scene in black and white.

"Just Like The Rose" (1909)
"Dreams, Just Dreams" (1910)

The Berlin/Snyder "Novelty Ballads"

For two years after Berlin took a position as staff lyricist at the Ted Snyder Company in 1909, he and Snyder collaborated on a succession of novelty songs intended for the vaudeville stage and, occasionally, for interpolation into musical shows; many of these pieces were well received in performance and reasonably successful in sheet-music sales. Lyrics are usually attributed to Berlin and the music to Snyder, although the men two undoubtedly collaborated on both.

Ballads were not a top priority for the young songwriting team, and none of their dozen or so songs of this genre attracted as much attention as their best pieces for the vaudeville stage. The protagonists of these ballads are youthful, and their expressions of affection or love are playful or coy, in contrast to the vows of passionate, enduring love found in such contemporary high-class ballads as Carrie Jacobs-Bond's "I Love You Truly" (1906) or the intense nostalgic aura of Tell Taylor's popular ballad "Down By The Old Mill Stream" (1910). In most of the Berlin/Snyder ballads a dramatic scenario is sketched in the third person in the verse; then one of the characters speaks in the first person in the chorus, as also happens in many novelty songs of the time.

Moon was slyly peeping from above, on a summer's night;
Sally Brown and Joe were making love, 'neath the pale moonlight;
Sally said, "I think I'd better go," as she rolled her eyes;
But foxy little Joe said, "There's a game I know called telling lies."
    Telling lies, Telling lies,
    Say you never want to be,
    Near to me, dear to me;

Figure 13. Cover of "Dreams, Just Dreams."

> Telling lies, close your eyes,
> Then a kiss or two I'll steal and give them back to you,
> While telling lies.

"Telling Lies"

As happens in many novelty songs, the performer is first cast in the role of a narrator, then is asked to speak in the voice of one of the song's characters. The "I" of the song is thus perceived as being neither the songwriter nor the singer, as happens in most ballads, but a character in the song, in this case Joe.

The only ballad of this group with a lyric in the first person throughout, "Dear Mayme, I Love You," has its text cast as a letter.

> Dear Mayme: I want to explain,
> Why I sat down to write you this note,
> Gee, Mayme, I do feel ashamed,
> It's the first letter I ever wrote,
> There's some little something 'way down in my heart,
> I haven't the nerve to say. . . .

The effect of this device is likewise to establish an emotional distance between the songwriter and the content of the lyric and to cast the singer in the role of representing an identified character rather than herself.

Because of the many features these pieces have in common with the novelty song, and because this fact led to their being performed on the vaudeville stage more often than were most ballads, I've coined the label "novelty ballad" for them.

There are several possible reasons for Berlin and Snyder's avoidance of the intense romantic sentiments of the high-class ballad, on the one hand, and the acute nostalgia of the popular ballad, on the other. Both men were young, in their twenties. Both were more drawn, at least in this period of their lives, to humor, irony, and satire than to directly expressed, deeply felt emotions. Berlin, as an immigrant and a city dweller, had no direct cultural ties to either the Victorian parlor, the environment of the high-class ballad, or to the bucolic Anglo-Celtic heritage that had spawned Moore's *Irish Melodies*, Foster's plantation melodies, and the later nineteenth-century nostalgic ballad.

The Berlin-Snyder ballads, and several others in the same style written by Berlin alone during this period, are set to mostly diatonic music serving as a somewhat neutral framework for the text, making little or no use of expressive chromaticism, climactic high notes, propulsive melodic sequence, or other devices derived from the classical repertory and associated with the high-class ballad, where they serve to underline or intensify the emotions expressed or implied in the lyric. (See excerpt from "Some Little Something About You" on facing page.)

I've met lots of girl-ies who were just my style,—
Oft' I've won-dered if an-oth-er boy like me,—

Girls whose charms most an - y boy would share,————
thinks there's some - thing sweet a - bout you too,————

Several of the Berlin/Snyder ballads are examples of other subgenres. "I Wish That You Was My Gal, Molly" and "Molly-O! Oh Molly!" are pseudo-Irish ballads in the tradition of William J. Scanlan's "Molly O!" of 1891. Three others—"Good-Bye, Girlie, And Remember Me" (coauthored with George Meyer, rather than with Snyder), "Christmas-Time Seems Years And Years Away," and "Kiss Me My Honey, Kiss Me"—are march ballads, in the style best epitomized by "Wait 'Til the Sun Shines, Nellie" (1905) by Andrew B. Sterling and Harry Von Tilzer, in which a romantic or sentimental lyric is sung in a brisk 2/4 tempo to an accompaniment bristling with fanfare-like and oom-pah figurations.

Exceptionally, "I Love You More Each Day" is an out-and-out nostalgic ballad, with a lyric mining the I-still-love-you-though-we're-old theme sounded most memorably in "Silver Threads Among the Gold" (Eben E. Rexford and H. P. Danks, 1873), set to music flowing along placidly in the style of a turn-of-the-century waltz ballad.

> Come, sit beside me darling, May, and look into my eyes,
> It seems as tho' 'twere yesterday I won you for my prize;
> The hand of time has turned your golden locks to silv'ry gray,
> The silver threads have drawn you closer to my heart each day.
> You were my queen at sweet sixteen,
> You're my queen at sixty three . . .

The song received little attention, and the two young songwriters were never moved to try another piece of this sort.

"Good-Bye, Girlie, And Remember Me" (1909)
"Some Little Something About You" (1909)
"I Wish That You Was My Gal, Molly" (1909)
"Next To Your Mother, Who Do You Love?" (1909)
"Christmas-Time Seems Years And Years Away" (1909)
"Before I Go And Marry, I Will Have A Talk With You" (1909)
"Someone Just Like You" (1909)
"Telling Lies" (1910)
"I Love You More Each Day" (1910)
"Kiss Me My Honey, Kiss Me" (1910)
*"When I'm Alone I'm Lonesome" (1911)
*"Molly-O! Oh, Molly!" (1911)
*"After The Honeymoon" (1911)
*"Bring Me A Ring In The Spring" (1911)
[*both words and music by Berlin]

Berlin's Post-Snyder High-Class and Semi-High-Class Ballads

In early 1911 several ballads for which Berlin had written both words and music were published by the Ted Snyder Company, and by the fall of that year the tremendous success of "Alexander's Ragtime Band" had freed him of the necessity of further collaboration with Ted Snyder; the two men never again wrote a ballad together. Berlin's own ballads soon became more openly expressive, suggesting that the emotional distancing so characteristic of the songs written by the two together had more to do with Snyder's temperament than with his own.

This new expressiveness is evident in three high-class ballads. "My Melody Dream," subtitled "A Song Poem," breaks completely with the usual introduction-vamp-verse-chorus format of the Tin Pan Alley song in favor of an ABA structure. The piano accompaniment flows and ripples, filling pauses and rests in the vocal line with countermelodies; chromatically altered chords are introduced for dramatic emphasis, the middle section changes key, and the vocal line moves inexorably to a climax on a sustained high note. The first-person lyric describes a melody that came to the protagonist in a dream, "to remind me of my love," then "vanished like my melody, like my melody dream," leaving him crying "come back, come back again." The song's somberness of expression is matched by the austere black-and-white front cover, bearing only the title, author's name, dedication, and publisher.

"He Promised Me" is a parody version of Reginald De Koven's "Oh Promise Me," one of the classics of the high-class ballad literature, introduced in the composer's operetta *Robin Hood* of 1890. In De Koven's ballad the protagonist asks his lover to promise that "someday you and I will take our love together to some sky, where we can be alone, and faith renew." Berlin makes pervasive use, in the song's introduction, verse, and chorus, of De Koven's familiar, distinctive opening motive, which begins with a leap of a major sixth. "Kindly stop that music from playing, 'Oh, promise me,' " pleads the female protagonist, "because it makes me sad, so sad."

> He promised me that some day he would marry me,
> He promised me a beautiful home,
> One down by the sea;
> He promised that he'd pay
> For the wedding day,
> On the first of May
> Then he moved away, and all he left,
> Were the promises he promised me.

Berlin distances himself from the song's sentiment by putting the words in the mouth of a protagonist of the opposite sex and setting her in a specific dramatic situation so that the song's "I" is an abandoned female, not the songwriter himself. Nevertheless, the emotional expression is much more direct and intense than in any of the Berlin-Snyder ballads.

"Spring And Fall" comes as close to an out-and-out art song as anything Berlin was to write. Through-composed in two sections corresponding to the two seasons of the title, the song changes in mood from the promise and happiness of spring at the beginning to autumnal melancholy, which concludes with an anguished cry (see musical example on following page):

> The sun had gone, the flowers died,
> And all nature look'd forlorn;
> It seem'd to me the angels cried,
> And I knew that you had gone.

With a vocal line encompassing a range of an octave and a fourth and a piano accompaniment filled with octaves and thick chords in the right hand and arpeggiated eighth- and sixteenth-note passages in the left, the piece looks (and sounds) almost nothing like most Tin Pan Alley songs.

These three high-class ballads are well-constructed and expressive specimens of the genre, suited for performance by refined women in their homes and on the recital stage by classically trained singers. Berlin had only limited interest in writing songs for these venues, however; his chief concern was now with the popular musical stage, and he set out to find a

more contemporary lyrical and musical expression of romantic love that would speak to audiences patronizing this venue.

"When It Rains, Sweetheart, When It Rains" is Berlin's first song to anticipate the style of such later classic waltz ballads as "Always," "Remember," and "The Girl That I Marry." The implied protagonist is a young male, and the emotional expression is so direct as to seem to be in the voice of the songwriter himself.

> I'll make ev'ry Monday a Sunday,
> I'll cover a wrong with a right,
> I'll still wear a smile in the morning,
> The smile that I wore last night.

I'll stick when the sunshine has vanish'd,
And darkness is all that remains,
I'll hold an umbrella up over your head,
When it rains, sweetheart, when it rains.

There are suggestions of the high-class ballad both in the lyric, even though it's written in vernacular rather than "poetical" language, and in the music. There's no vamp, for instance; melodic sequence is used for propulsion and dissonance for expressive effect, and the vocal line climaxes on a high, sustained note.

Most of the songs in this group also draw on elements of the high-class ballad, and in fact the publisher sometimes labeled them "semi-high-class ballads." As one can hear in period recordings of these pieces, they were sung in precise pitch and rhythm by performers with classically trained voices, with texts delivered in the pseudo British accent, complete with rolled "r"s assumed by actors of the day in "legitimate" theater.[25] "That's How I Love You" is typical: The lyric, a much more passionate expression of romantic love than that found in any of the Berlin-Snyder ballads, depicts the protagonist's love as being so intense that it will last "until the breath of life has gone." The final phrase of the first verse, "Let me say what's in my heart, for I want you to know," is a rhetorical device emphasizing the protagonist's earnestness in expressing the sentiment of the chorus: "I love you, darling, I love you, with a love as true as the heaven's blue." Musical references to the high-class ballad include the absence of a vamp, the virtuosic nature of the piano accompaniment, chromatically altered chords and expressive dissonances, and several abrupt shifts of tonality for dramatic effect.

Now——that my dream is re - al- ized,
Tell——me your love for me—— will grow

Now——that you love me so,——
Strong - er with ev - 'ry day,——

Berlin's biographers have singled out "When I Lost You" as his first mature, fully successful ballad. They have related the content of the lyric to the fact that in early 1912 Berlin married Dorothy Goetz, the sister of his friend and collaborator E. Ray Goetz, and that the bride died five months after their wedding of typhoid or pneumonia probably contracted during the couple's honeymoon in Havana. "When I Lost You," published several months after her death, has a lyric lamenting the loss of a loved one.

> I lost the sunshine and roses,
> I lost the heavens of blue,
> I lost the beautiful rainbow,
> I lost the morning dew;
> I lost the angel who gave me
> Summer, the whole winter through,
> I lost the gladness that turned into sadness,
> When I lost you.

It's not true that the song is "unlike any song Berlin had previously written" in being "an exceedingly simple and stately waltz employing a bittersweet harmony underneath the melody; diminished seventh chords added further melancholy."[26] As I have noted, some of his earlier high-class and popular ballads are characterized by precisely these elements. "When I Lost You" is distinguished from all previous songs by Berlin by its putative relationship to events in his own life, though. "He had had to write [the song]," explained his first biographer. "It gave him his first chance to voice his great unhappiness in the only language that meant anything to him."[27] And the song's first-person expression of grief was widely perceived as Berlin's commentary on this tragic event, when the piece was published and after, whether or not Berlin intended this; Dorothy's death had been so widely publicized that anyone hearing "When I Lost You" or singing it at home, could scarcely avoid connecting the event with the song. One biographer goes so far as to imply that Berlin cynically took advantage of the tragedy:

> The composer was too much a creature of Tin Pan Alley not to see the song's obvious commercial merit, and it was duly published by his company. . . . It began to sell, and by the following year, it became his first hit ballad as the public snapped up a million copies of his grief. . . . Dorothy's death, or to be more specific, Berlin's feeling about her death, was now one more item for sale on Woolworth's shelves.[28]

It should be noted, however, that nowhere on the sheet music and in none of the publicity generated by Berlin's publishing house is a connection made between the song and Dorothy's death. And, interestingly, Berlin seems to have first conceived the song with another text. Among the unpublished items in the Irving Berlin Collection in the Library of Congress, typed on Berlin's stationery and with inked holograph corrections, is a lyric titled "That's Just Why I Love You."

> A thousand times you've asked me
> Why I love you
> Come to my arms and I'll answer
> I'll tell you just why I do.
> > I love the flowers that bloom in the spring
> > I love the birds in the tree tops, that sing
> > I love the Church bells that solemnly [sic] ring
> > I love the sweet morning dew
> > I love the angel's [sic] who watch from above
> > I love the cooing of each little dove
> > I love the things "God" wants me to love
> > That's just why I love you.*

The structure of verse and chorus match the unusual formal design of "When I Lost You," and the text can be fitted to the melody with no changes beyond the repetition of several notes. Though one lyric is an expression of joy and the other of sorrow, the music works as well with one as the other.

If Berlin did indeed intend "When I Lost You" as a conscious expression of grief over his bride's death, then its first version, "That's Just Why I Love You," may record his very different emotions during his courtship of Dorothy and their brief marriage. For that matter, the slightly earlier song "That's How I Love You," copyrighted and presumably written during their brief time together, could be a similar expression of his emotional state before and during his marriage.

The important point isn't whether the connection between "When I Lost You" and Berlin's brief early marriage was deliberate but that he wrote his first ballads of convincing emotional expression during the time of his courtship, marriage, and bereavement.

> "When It Rains, Sweetheart, When It Rains" (1911)
> "My Melody Dream" (1911)
> "He Promised Me" (1911)
> "Spring and Fall" (1912)
> "That's How I Love You" (1912)
> "When I'm Thinking Of You" (1912)
> "When I Lost You" (1912)
> "If All The Girls I Knew Were Like You" (1912)

Berlin's First Rhythmic Ballads

Berlin himself once claimed that one of his important contributions to American popular song was the prominent role he played in the introduction of the rhythmic ballad.[29] His first experiments with this new subgenre date from 1911 and 1912, in several songs that are innovative in ways extending far beyond the use of syncopated rhythms in songs of romantic expression.

Although the first-person expression of personal sentiment in the lyric of "Stop, Stop, Stop (Come Over And Love Me Some More)" stamps it as a ballad, the song fits into neither of the two great traditions of the genre as it was known in nineteenth-century America and in the early years of Tin Pan Alley. The music of high-class ballads had drawn on styles and gestures of the classical repertory, and that of popular ballads had echoed the nineteenth century's notion of folk music. There was no reference in either type to any of the turn-of-the-century syncopated dances, which were still associated in the popular mind with African Americans and their culture and were used on the popular stage only in purportedly comic songs sung in blackface. But both verse and chorus of "Stop! Stop! Stop!" make immediate and repeated use of a common musical feature of cakewalk, "coon," and ragtime songs: the rhythmic tension between $3+3+2$ patterns in the melody and $2+2+2+2$ patterns in the accompaniment.

And although the song bears the ubiquitous tempo marking *moderato,* period recordings of this and other early rhythmic ballads by Berlin move at a pace approaching that of the syncopated dance music of the era.

The lyric is unlike that of earlier ballads in that it deals neither with romantic, enduring love nor with nostalgia for lost childhood or lost love, but rather with immediate physical attraction.

> Honey, there's something buzzin' 'round my heart,
> Something that must be satisfied,
> My dearie,
> See that Morris chair
> Standing over there,
> There's some room to spare,
> Now for some love prepare.

The word "love" is used in the chorus as an active verb rather than an emotional state, in fact: "Come over and love me some more." Another anomaly has to do with the use of the word "honey." As was discussed in Chapter Two, certain proper names or forms of address were associated with black protagonists in songs of this era; "honey" as a term of endearment was one such code words. "Put Your Arms Around Me, Honey" (1910) by Junie McCree and Albert Von Tilzer is a case in point; although the piece may not be thought of as a "coon" song nowadays, the verses, particularly the second, leave no question as to the ethnicity of the protagonist:

> Music am a playin' such a "lovin' glide,"
> That my feet keep a moving to and fro,
> And with you a swayin' I'll be satisfied,
> To dance untill *(sic)* we hear the roosters crow.
> I love seven 'leven, I love chicken too,
> Nearest thing to heaven is to be with you.
> For I'm spoony, moony, loony,
> But my love is true.

The term "baby" had a similar meaning, as in the title and text of "Hello! Ma Baby" (1899) by Joseph Howard and Ida Emerson, unequivocally a "coon" song with its lyric in dialect, including the word "coon," and a sheet music cover depicting a black couple talking by telephone.

Berlin's "Stop! Stop! Stop!," however, has no trace of dialect in the lyric beyond the use of the word "honey," Elida Morris's period recording[30] has no trace of "black" dialect or interpolated dialogue, and there's nothing on the sheet music cover or in the publisher's promotional copy to suggest a black protagonist. Even though both text and music of "Stop! Stop! Stop!" make some use of details usually associated with songs representing black protagonists, Berlin intends the characters in this song to be perceived as white, and the piece's references to the "coon" song, clear enough to contemporary audiences if not to us today, had the effect of giving the song an earthy flavor—of stripping it of the genteel aura that still clung to the ballad.

To appreciate the impact of songs such as this, one has only to look ahead at the flood of Tin Pan Alley ballads of the next two decades with texts in vernacular rather than "poetical" language, portraying playful or erotic interplay rather than high-flown romantic love and set to music that makes use of the rhythms of contemporary syncopated dances.

There is some slight ambivalence in the promotional copy for "Stop! Stop! Stop!" run by the Ted Snyder Company in *Variety*. The issue for 19 November 1910 claimed that the song had been "pronounced by all as a better song than 'Mendelssohn Tune,'" and on 14 January 1911 readers were told again that the piece was "bigger than 'Mendelssohn Tune' ever was." The reference is to Berlin's "That Mesmerizing Mendelssohn Tune," a "coon" song that had been his most commercially successful piece to that date, and the intent of relating "Stop! Stop! Stop!" to that particular song is to suggest the possibility of blackface performance. But there is no ambivalence about the race of the protagonist of "You've Got Me Hypnotized," which makes similar use of syncopated dance rhythms to underline a text that is not only shot through with "honeys" but also uses the word "blue" for perhaps the first time in a popular ballad. The lyric of "Cuddle Up" is an even more explicit invitation to physical intimacy than had been extended in "Stop! Stop! Stop!":

> Oh, my darlin' beau,
> I want to show I love you so;
> And if you want to know just how I love you, dear,
> Come and cuddle up now.

"Dog Gone That Chilly Man!," "You've Got Me Hypnotized," "Bring Back My Lovin' Man," "I've Got To Have Some Lovin' Now" (see following musical example), "Do It Again," "Goody, Goody, Goody, Goody, Good," and "He's So Good To Me" are all similar pieces with first-person lyrics in vernacular language set to music that makes some use of syncopated rhythms.

All these pieces have female protagonists who, rather than swearing romantic, faithful, and lasting love to their male partners, instead offer immediate,
willing, and enthusiastic physical gratification: "I've got to have some lovin'
now, won't you let me show you how," they beg, or "Hold me steady,
now I'm ready, Umm! . . . Do it again! do it again!" If spurned or abandoned by their man, they want him back.

> Bring back my lovin' man,
> Bring back my great big bunch of sweetness,
> Bring back them kisses sweet,
> Find 'em! Find 'em!
> The kisses with the steam behind 'em!

What emerges in these pieces is a type of ballad that differs from those of
the nineteenth century not only in stylistic details of music and text but
more broadly in the representation of women. The voice of the song is no
longer that of the songwriter, hoping to find (or expressing his delight at
having already found) a mate "just like the girl that married dear old Dad,"
to quote the famous line from a song by William Dillon and Harry Von
Tilzer, someone adept at keeping the house clean while tending to the
children and being faithful until death to her husband. Now the "I" of the
lyric is the singer, always a female, identifying herself as a woman who
wants to "cuddle up" and then "do it again"; afterwards she enthuses that
"it" was "goody, goody, goody, goody, good." There is no mention in these
songs of marriage or of children.

But just as surely as the portrait of the virtuous, faithful, cultured, patient wife/mother was a construct of male-dominated nineteenth-century
society, the new woman of the rhythmic ballad was a creation of the male
songwriters of Tin Pan Alley and of the male impresarios and producers
from whose stages these songs were sung.

None of Berlin's rhythmic ballads was a collaborative effort, not even
"Stop! Stop! Stop!," which dates from a time when most of his songs were
written together with Ted Snyder. Nor are there clear antecedents for these
pieces. There are no ballads of this sort from the first decade of the century;
none were written by George M. Cohan, Harry Von Tilzer, Paul Dresser,
or Charles K. Harris. Shelton Brooks came closest, with songs such as
"Some Of These Days" (1910):

> Some of these days you'll miss me honey,
> Some of these days you'll feel so lonely,
> You'll miss my hugging,
> You'll miss my kissing,
> You'll miss me honey when you go away.

Brooks's characters in such songs are not as unequivocally white as those found in Berlin's rhythmic ballads, particularly since singers and audiences knew that Brooks was black himself, and musically there were no more than hints of syncopation in these pieces. Nor did many of Berlin's contemporaries rush to get songs of this sort into print. Only Joe McCarthy, with such pieces as "Honey Man" (1911, with Al Piantadosi) and "You Made Me Love You" (1913, with Jimmy Monaco), and a handful of less noted songwriters—Jack Frost, for instance, with "Don't You Love Your Baby No More?" (1915)—approached the lyric and musical style of Berlin's rhythmic ballads. The heyday of the genre was to come later, in the 1920s, with "I'm Just Wild About Harry" by Noble Sissle and Eubie Blake, "Do-Do-Do" and " 'S Wonderful" by Ira and George Gershwin, "I Wanna Be Loved By You" by Bert Kalmar, Herbert Stothart, and Harry Ruby, and of course many songs by Berlin himself.

It appears that more than any other subgenre, the rhythmic ballad was Berlin's creation.

"Stop, Stop, Stop (Come Over And Love Me Some More)" (1910)
"Dog Gone That Chilly Man" (1911)
"You've Got Me Hypnotized" (1911)
"Bring Back My Lovin' Man" (1911)
"Cuddle Up" (1911)
"I've Got To Have Some Lovin' Now" (1912)
"Do It Again" (1912)
"Goody, Goody, Goody, Goody, Good" (1912)

Berlin's Ballads of 1913 and 1914

Berlin continued to write ballads in 1913 and 1914, although pieces of this genre make up a small fraction of his output for these two years and none of them enjoyed much success. Most of them are in styles that he had tried before. "Take Me Back," "God Gave You To Me," and "If I Had You" are semi-high-class waltz ballads, and new rhythmic ballads include "You're Goin' To Lose Your Baby Some Day" and "It Wasn't What He Said, But The Way He Said It!" Two others, "Kiss Your Sailor Boy Goodbye" and "That's My Idea Of Paradise," continue his rather clumsy struggles with the older-style, sentimental common-time ballad, and he also tried his hand at lyrics portraying women abandoned by their lovers, anticipating the torch song of the 1920s and 1930s, with "You Picked A Bad Time Out To Say Goodbye" and "I've Got To Catch A Train Goodbye."

In addition, after years of writing ballads with coy or suggestive texts, of often avoiding the direct expression of deeply felt emotions by putting the lyric in the voice of a protagonist who is clearly not the songwriter, and of incorporating the gestures of contemporary dance music into the ballad, Berlin now turned out a few ballads in styles more suggestive of nineteenth-century types. He had never before written, or at least never published, a "domestic" ballad, a subgenre of the popular ballad that celebrated the joys of a happy marriage and the deep and lasting affection among members of an extended family. The just-married couple in "Furnishing A Home For Two" have more on their minds than "cuddling": they're setting out to establish a permanent life and abode together.

> I'll hang a picture on the wall,
> You'll hold the chair so I don't fall, my honey,
> While I lay the carpet in the dining room,
> You'll be busy with a broom;
> I'll place the dishes on the shelf,
> You'll change them, dear, to suit yourself . . .
> We'll be such a happy pair,
> Furnishing a home for two.

The female child protagonist of "Somebody's Coming To My House" describes her family's excitement over the imminent arrival of another child: Her father "feels so happy he's jumping with joy, all he keeps saying is 'I hope it's a boy,' " her mother keeps crooning "He'll be president soon," and the entire family is "jumping with joy." "You've Got Your Mother's Big Blue Eyes!" is a father's paean to his seven-year-old daughter, and to his wife: "If you're half the lady that your mother is, I'll be mighty proud of you." And "Always Treat Her Like A Baby" is a gentle plea from a bride's mother to her new son-in-law:

> Treat her like a baby, for she's only a baby;
> When you take her with you lad
> You are taking all we had;
> I know she'll be a comfort to you like she's always been to me,
> So do be kind and keep unhappiness away;
> And when you find her golden hair is turning gray
> Continue to treat her like a baby.

Also for the first time in his songwriting career, Berlin wrote several rustic ballads, nostalgic reminiscences of a rural childhood he had never known himself, "Happy Little Country Girl" and "I Want To Go Back To Michigan." There is even an "inspirational" ballad, "We Have Much To Be Thankful For."

In order to understand why, in 1913, Berlin turned to types of songs that had never interested him before, two things must be kept in mind. First, as will be detailed in Chapter Five, his ambition was no longer to continue turning out songs for the vaudeville stage or the home circle but to write a complete show for the musical theater. Many of the pieces he wrote during this time, including his domestic, nostalgic, and inspirational ballads, were probably more in the nature of exercises to sharpen and broaden his songwriting skills for the shows he hoped to write than they were attempts to turn out hit songs, and some remained unpublished. Although none of his ballads of this period achieved the popular success of his earlier and later pieces, they contain passages that reveal Berlin's increasing technical mastery over melodic and formal materials. The final bars of "Always Treat Her Like A Baby," for instance, with their smooth sequential movement to a climax on the penultimate note of the song, have a flow found in none of his earlier songs but characteristic of many of his best later show songs and ballads.

A second factor was that Berlin's economic and social status had changed dramatically since he wrote his first song only six years earlier. By the end of

1912 he had written a number of major national and international hit songs; he had been a featured performer of his own songs in New York, London, and elsewhere; he was a partner in a thriving Tin Pan Alley publishing firm; he was a prominent and honored member of the Friars Club; and his economic status had permitted him to take an entire suite in a fashionable area of the city and to move his mother into a comfortable home in the Bronx, far from the Lower East Side where the family had lived for so many years. Berlin was no longer an alien and a cultural outsider; he was now a successful and accepted figure in New York City's world of entertainment, and beyond that as well. His first musical, *Watch Your Step,* starring Irene and Vernon Castle, would open in December 1914 as the most widely publicized show of the season, playing in a legitimate house before an audience that included many of New York's famous, well-to-do, and socially prominent, and the show would be reviewed in the *New York Times* and other "establishment" publications that had paid scant attention to his earlier career and accomplishments.

By 1914, then, Berlin was writing not for the working-class and ethnically marginalized audiences of the vaudeville houses but for a new and much more privileged audience that was finding the products of the American musical stage to be an enjoyable and socially appropriate alternative to grand opera and legitimate drama. This new audience would respond to a more sophisticated lyrical and musical style than Berlin had employed in his early songs, and many of his ballads of 1913 and 1914 show him working toward such a style by combining elements of his own earlier semi-high-class and rhythmic ballads.

"Down In My Heart" (1912)
"You Picked A Bad Day Out To Say Good-bye" (1913)
"Happy Little Country Girl" (1913)
"We Have Much To Be Thankful For" (1913)
"Somebody's Coming To My House" (1913)
"Kiss Your Sailor Boy Goodbye" (1913)
"Take Me Back" (1913)
"I Could Live On Love And Kisses" (1913) (unpublished)
"I've Got A Lot Of Love For You" (1913) (unpublished)
"I've Got To Catch A Train, Goodbye" (1913) (unpublished)
"You've Got Your Mother's Big Blue Eyes!" (1914)
"If I Had You" (1914)
"God Gave You To Me" (1914)
"I Want To Go Back To Michigan (Down On The Farm)" (1914)
"Always Treat Her Like A Baby" (1914)
"Furnishing A Home For Two" (1914)
"That's My Idea Of Paradise" (1914)

Chapter Five

Berlin's Early Songs for the Musical Stage

Irving Berlin has accomplished an Aladdin-like transition—from piano player in a Bowery dance hall to the authorship of WATCH YOUR STEP, a musical melange, which is attracting the elite of "sassiety" to the New Amsterdam.[1]

Watch Your Step, a "syncopated musical show in three acts" with a cast headed by Irene and Vernon Castle and the comedian Frank Tinney, had its first New York performance at the New Amsterdam on 8 December 1914 after tryouts in Syracuse and Detroit.[2] The book was by Harry B. Smith, the lyrics and the score—overture, songs, duets, ensembles, production numbers, incidental music—were by Berlin. Critical reception was positive; the review in the *New York Times* the morning after the show opened was typical:

> [It was] as gay, extravagant, and festive an offering as this city could possibly hope to see. . . . [It is a show] which the London dailies would describe as a "big, noisy, typically American entertainment," and which the London public would witness clamorously and with every evidence of high approval. As large a portion of the New York public as could be packed into the New Amsterdam last evening seemed uncommonly pleased, and with reason.
>
> More than to any one else, "Watch Your Step" belongs to Irving Berlin. He is the young master of syncopation, the gifted and industrious writer of words and music for songs that have made him rich and envied. This is the first time [he] has turned his attention to providing the music for an entire evening's entertainment. For it, he has written a score of his mad melodies, nearly all of them of the tickling sort, born to be caught up and whistled at every street corner, and warranted to set any roomful a-dancing.

Public reception was equally enthusiastic. The show ran for 175 performances, and a successful London production was launched at the Empire

173

Theatre well before the original production closed in New York. Although some historians of the musical stage have tended to downplay the show, others have seen it as a key piece in the Americanization of the musical comedy in the second decade of the twentieth century. Gerald Bordman, for instance, gives it a prominent place at the beginning of "Act Three" ("The Birth of the Modern Musical: 1914–1921") of his magisterial survey of the American musical theater.[3]

In order to assign *Watch Your Step* its proper place in the history of the American musical stage and in Irving Berlin's career as a writer of musical shows, one must first try to bring some order to the wide range of shows produced in the decade leading up to its premier and to determine where they fitted into the fabric of American society.

The American Musical Stage in the Early Twentieth Century

Although it would be a nightmarishly difficult job to construct a tidy taxonomy of the musical shows produced on the American stage in the first decade and a half of the twentieth century, some order can be brought to this repertory by approaching it not as a collection of discrete genres but rather as a collection of individual shows that fit at one point or another along a broad spectrum.

Opera stands at one end of this spectrum. Although it had been a semipopular form of entertainment in the first half of the nineteenth century, sung in English, produced in theaters offering a range of entertainment from legitimate drama to minstrel shows, and priced so as to be accessible to some of the working and clerical classes as well as to the more privileged, in the decades after the Civil War opera moved inexorably in the direction of becoming a diversion for the country's elite only. When the Metropolitan Opera House opened in New York City on 22 October 1883, it immediately became a bastion of "high culture" for America's "new elite centred on the leaders of the country's oligarchical industrial expansion, eager to assume the political and social roles played by aristocracies at other times and in other countries, including patronage of the arts."[4] Joseph Horowitz discusses how "the Gilded Age had produced a new stratum of fashionable New York wealth whose ambitions . . . included a Park Avenue apartment, a Newport villa, and—copying Old World prerogatives—a box at the opera,"[5] and Lawrence W. Levine summarizes matters in this way:

> By the end of the nineteenth century [opera], like Shakespearean drama, was no longer part and parcel of the eclectic blend of culture that had characterized the United States. More and more, opera in America meant foreign-language opera performed in opera houses . . . which were deeply influenced if not controlled by wealthy patrons whose impresarios and conductors strove to keep

the opera they presented free from the influence of other genres and other groups. . . . All forms of opera were deeply affected by the growing insistence that opera was a "higher" form of art demanding a cultivated audience.[6]

An evening's entertainment at the opera house usually consisted of a single work with continuous music by a single composer, written in the musical style of then-contemporary European classical music. The text of an opera, called a libretto, took the form of a dramatic narrative, almost always set in some distant time and place and usually melodramatic or tragic in mood. Spectacular solo singing by performers trained in a highly specialized style of vocal production were highlights of most operatic productions, but the stage spectacle created by lavish, expensive costumes, elaborate scenery and lighting, a large cast of principals, chorus members and extras for ensemble scenes, and often ballet or other dance sequences was also an important component of an operatic performance. The genre was understood to be a product of European culture; almost all operas performed in the United States at this time had been written by European composers, and pieces were sung in their original language, intelligible to only a few members of the audience. Like so much of the "high art" favored by the elite classes, opera was assumed to have little or no connection with the contemporary world of its audience.

Vaudeville, at the other end of the spectrum, contrasted with opera in virtually every way. As discussed in Chapter One, a vaudeville show was made up of a succession of acts or "turns," each by different entertainers, with no dramatic or musical unity from one event to the next. There were no resources in vaudeville houses for elaborate stage spectacles, and the audience was made up chiefly of immigrant and first-generation working-class people.

Between opera and vaudeville, occupying the two opposite ends of the spectrum, a complex middle field of genres, subgenres, and mixed genres flourished. It was here that the most successful and uniquely American forms of twentieth-century musical theater emerged.

Of the types of shows making up this in-between terrain, operetta—as exemplified by the works of Gilbert and Sullivan; Viennese classics such as *The Chocolate Soldier* (Oscar Straus), *The Merry Widow* (Franz Lehar), and *Die Fledermaus* (Johan Strauss); pieces by the European-born Victor Herbert *(Babes in Toyland* and *Naughty Marietta)*, Rudolf Friml *(The Firefly)*, and Gustave Kerker *(The Belle of New York)*; and an occasional show by an American-born composer such as Reginald De Koven *(Robin Hood)* or John Philip Sousa *(El Capitan)*—was closest to opera in style, structure, and audience. Although written also by a single composer, an operetta differed from an opera in several critical respects: Contemporary dramatic settings were much more common than in opera; narration was carried forward mostly in spoken dialogue, usually in English, rather than in sung recitative; plots were comic or romantic rather than tragic or melodramatic; the music required less technical skill to perform and was thus more amenable to semiprofessional or even amateur performance; and this music often drew on social dances of the day, such as the waltz, polka, or one-step.

Like opera, operetta was perceived as being European in origin, musical style, and singing technique. Performed in "legitimate" houses, operettas attracted the same sort of audience that patronized other attractions at these venues, as I will discuss later.

By far the largest number of works for the musical stage from this period were pieces variously called musical comedies, musical plays, or plays with music. These works were held together by a "book" of comic, sentimental, or burlesque character that served more importantly as a vehicle for introducing songs, choruses, dances, and ensemble numbers than to give the show much dramatic continuity or character development. The souvenir program's summary of Edgar Smith's book for the Lew Fields production *Hanky-Panky* (1911), a burlesque on George M. Cohan's hit show of the previous season, *Get-Rich-Quick Wallingford,* gives some sense of the nature of these shows.

> At the villa of Sir J. Rufus Wallingford, a recent addition to the British Peerage, are gathered William Rausmitt, a capitalist, Solomon Bumpski, an "angel"[an anarchist], Herman Bierheister, Rausmitt's partner, and Wallingford himself. With them are his stenographer, Clorinda Scribblem, Iona Carr, a former chorus girl, and the Wiggle Sisters, who are in vaudeville. Blackie Daw arrive to reproach his former pal—whereas Wallingford determines to raffle off his newly acquired "ancestral" mansion. Bierheister and Rausmitt win the house just in time to prevent Bumpski from blowing up the place with a bomb. In celebration, the whole party determines to go to America. But before they leave, Bumpski opens a mummy case which Bierheister has purchased—and out of it springs Cleopatra, who has been entranced for two thousand years, but who is now very much alive, and who recognizes Wallingford as the original Marc Anthony. After this surprising incident, the party sets sail; and in a final jamboree on the campus of the University of Chicago, Hanky Panks to its delirious conclusion.

Although the music for shows of this sort was usually written by a single composer or by several composers working as a team, performers often interpolated songs by other songwriters into the show, creating a mélange of musical styles. Unlike operas and most operettas, these pieces were set in contemporary and often urban America, the dialogue was in colloquial English, and the music was largely grounded in the styles of then-contemporary popular songs and social dances. *The Black Crook* (1866) is often taken to be the first show of this type; important successors included

A Trip To Chinatown (1891), the musical plays of George M. Cohan beginning with *Little Johnny Jones* (1904) and *Forty-five Minutes from Broadway* (1906), many of the shows produced by Lew Fields between 1904 and 1912, and the Princess Theatre shows, with music by Jerome Kern, from 1915.

Yet another type of show was made up of several discrete sections or "acts," each with its own cast of performers and with no dramatic or musical connections among the segments. The Weber and Fields shows at the Broadway Music Hall, beginning in 1894, which combined burlesque versions of popular operas, operettas, and dramas with a string of vaudeville acts, epitomized this type of show at the end of the nineteenth century, and the evening's entertainment that opened Joseph Lasky's Folies Bergere restaurant/theater in 1911, discussed earlier in connection with "Alexander's Ragtime Band," is a later example. The follies/revue show, which began with *The Passing Show* (1894) and continued with the annual *Ziegfeld Follies* and the Schubert-produced *Passing Shows,* was another variety, with a semblance of a plot or at least a theme or common setting within each act or section, if not for the entire show. These pieces had the resources for elaborate stage productions, and their principal performers appeared at different times during the evening, rather than in single turns as in vaudeville. Burlesque was somewhat similar, although more focused on takeoffs or parodies of other recently successful shows.

The spectrum of shows for the musical stage, then, encompassed the genres of opera, operetta, musical comedy, follies/revue, burlesque, and vaudeville, and any given show might fit somewhere along this spectrum without exhibiting the precise collection of characteristics commonly thought to define one or another of these genres.

The Changing Audience for the Legitimate Theater

Legitimate theaters were the venues for shows that fell anywhere between opera and vaudeville. Although statistics on the constitution of audiences for such theaters are meager, indirect and anecdotal evidence suggests that they made up a middle ground between the predominantly elite audience of the opera house and the predominantly working-class audiences of the vaudeville theater, with social custom and ticket prices favoring persons who were in the upper brackets of these "middling classes." In addition, as a neutral cultural space between opera and vaudeville, the legitimate theater sometimes attracted people who usually patronized one or another of these.

In a development that was to prove critical to the history of the American musical stage, the turn of the century saw vaudeville-style entertainment brought to the legitimate stage for the first time. Early in their careers, Joe Weber and Lew Fields had performed in vaudeville houses and other venues for variety entertainment in front of the predominantly working-class and immigrant/first-generation patrons of these places; much of their comedy took the form of parodying various ethnic groups, which had the effect of allowing their audiences to see themselves portrayed on stage. In 1896 Weber and Fields opened their Broadway Music Hall with the idea of attracting people from the more privileged classes by offering their shows in a theater rather than a vaudeville house. Continuing the strategy of offering comic and satirical depictions of their audiences, they introduced new characters from the upper classes. "No longer were immigrants the prime targets of their humor. The Music Hall's resident ethnics—Dutch (Weber and Fields, Sam Bernard), Irish (John T. Kelly), Jewish (David Warfield)—were the means to bring the dashing soldiers, saintly women, and other society folk who populated the stage down a peg."[7] All of this was done in the comic and musical styles of vaudeville, although sometimes the dramatic and musical repertories of the privileged classes were subjected to burlesque and parody treatment.

An excerpt from the final scene of Ziegfeld's *Follies of 1910* demonstrates how vaudeville-style parody and satire were directed at the privileged classes in the first decade of the century. As the scene opens, John D. Rockefeller has proposed to his fellow millionaires that they make it possible for new immigrants to go to college, to "benefit mankind by spreading knowledge." The chorus sings:

> Come on to Harvard, Izzy!
>   And come on to Princeton, Mike!
> We've got to spend this money,
>   So to College we will hike.
> We'll study Latin and French and Greek,
> And maybe English we'll learn to speak;
>   For we're all going to College, Boys!
>   Rah! Rah! Rah!

John D. Rockefeller Junior rushes in, dragging Kowalski, just off the boat from Europe.

(The Millionaires seize Kowalski, choke him, go through his pockets and find a large roll of bills. Kowalski struggles. They stand him on his head and shake coin out of his pockets. All scramble for it. The millionaires divide up the money.)

JOHN D. JUNIOR
This wretch has deceived us!

CARNEGIE *(Severely)*
How is it that you happen to have this money?

KOWALSKI

Vull, I just landed. I never met you gentlemens before.

(The Millionaires all have some of Kowalski's money and his pockets are turned inside out.)

JOHN D.

My poor man, you are now a worthy subject of charity. Take this and go and get a college education. *(Gives him a dollar)*

KOWALSKI

To hell with college. *(Exit L.)*

JOHN D.

Ah! How happy I feel when I have done a good action.

ALL

You are the greatest benefactor of the human race.

(They decorate John D. with wings and a halo. He soars upward like the apotheosis of Marguerite in "Faust," while they all sing the final Trio in "Faust.")

> All hail great John D.
> Ruler of all this land so free
> The people all adore thee.
> To thee we bend the knee
> All hail great John D.
> You are an angel we agree.

(TABLEAU. *All the millionaires as angels. John D. floating up to heaven. Red Lights*)

END OF SCENE[8]

It would be a mistake, I think, to see this on-stage ribbing of the privileged classes as sharp social criticism. Just as vaudeville had discovered that the very people parodied in ethnic novelty songs would come to the theater to see themselves portrayed on stage, even in caricature, so Fields, Ziegfeld, and the Schuberts used comic portrayals of the leisured and elite classes to help attract these very people to their shows.

In the first decades of the twentieth century, then, producers, writers, and composers for the musical stage, most of whom were immigrant or first-generation Americans, began creating shows not for their own kind, as they had done earlier, but for more privileged audiences. The ending of the scene just cited is instructive of their approach: The parodying of the opera *Faust* would be lost on a typical vaudeville habitué but not on a person moving in circles in which some knowledge of opera was assumed.

Composing for the Musical Theater

Composing for a musical comedy or for an extended sequence in a follies/ revue show was a different proposition from writing a song for the vaude- ville stage or the home circle. Most obviously, music other than songs for a single voice was needed: an overture and other scene-opening instrumental numbers to be played by the orchestra; music for dance sequences and incidental or mood-setting music to accompany stage action; pieces to be sung by the chorus and as duos and other vocal ensemble numbers by the principals; and music for the elaborate production numbers that came to be so characteristic of such shows.

Many composers for the popular musical stage, such as Victor Herbert, had formal training in music theory and classical composition. Others, like George M. Cohan, while lacking such training, knew how to write songs appropriate for the theater and to sketch the larger musico-dramatic and instrumental numbers needed for a work of musical theater as a result of their years of practical experience on the stage.

The pieces in musical comedies and follies/revue shows that required the most knowledge of the musical stage were the production numbers, the equivalent of ensemble scenes in opera, that brought together one or more principals with chorus and dancers in an extended sequence, often featur- ing elaborate costumes and scenic effects. Usually but not always positioned at the beginnings and ends of scenes and acts, these were set pieces, specta- cles for the eye and ear, often serving to parade attractive women before the audience.

The lyrics of a production number needed to be appropriate for stage action involving a number of people in group activity; thus, they could be neither an intimate expression of romantic, nostalgic, or moralistic senti- ments, as in the ballad, nor a third-person description of (or a first-person expression by) an individual, as in ethnic novelties and "suggestive" songs. Since the voice of a production number is a collective one, coming from the entire ensemble, the lyric must be either a third-person description of events taking place on the stage or, if written in the first person, cast as a message addressed by the ensemble to the audience—"we" singing to the plural "you." As for the music of a production number, it had to be capable of making musical sense when performed en masse by one or more princi- pals, the chorus, and orchestra; it was usually lively, extroverted, and suit- able for dancing of some sort.

Solo vocal numbers for the popular musical stage tended to be different in substance and style from songs written for vaudeville or the home circle. The principals in a book musical sing in the context of a drama, and no matter how flimsy the plot, the singers are identified with their stage roles; that is, when a song has a lyric in the first person, the protagonist (the "I") is the stage character portrayed by the singer, not the singer herself. These songs may take the form of a soliloquy, with the protagonist reflecting on the emotional state to which the events of the drama have brought her; they may be addressed by one character in the drama to another, or others; or they may be extraneous to the thread of the drama while still serving to suggest or develop the stage character portrayed by the singer.

As the popular musical theater reached out to more educated and "cultured" audiences in the early twentieth century, the musical style of songs written for these shows began to change. Most songs for the vaudeville stage and for earlier musical comedy were written in a syllabic style, in a number of strophes each followed by a brief chorus. The chief emphasis was on the text, as the performer sketched and developed a comic or satirical vignette, often in dialect; although the music might color the lyric with hints of an appropriate ethnic style or develop a catchy refrain that would stick in the listener's memory, its most important function was to serve as a frame for the lyric. Stage songs of the period, by contrast, began to take on more musical autonomy, as in opera and operetta. That is, although the music of a song might be appropriate in general style and mood for the dramatic moment sketched in the lyric, it could also take on a life of its own, unfolding according to purely musical considerations through the use of sequences, goal-oriented melodic and harmonic patterns leading to climaxes and then subsiding from these, sustained legato lines and climactic high notes designed to display the singer's vocal technique to best advantage, and the placing of emphasis on the chorus of a song rather than on the verse.

Patrons of the legitimate theater were quite aware of the off- and on-stage identities of the leading performers, and they often came to the theater as much to see and hear these stars as for the dramatic offering itself. Accordingly, it was common practice for principal singers, at one point or another during the show, to move forward to the footlights, literally and figuratively stepping out of the drama in progress and their roles in it, in order to address a set piece directly to the audience. These interpolated songs had nothing to do with either the plot of the show or its music and were, in fact, often the work of a songwriter other than the show's chief composer(s). Selected not by the producer or musical director of the show but by the performers themselves to display their distinctive musical and interpretive skills, they could be of whatever genre or style the performers felt they could do most effectively—sentimental or nostalgic ballads, "suggestive" songs, "coon" songs, or other ethnic novelties. They were interruptions not only in the show's dramatic flow but also in whatever musical unity the show might have.

In order to sketch a fuller picture of the state of the popular musical stage immediately before *Watch Your Step* and to examine how Berlin gradually came to grasp the nature of writing for the musical stage during these years, in the rest of this chapter I will discuss briefly each of the shows to which he contributed one or more pieces of music, as well as the songs themselves.

Berlin's First Show Song

Berlin was still a teenager when "She Was A Dear Little Girl," which he wrote in collaboration with Ted Snyder, was interpolated by Marie Cahill into the musical comedy *The Boys and Betty*. The show, with a book by George V. Hobart and a score by Silvio Hein, opened at Wallach's on 11 February 1909 and enjoyed a moderately successful New York run of seventeen weeks before being taken on the road.[9] As was customary, the song's publisher, the Ted Snyder Company in this case, attempted to capitalize on its inclusion in a stage production by featuring a large portrait of the star who sang it, with reference to the show itself, on the sheet music cover.

Having a song interpolated into a Broadway show by one of its stars was no mean accomplishment for a young songwriter with no more than a dozen published songs to his credit, although the song was probably in the show because its coauthor was the more veteran songwriter Ted Snyder. Cahill was an established star of the musical stage; high points of her career to this point included the title role in *Sally in Our Alley* (1902), in which she introduced Bob Cole's "Under The Bamboo Tree," and the star role in *It Happened in Nordland* (1904), with a score by Victor Herbert, which opened the new Lew Fields Theater on 42nd Street. In a period when it was common enough for principals to interpolate songs of their own choosing into a show, Cahill was particularly noted for this practice. As early as 1902 she had caused a controversy by interpolating the song "Nancy Brown" into *The Wild Rose* against the wishes of the composer of the show, Ludwig Englander, and she eventually left the cast of *It Happened in Nordland* after a dispute with Herbert, who didn't want his score interrupted by the music of other composers.

The lyric of "She Was A Dear Little Girl" has nothing to do with Hobart's book, which is concerned with the adventures of an American woman who goes off to Paris to create a new life for herself. The style of its text and music places it in the genre of the "suggestive" song, discussed in Chapter One. The third-person lyric narrates a titillating story, which goes against the grain of Victorian morality: A young woman accepts the advances of "the son of some millionaire" in return for being wined and dined in high style; "dear" refers both to her personal traits—"dear little eyes, dear little size, dear little golden curls"—and to her expensive taste: "Seven waiters worked hard that night, serving what she called a bite . . .

Figure 14. Cover of "She Was A Dear Little Girl." (Lester L. Levy Collection of Sheet Music, Special Collections, Milton S. Eisenhower Library, The Johns Hopkins University)

to a check his pen was introduced, but then, she was a dear, dear little girl."

The song's protagonist, Betsy Brown, is not even a character in the show. The piece served as a set piece for Cahill, who stepped out of her role as Betty Barbeau to deliver a comic monologue directly to the audience—as Marie Cahill, whom the audience had come to the theater to see and to hear. It was written in a pervasively syllabic style to allow the singer to project the text easily.

It was a song for a specific performer, not a specific show.

The 1909–1910 Season

Several other songs by Berlin were interpolated into shows during 1909–1910; more important, the season brought his first involvement in a high-profile production by one of the popular theater's major impresarios.[10]

There was, first, "Oh How That German Could Love," interpolated by Sam Bernard into *The Girl and the Wizard*, a "comedy with music" with a book by J. Hartley Manners and a score by Julian Edwards that ran for twelve weeks at the Casino Theatre after opening on 27 September 1909. Bernard, one of the great dialect comedians of the day, was born in Birmingham, England; specializing in "Dutch" and "Hebrew" characters, he had been a mainstay of Weber and Fields productions for many years. The song, another joint effort by Berlin and Ted Snyder, differed from "She Was A Dear Little Girl" in being sung in character. That is, even though the lyric has nothing to do with the story line of the show, Bernard, in the role of Herman Scholz, sang the piece in the same "Dutch" dialect that he assumed throughout the show and even referred to himself as "Herman" in the lyric. A German ethnic novelty song of the sort discussed in Chapter One, the piece fit Bernard's stage character in musical style as well, and the singer was pictured on the sheet music cover in his stage role as a dealer in gems.[11]

Later in the season, Berlin and Snyder's "I'm Going On A Long Vacation" was performed by Beth Tate in *Are You A Mason*, Leo Ditrichstein's adaptation of the German farce *Die Logenbrüder* by Carl Laufs and Kurt Kraatz, a play first mounted on Broadway in 1901. After playing in various provincial theaters in the spring of 1910, *Are You A Mason* began a run at Chicago's Garrick Theatre on 6 August. Described in the *Chicago Tribune* for that day as a play that "pats masons on the back and makes those who are not wish they were," the show closed after only several weeks and never played in New York. An interpolation in a play rather than a musical show, the Berlin-Snyder piece is a "suggestive" song in style and content, narrating an attempt by a lecherous boss to take his young secretary away for a weekend; his scheme is thwarted by the office boy, who then goes off with the young woman himself. The show was coproduced by Sam H. Harris, bringing Berlin into contact for the first time with a man who would play an important role in his own ventures in the years to come, not least the Music Box Revues.

The 1909–1910 season was dominated by Lew Fields, who mounted no fewer than nine productions. At a time when the style of Viennese operetta, with its "coherent stories and soothing melodies, promis[ing] an orderly world where romance ruled and sentimental gestures were taken seriously," was threatening to take over the American musical stage, Fields's shows grew out of a more characteristically America tradition. A "constantly changing collage of borrowings and found fragments, a hybrid of high and low stage traditions," their expressive nature tended to the "chaotic, flippant, sometimes even corrosive."[12] Put another way, they had much more to do with the disjunct, satirical, irreverent, sometimes boisterous character of vaudeville than with the Europeanness of *The Merry Widow* and *The Red Mill*.

Berlin's first contribution to a Fields production came with *The Jolly Bachelors*. Planned first as a major winter review with a large cast of vaudeville headliners—Stella Mayhew, Joe Welch, Josie Sadler, John T. Kelly, Emma Carus, Topsy Seigrist, Gertrude Vanderbilt, and Ed Begley—and a chorus of more than a hundred, the show went into rehearsal early in the fall. But after a disastrous preview performance in New Haven, Fields shut down rehearsals, asked Glen MacDonough to do a completely new book, and eliminated or replaced many of the star performers "whose desire to shine in their own specialities [had] played havoc with the story."[13]

Finally opening in New York at the Broadway Theatre on 6 January 1910, *The Jolly Bachelors,* billed as "A Musical Spectacle in Two Acts," was the most lavish and expensive production ever undertaken by Fields. It became a box-office success not because of a tight-knit plot or any character development of its principals but because of its spectacular stage settings and costumes, well-choreographed production numbers, and effective musical numbers interpolated into Raymond Hubbell's score, including "Has Anybody Here Seen Kelly" sung by Nora Bayes,[14] a male chorus clogging to "We'uns From Dixie," and Stella Mayhew's rendition of "Stop That Rag" by Berlin and Ted Snyder. The last piece, performed in blackface by Mayhew in the role of "a colored chorus lady" named Veronica Verdigris Jackson, was tailored to Mayhew's "coon shouting" and dancing talents. It was no different in style and content from other "coon" songs sung on the vaudeville stage, where in fact it subsequently enjoyed considerable popularity.

In an illustration of the vicissitudes of composing for the musical stage, none of the three other songs written by Berlin and Snyder for *The Jolly Bach-elors* survived to the New York opening. "Oh, That Beautiful Rag" was dropped at some point, then put into a later show, as I will discuss later. The other two, "Sweet Marie, Make-a Rag-a-Time Dance Wid Me" and "If The Managers Only Thought The Same As Mother," were written for Emma Carus while she was a member of the cast; when she left the show in November, before the New York opening, the songs were dropped. Even so, both were later published with sheet music covers featuring a large portrait of Carus and much smaller oval portraits of the two songwriters and claiming that they had been introduced by Carus in the show.

"Sweet Marie" is a hybrid piece in style and content, an Italian novelty/ragtime song that found a home on the vaudeville stage after being dropped from the show. "If The Managers" is a different matter, specifically tailored for the legitimate stage rather than vaudeville. The lyric has to do with the stage itself:

> There's no mistake that I can act,
> I'm talented and that's a fact,
> I know because my mother told me so;
> She kept a house for actor folks,
> And listened to their funny jokes,
> So now I guess my mother ought to know;
> But managers are awful dense,
> It seems to me they have no sense . . .
> And all they say is, "Go somewhere and die."

The lyric goes on to mention actresses of the day to whom the first-person protagonist's mother compares her—Margaret Illington, Margaret Anglin,

Leslie Carter, even Sarah Bernhardt—and producers who haven't the sense to recognize her talent, among them Charles Frohman, Henry Miller, and the Schuberts.

The "I" of the lyric is Emma Carus herself, stepping out of her role in the show to address an audience that has come to the theater at least in part to see and hear her, an audience aware that she had taken dramatic as well as musical roles and had often been criticized for the former and that knows enough about the legitimate stage to recognize the names of the actresses and producers mentioned in the lyric. The music moves along in 6/8 meter at a moderately fast tempo, with the singer spitting out the words quickly, almost in the style of a patter song; there is no particularly memorable melodic material and no vocal climax to distract the listener from the lyric.

Berlin and Snyder had created a piece for a specific performer, Emma Carus, to sing to a specific audience, that of the legitimate theater. If the piece had been performed by another singer in another setting, the effect would not have been the same.

The 1910–1911 Season

Berlin's first collaboration with Florenz Ziegfeld came with the *Follies of 1910,* fourth in the series, which opened at the Apollo Theatre in Atlantic City in mid-June in a "blaze of brilliancy." Described in *Variety* as "teeming with novelties, dressed in the most gorgeous costuming, replete with catchy music, brilliant with pretty girls and a cast of stars," the show had its New York opening at the Jardin de Paris Theatre on 20 June. Typical of shows of this sort, it fell somewhere between vaudeville and legitimate musical theater. While many of the individual acts were similar in style and content to vaudeville turns and many of the performers were veterans of vaudeville, Harry B. Smith's book gave the three acts a semblance of dramatic unity, or at least a theme, and the elaborately costumed and choreographed production numbers brought principals, chorus, and dancers together in extended sequences unknown in vaudeville. The show introduced both Fanny Brice and Bert Williams, the latter becoming the first black entertainer to be featured in the Follies when he sang three songs in the course of a sketch entitled "The Watermelon Patch."

Berlin was one of a number of songwriters—others were Will Marion Cook, Jean Havez, Harry Von Tilzer, Will D. Cobb, and Ballard MacDonald—to contribute additional pieces to the score by Gus Edwards and "who insisted upon having their names tacked to the interpolations [in the program], which isn't a bad idea since one can't be blamed for the other under this system."[15] His "Good Bye, Becky Cohen" and "Wild Cherry Rag" were both sung by Fanny Brice, whose performance of "Lovie Joe" by Will Marion Cook and Joe Jordan was a highlight of the show. Even though her rendition of "Becky Cohen" didn't go over nearly so well with audience and critics, the song was kept in the show throughout its New York and road runs. Berlin chose not to publish the song, however, and neither its music nor its lyric has been preserved, making it impossible to say anything about the piece beyond the fact that it was a Jewish novelty song. "Wild Cherries" was one of eight songs included in a "Reminiscent Ragtime Revue" in the show's second act. Based on a piano rag by Ted Snyder, this ragtime song had been published, performed in vaudeville, and recorded the previous year and was thus a song sung in a show rather than a song written for a show.

Like many shows of the time that were advertised as musical comedies, *Up and Down Broadway,* a Lew Fields production opening at the Casino on 18 July 1910, consisted of a string of episodes held together by a semblance of a story line. Subtitled "A more or less incoherent resume of current events, theatrical and otherwise," the show had a book by Edgar Smith, lyrics by William Jerome, and music by Jean Schwartz. Apollo and the other gods, members of the High Brow Club on Mount Olympus, are alarmed by reports of the low state of culture in New York City. Led by Momus (Eddie Foy) and Melpomene (Emma Carus), they descend to earth to "highbrowize Broadway"; after visiting Herald Square, the Polo Grounds, Chinatown, the Tabloid Opera House, and the Cafe d'Lobster, they conclude that contemporary American culture is in good shape. Without making too much of an evening of light entertainment, the show can nevertheless be seen in the context of the culture wars of the time, in which popular music and theater were being attacked in some quarters for allegedly degrading public taste and morality and defended in others as being distinctively American and democratic.

The show was the most important showcase for the talents of Berlin and Snyder to date. In one scene the gods visit the Cafe d'Lobster, where the young songwriters are cast as house entertainers, performing two of their own songs, "Sweet Italian Love" and "Oh, That Beautiful Rag." *The Evening World* for 19 July reported that "a dark-eyed youth won great favor with 'Italian Love' while his boon companion at the piano managed to put in a word or two about 'That Beautiful Rag.' It was impossible to tell which was Berlin and which Snyder." But there was no mistaking their success, according to *The Morning Telegraph* for 23 July:

> The screaming big hit of the evening, however, must be put down to the credit of Irving Berlin and Ted Snyder. . . . The songs were two of the catchiest that Broadway has heard in years, and when to that was added their peculiar proficiency for "putting them over," something eventuated which is rare: after half a score encores the lights were turned off to set another scene, but the applause continued so steadily through the scene setting that when the theatre became luminous again Messrs. Snyder and Berlin were forced to appear in the next set and bow their thanks to their thousand or so newly-made friends.

Both songs were ethnic novelties, a "wop" song and a "coon" song, written and sung in the style of these subgenres, both of which were popular at the time in vaudeville.[16] Even though Berlin and Snyder wrote and performed the songs together, a full-length portrait of Berlin alone decorates the sheet music covers of both pieces.

One of the three different sheet music covers for the Berlin-Snyder song "Kiss Me My Honey, Kiss Me" features a portrait of Emma Carus with the claim that she sang the piece in *Up and Down Broadway*, but the song is not listed in any of the programs for the show that I've seen. Although it was possibly interpolated at some point in the run, the piece will be discussed later in connection with another show.

Figure 15. Cover of "Sweet Italian Love."

Not all the shows for which Berlin and Snyder wrote songs during this season were as successful as *Up and Down Broadway*, which ran for several months in New York and then played on the road for another half year. "Oh, That Beautiful Rag" was first interpolated into *The Girl in the Kimono*, a show described in *Variety* for 25 June 1910 as "light and frothy, perfumed with the aroma of cleanliness and innocence" and as "a sort of musical comedy sundae, palatable and refreshing at the time, but unsatisfying to a thirst for greater and deeper draughts of amusement." A Florenz Ziegfeld production with a book by Helen Bragg, lyrics by Harold Atteridge, and music by Phil Schwartz, the show opened at Chicago's Ziegfeld Theatre on 25 June but closed after only a brief run.

Jumping Jupiter, a "Farce, in Three Acts, with Music" with a score by Karl Hoschna, opened at Chicago's Cort Theater on 4 August 1910 as a vehicle for the comical and musical talents of Richard Carle. The show was popular in London and Chicago but less well received in New York.[17] Percy Hammond wrote of the show in the *Chicago Tribune* for 5 August 1910: "To the framework of an old time farce by Mr. Sydney Rosenfeld, Mr. Richard Carle, a dextrous adapter and tinkerer in plays with music, has added song and dance and color." Two of these songs were by Berlin: "Kiss Me My Honey, Kiss Me," an old-style march ballad that had been published earlier with a cover picturing Little Amy Butler, by whom it had been "sung with great success in vaudeville," and "Thank You, Kind Sir! Said She," a "suggestive" song performed in the show by Carle himself. Both were published with a collective cover for the show dominated by a large portrait of Carle. After a well-received run of some months in Chicago, *Jumping Jupiter* was taken on the road and then brought to Broadway, where it ran for only a few weeks after opening at the New York Theatre on 6 March 1911. Berlin's "It Can't Be Did!" and "Angelo," both ethnic novelty pieces, are listed in various sources as being used in *Jumping Jupiter* as well,[18] but I've been unable to verify their appearance in the show. Both were copyrighted, atypically as lead sheets, on 13 April 1910, some four months before the show opened, with no mention of *Jumping Jupiter;* neither was published.

Berlin and Snyder's "Herman Let's Dance That Beautiful Waltz" was sung by Belle Gold in William Brady's production of *The Girl and the Drummer,* William Broadhurst's own adaption of his play of 1897, *What Happened to Jones,* made into a musical comedy by the addition of a score by Augustus Barrett. The show opened in Chicago, at the Grand, on 4 September, running for only a few weeks and never making it to New York. Curiously, although Gold was cast in the role of Miss Ethel Johnson, a "dancing Scandinavian," her interpolated Berlin-Snyder song is a German (or "Dutch") novelty piece, with a lyric recounting the attempted seduction, at a ball, of "Mister Herman, a sweet little German" by "Miss Lena

Kraussmeyer with hair red as fire," set to music with the movement and feel of a ländler.

The same song was subsequently interpolated by Belle Gold into a Schubert production, *Two Men and a Girl,* with a book by Julian Edwards and Ralph Skinner and a score by Charles Campbell. The show opened at Chicago's Cort Theatre on 4 December 1910 to enthusiastic popular and critical acclaim; as Richard Henry Little wrote in the *Chicago Tribune* for 6 December:

> At last we have the ideal show for that much discussed person, the "tired business man." This impressive personage who always is dragged into every discussion of what sort of things should be presented on the stage and who always is referred to as demanding relaxation and entertainment and an opportunity to laugh and as being opposed to grand opera and problems and the presentation of the sad and sordid side of life no longer can complain that managers do not cater for his especial entertainment. [The] new musical comedy at the Cort theater seems to have been especially created for the aforesaid tired business man. And for everybody else, for that matter, that likes to go to the theater for the sake of laughing. For "Two Men and a Girl" bubbles and froths like a freshly opened bottle of champagne. It's all nonsense, sheer, utter nonsense, but the funniest and most rollicking nonsense.

Belle Gold's German dialect role as Wilhelmina Lamb was appropriate for her singing of "Herman Let's Dance That Beautiful Waltz," and "Wishing," a sentimental ballad by Berlin and Snyder, was interpolated into the show by Elsie Ryan, who according to the *Tribune* "carried the love sentiment of the piece in a bewitching manner." But despite all this enthusiasm in the press, the show closed after only a moderate run and was never brought to New York.

"Bring Back My Lena To Me," another "Dutch" novelty song written for Sam Bernard, fared better. Interpolated into Sam and Lee Schubert's *He Came from Milwaukee,* a musical comedy with a score by Ben Jerome and Louis Hirsch that ran for some four months on Broadway after opening at the Casino on 21 September 1910, the song was extraneous to the dramatic action, but was sung in character. Herman von Schellenvein, the character portrayed by Bernard, laments his abandonment by "sweet little neat Lena Kraus," who has left him with an empty stomach and memories of her "sweet sauerkraut that would swim in your mouth, like the fishes that swim in the sea"; the song is sung to stage "Dutch" music moving in a ländler rhythm with an oom-pah-pah accompaniment.

Several mysteries surround Berlin's contributions to a play by Booth Tarkington and Harry Leon Wilson, originally called *Mrs. Jim* but retitled *Getting A Polish* for its opening at Wallach's Theatre on 7 November 1910. May Irwin, in the role of a miner's widow who goes off to Paris to become "cultured" after gold is found on her late husband's claim, "inserted several of her lusty songs" into the show, as was her custom when appearing on the legitimate stage.[19] The sheet music cover for Berlin's "That Opera Rag" gives the titles of three songs written by him for the show. One of these, "He Sympathized With Me," was never copyrighted or published and was apparently never used in the show. Another, "My Wife Bridget," was purchased outright by Irwin from Berlin. As one journalist told the story:

> [May Irwin] is to go out in "Mrs. Jim," a new farcical play, within a few weeks. . . . She knows that with one good song, the audience wouldn't care if she wore a pale green silk with solferino flounces, a Garibaldi jacket and a widow's bonnet of before the war vintage. So the minute she signed her contract Miss Irwin started on a still-hunt for a successor to the famous ditties that caroled her into fame. After she had driven all the composers of Tin Pan Alley crazy by pronouncing their stuff utterly useless, she came across a young man named Irving Berlin. He was singing his "latest composition," which he called "My Wife Bridget," and the moment Miss Irwin heard it she sat down in the nearest rocking chair and rocked away until she was rested. Then she said she liked the song and wanted to sing it. Mr. Berlin said that would be all right, and a good ad, for the song as well.
>
> It was then that the future "Mrs. Jim" explained herself. She said she wanted to buy the song outright. Mr. Berlin was won over by a check for $1,000. It sounds like a big sum for a small tune, but it isn't much when the profits from popular songs are considered. And that's what has moved Miss Irwin to purchase. She admitted in New York on Tuesday that she would get her thousand dollars back in royalties in a very few weeks, if the song pans out as well as she thinks it will. "I don't pay one thousand large, round silver buttons for fun," said the actress. Then she added that she was Scotch.[20]

The song was never copyrighted or published under anyone's name, however, and only "That Opera Rag" survives of the three songs for the show. Written to display Irwin's "coon shouting" talents, it narrates the adventures of "op'ra mad" Sam Johnson who becomes so excited upon hearing a German band play operatic excerpts while he's painting a house that he falls from his ladder. Although the piece has nothing to do with the plot of the play or the development of the character portrayed by Irwin, it was written for an audience that could be expected to know the operatic repertory and hence appreciate a burlesque treatment of it.

The Fascinating Widow, a "Comedy with Music" starring the female impersonator Julian Eltinge in the dual role of Mrs. Monte, the widow of the title, and Hal Blake, an undergraduate student at K. College, had a book by Otto Hauerbach and a score by Kerry Mills. The show opened in Chicago on 5 December 1910, at the Illinois Theatre, then played on the road for a while before beginning a New York run at the Liberty Theatre on 11 September. Berlin's "You've Built A Fire Down In My Heart," interpolated by Margaret (Winona Winter), was one of his first romantic ballad with a bit of syncopation in the music. The first-person lyric is addressed to a second party.

> You've built a fire down in my heart,
> Dearest, it's burning higher than any house on fire,
> Just like a live, live wire, right from the start.

Whether or not the "you" in question is actually present on the stage when the song is delivered, the gesture is internal to the production; that is, the piece is addressed by one member of the cast to another, not to the audience, and is heard as being in Margaret's voice.

A second song in the show, "Don't Take Your Beau To The Seashore," which Berlin cowrote with E. Ray Goetz, is another song tailored to the talents of a specific performer, in this case Eltinge, an old hand at projecting slightly off-color humor in a "drag" role. Cast musically (and satirically) as a march ballad, the lyric warns girls with "nothing to show" to leave their beaus at home when going to the beach, because "bathing suits reveal what petticoats conceal, and if there's a slight defection, you will never stand inspection." The piece was done as a production number, with Eltinge (as the widow) in a bathing suit, singing to and being echoed by a dozen or so chorus girls—obviously selected because of having plenty to show—in similar attire.

One of the season's major events was the opening of the Schubert's new Winter Garden on 20 March 1911 with a show titled *La Belle Paree.* After starting off with "Bow Sing," a pseudo-Chinese opera by Manuel Klein, the show got down to business with an extended vaudeville-like sequence titled "Jumble of Jollity," with a score by Frank Tours and Jerome Kern. At one point in the evening Dolly Jardon sang a pseudo-Spanish song, "Sombrero Land," cowritten by Berlin, Ted Snyder, and E. Ray Goetz, but like most of the evening's other events, the piece was overshadowed by Al Jolson's success in the first of his many Winter Garden appearances.

As mentioned in Chapter Three, Berlin wrote three songs for *Gaby,* the final segment of the three-part show that opened Joseph Lasky's new restaurant-theater, the Folies Bergere, on 29 April 1911. Modeled after fashionable French establishments and entertainments, the show was targeted at the "tired business man" who could afford an expensive evening out in opulent surroundings. This audience was quite different from the working-class and immigrant/first-generation patrons of vaudeville houses, and Berlin's songs for the show were consequently quite different in style and content from those he had written, and was still writing, for vaudeville. "Spanish Love," coauthored with Vincent Bryan and Ted Snyder, was a vehicle for the star of the show, Ethel Levey, brought over from England to take the role of Gaby Deslys, whose highly publicized affair with the king of Portugal gave the show its story line. The song comes as close to the style of European operetta as anything Berlin had written: Set in a minor key and spiced with Iberian rhythms, it was a set piece for the classically trained Levey, who could do justice to the sustained, legato vocal line and the high-note climaxes that were deemed appropriate for the "cultured" clientele expected to patronize the Folies Bergere.

"I Beg Your Pardon, Dear Old Broadway," also sung by Ethel Levey and for which Berlin wrote both words and music, invokes the snappy, jingoistic stage songs of George M. Cohan, particularly his "Give My Regards To Broadway":

> I beg your pardon, dear old Broadway,
> For list'ning to a foreign song;
> I thought I'd find a street with which you could compete,

> I only found that I was wrong.
> My hat's aloft to you, old Broadway,
> You're in a class alone today . . .

This is another front-and-center number, delivered by a singer who steps to the footlights and addresses the audience directly in the first person, not as a character in a drama but as herself—a famous, American-born performer, once married to George M. Cohan, who had made a success in London and had come back to New York to star in this show.

Although the sheet music cover of a third song, "Down To The Folies Bergere," written by Berlin, Snyder, and Bryan, claims that it too was sung in *Gaby,* the song must have been dropped before the New York opening, since it's not listed in the show's program or mentioned in reviews. It seems to have been intended as a production number, perhaps to open the show, since its hortatorical lyric written in the first person plural and its extroverted music make it appropriate for delivery from an ensemble to an audience.

> Why do they rave about beautiful France,
> Where the wine flows and the maidens entrance,
> Why go to Berlin, Vienna or Rome,
> We can enjoy all their joys here at home.
> In old New York up at Long Acre Square . . .
> Two doors from Heaven, the Folies Bergere.

Also as I mentioned earlier, the week before the show opened, Berlin was pressed into service to help write a replacement number for the opening segment of the evening's show, *Hell.* The program lists this piece, "Keep A Taxi Waiting, Dear," as being performed by "Leslie Leigh, Lonely Maidens and Messengers." From this, and from what reviewers said about it, we know that it was a production number, a costumed and choreographed sequence involving one or more of the show's principals supported by chorus and dancers. Since only a fragment of the lyric and none of the music has been preserved, nothing can be said about the number beyond the fact that it and "Down To The Folies Bergere" were Berlin's first attempts at writing production numbers.

The season ended for Berlin with an appearance in the fourth edition of the *Friars' Frolic,* which opened at the New Amsterdam on 28 May, in which he himself sang "Alexander's Ragtime Band" and "Ephraham Played Upon The Piano." Even though "Alexander" had been written for vaudeville, as discussed in Chapter Three, and the *Friars' Frolic* itself was a revue, the song proved to be an important step in his writing for musical comedy; as I will detail later, the come-listen-to-the band gesture of "Alexander" 's lyric combined with similarly exuberant music became a model for a series of later production numbers in which the ensemble on stage exhorted the audience to come join in the fun.

In summary, the theatrical season of 1910–1911 represented a turning point in Berlin's career. When the season opened, he had just turned twenty-one, was the author of a handful of songs that had enjoyed modest success on the vaudeville stage, and with a single exception had never contributed a song to a high-profile musical show. In the course of this season he contributed well-received songs to shows produced by two of the major entrepreneurs of the popular musical theater, Lew Fields and Florenz Ziegfeld, and to the season's most spectacular single event, the opening of the Folies Bergere; his songs were performed in these and other shows by such stars of the musical stage as Sam Bernard, Stella Mayhew, Emma Carus, Fanny Brice, May Irwin, and Ethel Levey; and, with Ted Snyder, he made a well-received appearance on the musical stage himself. These successes brought an invitation to become a member of the prestigous Friars Club, and by season's end he was not only a participant in that club's *Friars' Frolic* but was one of the stars of the show, as a singer-songwriter. Almost all of his songs for the musical stage this season were interpolations; although some of these were similar in style and content to songs for the vaudeville stage, others were written for specific singers in specific shows. Finally, near the end of the season, he collaborated for the first time in the writing of several production numbers.

The 1911–1912 Season

The new season began for Berlin with the *Ziegfeld Follies of 1911,* the first edition in the series to bear Ziegfeld's name in the title. Opening at the Jardin de Paris on 26 June, the show brought back many of the stars who had made their first appearances in the previous year's show, including Bert Williams, Fanny Brice, Lillian Lorraine, and Berlin himself.

According to the collective sheet music cover for the show, Berlin contributed four songs. "Woodman, Woodman, Spare That Tree!" was a vehicle for Bert Williams, a comic monologue delivered directly to the audience in that entertainer's inimitable half-speaking, half-singing style.[21] "Ephraham Played Upon The Piano," written in collaboration with Vincent Bryan, had been sung by Berlin himself in the *Friars' Frolic of 1911* several months earlier; technically a "coon" song because of its black protagonist, the piece is a third-person description of a black musician, narrated by the singer to the audience. "Dog Gone That Chilly Man" is one of Berlin's first rhythmic ballads, and its presence in this show suggests that Berlin's attempt to find a more contemporary lyrical and musical style for the expression of romantic sentiments was linked to the fact that he was now addressing a more educated and "cultured" audience than that of the vaudeville house, but one too sophisticated and modern to respond to an old-fashioned Victorian ballad.

Figure 16. Cover of "Ephraham Played Upon the Piano" and other songs from the *Ziegfeld Follies of 1911*. (Lester L. Levy Collection of Sheet Music, Special Collections, Milton S. Eisenhower Library, The Johns Hopkins University)

The fourth song intended for the 1911 Follies but apparently never used in the show, "You've Built A Fire Down In My Heart," had already been performed in *The Fascinating Widow,* as noted earlier.

The Never Homes, another Lew Fields show, opened at the Broadway Theatre on 5 October. Berlin contributed a single song, "There's A Girl In Havana," written in collaboration with the two composers of the score, E. Ray Goetz and A. Baldwin Sloane.[22] Performed as a duet by Will Archie and Helen Hayes, the song represents "the only tenderness between the sexes" in a show otherwise concerned with gender tensions brought about by the actions of militant suffragets.

> [He] offers [her] a bite of his raspberry tart; she tries it, then argues with him about what flavor it is, whether it's good for her, etc. She takes a few more bites to prove her case, until the tart is gone. To show her thanks, she wipes her sticky fingers on his sleeve. Jimmy is enthralled, and together they sing "There's A Girl In Havana."[23]

Two things are worth noting about this song. First, it's a catalogue of male conquests: Although the protagonist's first words are "I'm in love with you," he hastens to add that he's told "lots of girls" the same thing, and he proceeds to identify some of them. Second, the piece was performed on stage as a duet, with the two principals singing to one another, alternating lines of the text in the verses and then joining in unison or parallel thirds in the chorus, but the sheet music presents the song as if it were to be sung by the male character alone, underlining how misleading it can be to approach songs of this period from their published versions alone.

Lew Fields's *Hanky-Panky,* "A Jumble of Jollification" with a book by Edgar Smith, score by A. Baldwin Sloane, and lyrics by E. Ray Goetz, opened the new American Music Hall in Chicago on 31 October 1911. The show made little pretense of having a plot or cohesive score; as had been the case with many of the earlier Weber & Fields Music Hall shows, the opening section was a vaudeville olio that was changed weekly.[24] As Percy Hammond observed in the *Chicago Tribune* for 1 November 1911:

> Mr. Lew Fields has established a song and dance institution [the American Music Hall] calculated to divert the well fed and not particular and to bestow upon them the feeling that they are observing an entertainment a bit fleet but not, in a manner of speaking, intended to deprave. It is one of those airy exhibitions contrived deliberately to divert the sophisticated, and if all evidences are to be depended upon, it fulfilled last evening its function. . . . Mr. De Haven, it is generally known, impersonates upon the stage those persons who drink champagne and call it wine—singing of midnight and taxicabs and other naughty elements of our civilization.

After running in Chicago until the following May, the show was taken on the road, then opened in New York at the Broadway Theatre on 5 August 1912, playing there until November. Moving to another theater in New York and then taken on the road again for another 32 weeks, *Hanky-Panky* ended up as "the most profitable of Fields' productions, excluding the Jubilee." [25]

Variety for 9 August 1912 found it to be "a big show, with lively numbers, thirty pretty chorus girls, ten chorus men and plenty of action." Singled out for particular mention were Berlin's "Ragtime Opera Sextet" and "The Million Dollar Ball." The lyric of the "Sextet" tells the story of an "op'ra darkey" who haunts the opera house to hear Caruso sing, then buys a score of Donizetti's Sextet from *Lucia di Lammermoor* and persuades four friends to sing through the piece with him, with disastrous results. Berlin must have known the sextet from one of the many transcriptions for voice and piano in print at the time.

Donizetti's music is recognizable in Berlin's parody version, even though meter, pitch, phrasing, and other details are treated freely. The first piece by Berlin published in an arrangement for more than a single voice, it is written for five voices, as part of the joke, although six singers are listed in the program: Florence Moore, Christine Nielsen, Harry Cooper, Bobby North, Max Rogers, and Hugh Cameron. It was published, all sixteen pages of it, in two versions, even though it hardly figured to sell well as sheet music—in small format with a plain black and white cover and in the usual large format with a collective cover for the show.

"The Million Dollar Ball," cowritten with E. Ray Goetz, was staged as a production number featuring Carter De Haven, Christine Nielsen, and the show's ensemble. The lyric has the same "come-on-and-hear-the-music" gesture as "Alexander's Ragtime Band," nominally addressed by the protagonist to a second person but serving equally well as a collective exhortation to the audience voiced by the entire ensemble. In keeping with the show's targeted audience of the well-fed and the sophisticated, the song's invitation is to an event quite different from a performance by Alexander's band, with its "fiddle with notes that screeches like a chicken" and a "colored pet" of a clarinetist in a public bandstand.

> Come on down, there's a million dollar ball in town,
> Just chase away that frown,
> Come on down,
> You'll be the best little, dress'd little lady, with your diamond crown;
> And your pretty little satin gown. . . .
> Come with me,
> And hear that most appealing harmony.

The music is exuberant, extroverted, syncopated, a bit noisy, just right for a stage filled with an elaborately costumed ensemble.

"Cuddle Up" has a collective sheet music cover for the show *A Real Girl,* a production of the Bonita Amusement Company starring Bonita and Lew Hearn, with a large portrait of Bonita and a list of nine songs featured in the show, four of them by Berlin. The production was intended as a vehicle for Bonita's singing. "Cuddle Up" was the only song by Berlin written specifically for the show; the other three—"When You're In Town," "That Mysterious Rag," and "One O'Clock In The Morning I Get Lonesome"—had been performed in vaudeville and published with sheet music covers making no mention of *A Real Girl* well before the show went into rehearsal in the late fall of 1911 and were thus songs performed in a show as opposed to being written for a show. "Cuddle Up" is another of Berlin's new rhythmic ballads, a type of song he was developing for audiences of the legitimate stage.

The fate of the show was related in a dispatch to *Variety* for 9 December 1911, from Richmond:

> "The Real Girl" company, which presented Bonita and Lew Hearn as its star features, closed its road trip suddenly here last week amid great excitement. About 500 college boys packed the Granby theatre Friday night. As their hearts seemed overflowing with Thanksgiving joy, they made an outward demonstration when Bonita appeared. It did not please the star one bit. She quickly retorted with some remarks which the students took as a cue to hoot, howl and yell. Bonita made a hurried exit, and did not appear again until the second act. During the intermission the university lads made some quick purchases of articles which were hurled stageward when Bonita reappeared. Fearing for the safety of the woman, and wishing to avoid a scene not down on the bills, the management had the curtain rung down. When the chorus girls left the theatre, they were boldly kidnapped by the college boys and escorted to an eating parlor, where they were treated to the best obtainable.

The Hearns were unsuccessful in booking the show elsewhere, and the three previously published songs by Berlin were never brought out again with new sheet music covers linking them to the ill-fated show.

She Knows Better Now, starring May Irwin, was yet another show that didn't make it to Broadway. Berlin and Snyder's "I'm Going Back To Dixie" and Berlin's "Ragtime Mocking Bird," both written to showcase Irwin's "coon shouting" prowess, were published with a collective sheet music cover for the show.[26] After opening in Chicago, the show moved to Boston's Plymouth Theatre, where *Variety* for 13 January 1912 tartly noted that " 'She Knows Better Now' is not the attraction. It is May Irwin who gets the billing and the receipts." The show died there, but "I'm Going Back To Dixie," reprinted with a new cover and the new title "I Want To Be In Dixie," became a popular item not only in this country but also in England, where it was featured in the revue *Hullo Ragtime,* and in France, where it was published both as a song ("Dans Mon Pays") and in piano arrangement.

A high point of the New York theatrical season came on 8 February 1912 when *Hokey-Pokey,* a show reuniting Lew Fields and Joe Weber for the first time in seven years and also bringing back Lillian Russell, Fay Templeton, John T. Kelly, and other performers from the Weber and Fields shows of the previous decade, opened at the Broadway Theatre. The evening's final segment, "Bunty, Bulls and Strings," a burlesque version of Edgar Smith's popular Scottish comedy *Bunty Pulls the Strings,* included a production number sung and danced by Fay Templeton and the ensemble. The number was called "Alexander's Bag-Pipe Band" and was a parody by Berlin, E. Ray Goetz, and A. Baldwin Sloane of the Berlin song that had swept the country six months earlier. Although published only in a version for one voice with piano accompaniment, it's easy enough to see how the piece would have been done as a production number. Templeton would have addressed the narrative, third-person verses to the theater audience:

> Last week when Alexander McIntosh
> Returned from a trip to Yankee Land,
> He got a half a dozen pipers with their bagpipes
> And organized a band.

The ensemble would have joined in the chorus, making it a collective exhortation to the audience:

> Come on and hear the bagpipes raggin' up a tune,
> In Alexander's bagpipe band.
> Come on and see McPherson acting like a coon,
> In Alexander's bagpipe band.

Near the end of the season, Berlin was asked to contribute to yet another major production, this one a three-part entertainment opening at the Winter Garden on 5 March 1912 and starring Al Jolson. The first segment, "A Night with the Pierrots," was a ragtime burlesque of a show from earlier in the season, *Sumurun,* a pantomime with an Arabian Nights theme written by Friedrich Freska and produced by Winthrop Ames. Berlin's "Rag-time Sextet," used earlier in *Hanky-Panky,* was sung in this show by José Collins, Stella Mayhew, Jolson, Billee Taylor, Willie Howard, Eugene Howard, and Ernest Hare, and two other songs by Berlin—"I Want To Be In Dixie," performed by the Courtnay Sisters, and "Lead Me To That Beautiful Band," sung by Willie Weston—were interpolated into this part of the show. In addition, Berlin's "Society Bear" was sung by Mayhew in the show's second segment, a revue titled *Whirl of Society,* described in the program as "A Musical Satire of Up-to-Date Society." The song is an irrev-erent fantasy in which members of New York's "rich four hundred" are imagined to cavort to the vernacular dance music of the day.

> Carnegie did the Turkey Trot,
> For an hour with a chicken that
> Egged him on 'til he most forgot to care
> A snap about his libr'ry, doing that rich Society Bear.

At some point in the season, Happy Lambert interpolated Berlin's "Lead Me To That Beautiful Band," cowritten with E. Ray Goetz, into the *Cohan and Harris Minstrels,* a show that had first opened in New York on 3 August 1908, been revived on 16 July 1909, and then been taken on the road. The song is yet another come-on-and-hear-the band exhortation, very much in the spirit of "Alexander's Ragtime Band." But even though the piece was undoubtedly sung in blackface in this show, the sheet music cover shows a white couple cavorting to the playing of equally white musi-cians, and the cover nowhere acknowledges that the song had been intro-duced in a minstrel show.

In summary, 1911–1912 brought more of the same for Berlin: songs interpolated into successful and not-so-successful shows, with some of these pieces staged as production numbers, but no invitations to write the score for an entire show.

The 1912–1913 Season

The season of 1912–1913 began for Berlin, on 22 July 1912 at the Winter Garden, in much the way that the previous one had ended, with one of his songs performed in a high-profile show for which most of the music had been written by someone else. In this case it was the *The Passing Show of 1912,* the first of the Schuberts' challenges to Ziegfeld's *Follies,* with a score by Louis Hirsch. The show opened with *The Ballet of 1830,* imported from the Alhambra in London, then continued with the ragtime-flavored *Passing Show* itself, which contained such production numbers as "The Wedding Glide" (with "everyone on stage, including minister, bride and groom, indulging in a rag motion"), "The Metropolitan Squawk-tette" (another parody on grand opera), and "The Bacchanal Rag." At one point in the show Berlin's song "Everybody's Doing It Now" was played by the pit orchestra to support a bit of stage action. His chief contribution, however, was "The Ragtime Jockey Man," sung by Willie Howard. According to the *Boston Evening Tribune* for 19 November 1912, it was the "best song in the show," with "a swing and dash that caused it to be encored several times." It was the first of several Berlin songs from this period to be set at a sporting event, with the singer cast in the role of narrating the action to the show audience.[27]

> Down upon the track,
> On a horse's back,
> Warming up his fingers, sits the ragtime jockey.
> Smile upon his face,
> Ready for the race,
> In his colors so gay.
> See 'em spread apart,
> Now they're goin' to start. . .

The piece had been published a month before the show's opening, and even though it went over well on stage, it wasn't reprinted with a new sheet music cover linking it to the show.

Berlin's "Follow Me Around" was interpolated by Maude Raymond into Harry B. Harris's *My Best Girl,* a "musical play" with book and lyrics by Channing Pollock and Rennold Wolf and score by Clifton Crawford and Augustus Barratt, at some point after the show opened at the Park on 12 September 1912. The piece, sung by Daphne (Maude Raymond) and "the Girls," repeats the "come-on-along" gesture of "Alexander's Ragtime Band" yet another time:

> Tell me, dear, would you like to see the town a bit?
> Would you like to go around? . . .
> I've got the key to most ev'ry cabaret,
> Where there's an hour of joy we can grab away,
> We'll discover places that Columbus never found.

The season's installment of the *Ziegfeld Follies* opened at the Moulin Rouge on 21 October 1912, with a book by Harry B. Smith and a score by Raymond Hubbell. Berlin's "A Little Bit Of Everything" was brought out with a sheet music cover linking it to the show, although the piece is listed in none of the programs and mentioned in none of the reviews that I've seen. With its invitation to a second person (and, in effect, to the audience itself) to come and enjoy a night on the town, including a visit to a ball where "we'll hear a band that's a dream, you bet" playing songs "that'll make you sad [and] make you glad," the piece is still another trope on "Alexander's Ragtime Band."[28]

The Sun Dodgers, subtitled "A Fanfare of Frivolity," was not one of Lew Fields's more successful shows. With a book by Edgar Smith parodying "leisure-class behavior"[29] and a score by E. Ray Goetz and A. Baldwin Sloane, it underwent major cast changes and alterations during rehearsals and tryout performances in Philadelphia, Albany, and Pittsburgh before finally opening in New York at the Broadway Theatre on 30 November 1912. Berlin and E. Ray Goetz contributed a production number, "At The Picture Show," staged so that "a moving picture was projected on a transparent gauze screen, behind which the chorus sat, while in front of the screen a couple danced and sang."[30] Although the piece was published only as a song for a single voice with piano accompaniment, it's obvious that the couple, Trixie (Maud Gray) and Lamb (Harry Clark), sang the verses to one another:

> Hurry up, hurry up, buy your ticket now,
> Hurry up, hurry up, better come some how;
> Evr'ybody's going, all tiptoing,
> To the picture show.

The ensemble then sang the chorus, with the images of the projected movie coordinated to the lyric:

> At the picture show,
> At the picture show,
> Come and see the villain gay,
> Steal the hero's girl away,
> Or ponies racing,
> Just see them chasing . . .[31]

Closing after only eighteen performances, once again subjected to rewriting and cast changes, then given a trial run in Boston in its new version, the show returned to New York, but with not much more success. At some point in the show's brief and troubled history, Berlin collaborated with Goetz on another production number, "Hiram's Band," a burlesque treatment of a small town and its band. Exceptionally, the piece was published in an arrangement that gives some idea of how it was performed on stage as a production number: The verses are given to a solo voice, the chorus is sung by a four-part mixed ensemble, and the town band is heard in instrumental interludes in the second and third choruses, playing wrong notes and almost atonal passages.

George M. Cohan's *The Little Millionaire,* a "New Musical Farce," ran for 192 performances after opening on 25 September 1911, then was taken on the road. Sometime in 1912 Berlin's "Down In My Heart" was interpolated into the show by Charles King, not a member of the original cast, who apparently brought the song with him when he joined the show. It was Berlin's first song published with instructions for performance by two voices: The first verse and chorus are sung by the "Boy" to the "Girl," who reciprocates by addressing the second verse and the chorus to him. Thus, for the first time in a song by Berlin, stage characters sing to each other rather than to the audience. Written in the style of Berlin's new rhythmic ballads, the music is more flowing and goal-oriented than that of most of his earlier songs, with a melody often moving by sequence to a sustained note. Put differently, in this song Berlin has begun combining the "jumpy," slightly syncopated, American style of ragtime song with operetta-like, more European techniques.

Berlin's music was first sung on the British legitimate stage, as opposed to in the music hall, on 23 December 1912, when "I Want To Be In Dixie" was included in the revue *Hullo, Ragtime!*, with a score by Louis Hirsch, which ran for 451 performances at London's Hippodrome Theatre. Berlin himself performed in the show later in its run, offering a selection of his newest songs and then, in response to requests from the audience, singing several older hits such as "Alexander's Ragtime Band" and Everybody's Doing It Now." As *The Encore* reported the event on 10 July 1913:

> That successful revue, "Hullo, Rag-time!" still continues to draw crowded houses to the London Hippodrome and for the third edition several additional attractions have been added to the already strong cast. Irving Berlin, the gifted composer of ragtime songs, met with a most enthusiastic reception on Monday evening when he sang a new number entitled "The International Rag," following on with "Snooky Ookums," a ballad entitled "When I Lost You," and one of his most popular rag songs, "Dixie" [i.e., "I Want To Be In Dixie"].

Hullo, Ragtime! was a revue, not a book musical, and Berlin's appearance in it was, in effect, a vaudeville turn; his songs were addressed to the audience, with no connection to anything before or after he sang. His singing style was nondramatic and even intimate, according to a review in *The Times* for 8 July 1913:

> It is not only that he sings his rag-time songs with diffidence, skill and charm. In his mouth they become something very different from the blatant bellowings that we are used to. All their quaintness, their softness, their queer patheticalness come out; they sound, indeed, quite new, and innocently, almost childishly, pleasingly, like a negro's smile.

The 1912–1913 season ended for Berlin as it had begun, with several songs written for interpolation into major productions. Lew Fields opened his new Forty-fourth Street Roof Garden on 5 June 1913 with *All Aboard*, a "Musical Panorama" produced in collaboration with the Schuberts, with a book by Mark Swan and music by Malvin Franklin and E. Ray Goetz. Fields took the role of Jan Van Haan, a sailor who "goes to sleep on the dock and dreams of enough vaudeville turns to fill out the evening."[32] *Variety* reported on 13 June that "for three solid hours there were song and dance numbers with innumerable changes of scenery, liberally besprinkled with comedy lines and situations, mostly new, but a few hoary with age," that "provide a pleasant evening's diversion," but added that "it is doubtful if there is a single musical number that will attain sufficient popularity to be hummed about town."

Berlin contributed "The Monkey Doodle Doo," staged as a production number with "a real simian perched on the shoulder of each chorus girl. According to a memo from J. J. [Schubert], the monkeys gave 'the house a very unhealthy smell and will bring the Board of Health down upon us.' "[33] The lyric is yet another variant on the hortatory gesture first used by Berlin in "Alexander's Ragtime Band," with the protagonist urging his "honey" to "come and hurry to the Zoo" to hear "that pure little monkey overture, coming from the little monkey band" led by the simian equivalent of Alexander—"See that monkey on that bench, lead the band with a monkey wrench." "Take Me Back," which according to the sheet music cover was sung in the show by Claire Rochester, is a lyrical love ballad with a chorus in waltz time; it was apparently dropped before opening night, since there is no mention of the song, or for that matter of Miss Rochester herself, in the program or in reviews of the show.

Three other songs by Berlin intended to be used in the show were dropped at one point or another. "Abie Sings An Irish Song," an ethnic novelty song, was copyrighted but never performed or apparently even published, since no sheet music cover exists. According to Dave Jay[34] and others, "Somebody's Coming To My House" and "The International Rag" were sung in the show, but there's no trace of either in any programs or reviews.

In summary, during the season of 1912–1913 Berlin became less interested in writing songs for individual singers to interpolate into shows and more interested in writing pieces, in collaboration with E. Ray Goetz and other men more experienced in writing for the musical stage, suitable to be mounted as production numbers.[35] He wrote his first show songs in which characters on stage address each other, rather than the audience. And he began assimilating musical elements associated with operetta into his show songs to make them more appropriate in style for audiences of the legitimate theater.

The 1913–1914 and 1914–1915 Seasons

Berlin was almost invisible as a writer of show songs during the 1913–1914 theatrical season. He contributed no songs to the *Ziegfeld Follies of 1913, The Passing Show of 1913*, the several new Lew Fields productions, or any other shows of the sort that he had written for in previous seasons. Over the entire season only three new songs of his were performed in shows, and none of them caused any great stir. A romantic duo, "If You Don't Want Me (Why Do You Hang Around)," was sung by Henry Bergman and Gladys Clark in Jesse Lasky's vaudeville production *Trained Nurses* at the end of the summer. "Follow The Crowd," his latest spinoff of the come-on-and-hear-the-band gesture of "Alexander's Ragtime Band," was staged as a production number in *The Queen of the Movies*, a musical comedy with a book by Glen MacDonough and music by the German composer Jean Gilbert, which opened at the Globe on 12 January 1914.

You'll hear a jew'l of an orchestra!
Best of the rest in America!
Each syncopated beat
Just goes right to your feet.
Heirs, millionaires, all the best of them,
Glide side by side with the rest of them.

A review of the show in the *Boston Evening Transcript* for 14 April 1914 was a reminder that American songwriters still had to contend with Euro-centric attitudes in some quarters:

> No fancy tunes in the whole list: nothing but waltzes and two-steps as it used to be in the Sousa days of American operetta. But what tunes! . . . And they went in open competition with Irving Berlin, whom Europeans consider the Roosevelt of music. Berlin had an interpolated song, "Follow the Crowd"—a rather sick affair, a plain imitation of "The International Rag," and not very lively even then. And there was a tango or a maxixe or something interpolated after one of the songs. But these American things couldn't hold up their heads beside Gilbert's tunes.

Berlin's third song performed on the stage during the season was a roman-tic ballad, "Along Came Ruth," interpolated into Henry Savage's produc-tion of Holman Day's play of the same name, which opened at the Gaiety on 23 February 1914. And the season of 1914–1915 started off even more quietly for Berlin, with no new songs in shows during the summer season, not even in *The Ziegfeld Follies of 1914* and *The Passing Show of 1914*. The fall brought only two more duos for Bergman and Clark, "Furnishing A Home For Two" and "That's My Idea Of Paradise," written for another of Lasky's vaudeville productions, *The Society Buds,* in October.

Thus, over the eighteen-month stretch between 5 June 1913, when *All Aboard* opened in New York, and 8 December 1914, when *Watch Your Step* had its first New York performance, only five new songs by Berlin were introduced on the stage, none of them in major productions. But these few pieces, particularly the three written for Bergman and Clark, sung on stage as duos with the two characters speaking to one another rather than to the audience, underline that Berlin was continuing to hone some dramatic and musical techniques more appropriate for the legitimate stage than for vaudeville or the home circle. Although these duos were published in the customary arrangement for one voice with piano accompaniment, a holograph sketch of the chorus of "Furnishing A Home For Two" shows how the piece played on stage for two characters:

I'll hang the picture on the wall,
You'll hold the chair so I don't fall, my honey,
While I lay the carpet in the dining roon,
You'll be busy with a broom; . . .

We'll be such a happy pair,
Furnishing a home for two. *[as published]*

> HE: I'll hang the pictures on the wall
> SHE: I'll hold the chair so you don't fall
> HE: You'll stand by while I lay the carpet
> SHE: When that's done, I'll unpack the crockery carefully . . .
> HE: We'll be such a happy pair
> BOTH: Furnishing a home for two. *[holograph sketch]* [36]

Musically, these duos feature flowing melodic lines, often unfolding in sequential patterns, somewhat in the style of operetta, albeit spiced with hints of syncopation.

Not only did Berlin write few new pieces for the musical stage during this period; his productivity in general, as measured by new songs copyrighted and published, dropped off as well. Only thirty-two new songs were copyrighted in his name between 5 June 1913 and the end of 1914, compared to ninety during the calendar years 1911 and 1912. His trip to England probably contributed to this decline, as did business matters that had to be attended to now that he was a partner in a publishing company; more important, however, his focus as a songwriter was in a transitional state. In the spring or early summer of 1914 he began working intensely on his first musical comedy to the virtual exclusion of individual songs.

Although songs by Berlin had been inserted into high-profile shows for some years now, he had never written a score for the musical stage himself, and doing so became a top priority for him. Rennold Wolf reported that Berlin planned "to write an opera in rag-time, if you please. He argues, and argues soundly, that rag-time is our only distinctively characteristic music, and he feels that, treated seriously, the possibilities for a classic in that form of rhythm are unlimited."[37] Berlin himself said that "my readers will perhaps smile when I tell them that I am writing an opera in ragtime; the whole of the libretto as well as the music. The idea is so new and ambitious that it may be a great big failure, and certainly such a thing has never been tried before."[38] In an interview with Frederick James Smith, he repeated that "I shall write an opera completely in ragtime," adding that "I have snatches—here and there—of the score completed, but the actual work of the opera is yet to be done."[39] The *Chicago Tribune* for 24 January 1914 reported that "Berlin is absolutely serious in his determination [to write an opera with a ragtime setting], and his wide acquaintance with theatrical producers makes the immediate production of his operatic effort certain."

Berlin hadn't been asked to write a show score for good reason. He had no formal training in music, and his limited pianistic skills, although adequate for songwriting, accompanying, and coaching, were a potential handicap when it came to writing such things as an overture and ensemble numbers. And unlike George M. Cohan, he had no direct experience with the workings of musical theater, aside from his cameo appearance in *Up and Down Broadway* and his coaching of singers for other shows.

By 1912, however, Berlin was taking steps to overcome these limitations. Dependent to this point, like so many of his Tin Pan Alley peers, on staff musicians to notate his songs and to help with harmonizations and piano accompaniments, he hired a young musician, Cliff Hess, away from a position as a house pianist in a Chicago music publishing house to be his personal "musical secretary," as noted in the Introduction. "The two are virtually inseparable," reported Rennold Wolf. "Hess resides with Berlin at the latter's apartment in Seventy-first Street; he attends to the details of the young song-writer's business affairs, transcribes the melodies which Berlin conceives and plays them over and over again while the latter is setting the lyrics."[40] Having an accomplished musician available to work with him and with him alone made it easier for Berlin to undertake longer and more complex pieces.

Also, by 1912 Berlin had begun writing show songs with E. Ray Goetz, Vincent Bryan, and A. Baldwin Sloane, men who had much more experience in writing for the musical stage than did his earlier collaborator, Ted Snyder. In addition to the pieces I have noted that reached the stage in one show or another, a number of Berlin's unpublished sketches from this period were obviously intended for the musical theater. "Beautiful Chorus Girls," for instance, has just the sort of third-person lyric, describing the stage action, that would make it work as a production number:

> Beautiful dancing, most entrancing, chorus girls
> What would the managers do without Marie's and Pearl's
> Gwendlyn, Polly, Estelle and Cora
> Figured a little in Floradora
> Many's the mess was made success,
> By Beautiful Chorus Girls.[41]*

Other unpublished pieces have characters singing to one another, rather than to the audience:

> HE: I could live on love and kisses in a furnished four by two
> SHE: I would have to wash the dishes
> HE: You'd be glad to do it too
> SHE: Could you walk the floor with baby if it cried the whole night thru
> HE: I could even live in Brooklyn with a beautiful girl like you[42]**

During this period of apparently reduced productivity, then, Berlin was in effect serving a second apprenticeship as a songwriter in preparation for writing for the musical theater. He was learning what kinds of lyrics and music worked best on stage, he was writing show songs in collaboration with more experienced writers, and he was expanding his technique by experimenting with types of pieces he'd never written before.

Although there's no record of exactly when Berlin began working with Harry B. Smith on *Watch Your Step,* a note in *Variety* for 19 September reported that "Irving Berlin has finished 22 numbers for 'Watch Your Step,' the new Dillingham show scheduled for an early production." A folder in the Irving Berlin Music Company contains sketches and early drafts of lyrics and music for various numbers in *Watch Your Step,* many of them never used in the show; one of these, "There's A Girl On My Mind," is dated 13–14 July, suggesting that Berlin's concentrated work on the show was under way no later than early summer. The incubation period may have extended back considerably before that: A preliminary typescript of Smith's book for the *Ziegfeld Follies of 1912* includes an extended draft of a scene set in the Metropolitan Opera House, concluding with an ensemble entitled "Old Operas in New Ways," which never reached the stage in the *Follies* but eventually became the second act finale of *Watch Your Step.*[43]

The latter show was filled with pieces that demonstrate how effectively Berlin had learned to write for the musical stage over the previous two years.

- In addition to the innovative and effective potpourri overture, his first extended instrumental composition, there are several entr'actes and various bits of instrumental music, such as the sixteen bars accompanying the "Entrance of the Relatives" in the first act.
- The opening section is a complex, extended production number. The lyrics describe office workers "keep[ing] alive from nine to five"; members of the ensemble pantomime their daily tasks while singing to music that moves through three different keys and four different meters and tempi; the scene ends with a syncopated dance for the entire company. Other production numbers include a Berlin signature piece, "Let's Go Around The Town," yet another of his "come-on-along" numbers tracing its ancestry back to "Alexander's Ragtime Band." Six of the show's principals take alternate lines in the verses, then join the chorus in an exhortation to anyone within earshot—the audience, that is:

> Let's go 'round the town,
> And where a band is playing,
> We'll go hip-hurraying . . .

- There are several numbers in which the principals sing to one another in character, rather than to the audience. In the duo "Settle Down In A One Horse Town," Stella sings the first verse to Algy, he sings the second verse to her, and they sing the chorus together, with the "I" of the verses becoming "we."
- Act III concludes with another elaborate production number in which a series of standard selections from the operatic repertory are parodied in the styles of popular social dances of the day. Verdi appears on stage, protesting the "ragging" of his music against the jeers of the ensemble. (See musical example on facing page.)
- The finale of Act III brings the entire cast on stage for a syncopated dance as the chorus and principals sing directly and collectively to the audience:

> Look at 'em doing it
> Look at 'em doing it
> That syncopated walk
> What do you think of it
> What do you think of it
> We really hope you like it . . .

- Throughout the show, Berlin's music is written in a style combining the rhythmic vitality and freshness of the day's syncopated dance music with more sophisticated compositional techniques derived from operetta, and his lyrics are written in a colloquial language that nevertheless manages to appear more sophisticated than his earlier material for the vaudeville stage.

Summary

Between early 1909, when his first song was interpolated into a show, and late 1914, when his own first complete musical comedy was completed and produced, Berlin slowly but surely mastered the techniques of writing for the legitimate theater as opposed to the vaudeville house or the home circle. Much more was involved than mere technical details of lyrics and music; Berlin had to learn how to address an audience that was quite different from the one he had written for in his early days as a songwriter. This process was aided by the fact that, as a result of the national and international success of his songs, his own financial and social status was approaching that the people for whom musical comedies were now written: audiences for the legitimate theater.

Epilogue

In their material form as published sheet music, virtually all of Berlin's songs written between 1907 and the end of 1914 resemble one another closely in being brief pieces for one voice with piano accompaniment, written in verse-chorus format and making use of a limited harmonic, melodic, and rhythmic vocabulary. Given such apparent simplicity and homogeneity, it would seem difficult to make judgments as to their quality, their stylistic and expressive progression during this span of time, and their relation to apparently similar contemporaneous pieces by other songwriters.

This book has proposed, however, that there are in fact considerable differences among these songs despite their apparent homogeneity and that an understanding of these differences is essential to an assessment of them and of Berlin's role in the development of American popular song and musical theater. These differences come most sharply into focus if one examines the meaning of these pieces for Berlin's performers and audiences, taking into consideration not only their musical and textual content but also the environment in which they were performed. Such an approach leads inevitably to the broader issue of strategies adopted by the turn-of-the-century immigrant/first-generation community of New York City, the group most responsible for the composition and dissemination of popular songs of this period, in their interactions with an established American society that considered them outsiders.

Berlin must have known the music of Jewish services and rituals in his childhood, and perhaps also songs of the Yiddish theater. This was the music of a single group, and when he began singing for money on Lower East Side street corners and in saloons, he understood that his audience (and potential benefactors) cut a wide swath in New York City's radically multiethnic population and was thus likely to be more responsive to songs generally reflective of America's urban culture of the day than to those of one of its constituent subcultures. Accordingly, Berlin's repertory consisted mostly of pieces by Tin Pan Alley songwriters, written in a style that had become the lingua franca of turn-of-the-century urban America. When he turned to writing songs himself, this style was his own starting point.

American popular song of the nineteenth century had been an important component of an emerging national culture. For most of the century influential and successful songwriters had lived and worked in various parts of the country, and their songs had been published in Chicago, Boston, Philadelphia, New York, and many other cities and towns. Although much of the popular-song repertory from the early decades of the century was the work of European and immigrant composers, in the 1840s and 1850s a native school began to emerge that included the Hutchinsons, Dan Emmett, Stephen Foster, George F. Root, and Henry Clay Work. Although the musical idiom of these songs is traceable to a variety of sources—oral-tradition music from the British Isles, Italian opera, German lieder, British comic opera, the music of African Americans—this repertory struck the ears of listeners in America and abroad as distinctively American, and the lyrics dealt with American concerns, particularly those having to do with rural and small-town life.[1]

As the nineteenth century drew to a close, New York City increasingly became a mecca for those with a commercial interest in popular music. Aggressive new publishing companies based there began specializing in popular music and developing new tactics for the dissemination and marketing of their songs, the city became the country's most important center for performance venues, and songwriters from elsewhere flocked to New York.

The music of Tin Pan Alley, as the new urbanized, New York–centered style of popular song came to be called, did not represent a complete break with the older traditions of American song. To the contrary, it accommodated and assimilated the styles and genres of pieces written throughout the second half of the nineteenth century for the American home circle and the musical stage. But as popular music came to be dominated by immigrant and first-generation Irish, Italian, and particularly Jewish songwriters, performers, impresarios, and publishers, the received content and style of nineteenth-century song were gradually modified. Urban settings began to replace rural ones in the miniature dramas developed in song lyrics, the protagonists in these dramas were increasingly characters from the streets of New York rather than the farms and villages of Indiana, and echoes of ethnic musics brought to the New World by the latest immigrants often spiced the musical style.

Berlin wrote his first songs as a teenager making his way on the sidewalks and in the saloons of lower Manhattan just as these changes were taking place. Most of these new Tin Pan Alley songs were written about (and for) the "great conglomeration of men from ev'ry nation"[2] who populated this world, this "stirring and seething [of] Celt and Latin, Slav and Teuton, Greek and Syrian—black and yellow—Jew and Gentile,"[3] to quote David Quixando in *The Melting-Pot*. However disparate their national or ethnic backgrounds, together these new Americans were forging a common public culture in the songs, dialogues, and skits of the popular stage. Although Berlin's early songs for the vaudeville stage, like those of his peers on Tin Pan Alley, in some ways drew on older American models, they had a different intent: to amuse and empower the various outsiders who made up their audiences in saloons, burlesque theaters, and vaudeville houses, people whom the dominant culture sought to keep in check. In using these people as their protagonists, Berlin's ethnic novelty songs acknowledged their existence and the stuff of their lives, and his "suggestive" songs accomplished the same purpose by satirizing the behavior of the more privileged classes. Berlin wrote these pieces for his own community, the people he observed, knew, and associated with in multiethnic New York City, and the fact that many of these pieces were also accepted and enjoyed elsewhere simply meant that ethnic identity and urban life were matters of growing concern to the country at large.

But even though these songs draw their protagonists and musical styles from the various "races of Europe" that had found their way to the United States, they show little evidence of the cultural process of "melting and reforming" envisioned by Zangwill. Their characters are still German or Italian or Jewish or black; their lyrics, and the music to which these are sung, are written so as to distinguish these "races" from each other, if only at the level of comic caricature. While it's true that the various people represented on the vaudeville stage share the common feature of being newcomers to an entrenched society reluctant to accept them into full membership, each group maintains its own identity both on the stage and among the multiethnic audiences of the popular theater. There was little sense that all concerned were moving in the direction of becoming generic Americans.

These first songs of Berlin appear to be little different from those of other songwriters of the day; even though on closer inspection some of them do exhibit mannerisms that distinguish them from those by other writers—an interior phrase that shifts abruptly to a new key without modulation and just as abruptly jumps back to the tonic, for instance, or a phrase that is compressed or extended beyond the usual four-bar length—

such details are stylistic minutiae and were probably undetectable by most listeners. Popular music is, after all, a genre in which communication takes place in the context of a shared idiom, and as Berlin himself pointed out more than once, any piece that strikes its intended audience as too "original"—i.e., too removed from the stylistic norms of the day—runs the risk of being rejected.

Berlin also wrote songs other than ethnic novelties and "suggestive" pieces in his first years of songwriting. A few of his early ballads tried, with little success, to emulate two well-established strains of American song: the pseudo-folk popular ballad, best epitomized by Stephen Foster's enduring songs, and the high-class ballad, with roots in classical music. Berlin became a successful writer of ballads only after he had assimilated and reshaped elements of these two older styles into several new subgenres more suitable for his own time and for venues other than the nineteenth-century home circle, where most ballads had been sung.

The Berlin-Snyder ballads, in which a more youthful sentimentality leavened with humor replaced the intense emotionalism of the nineteenth-century ballad, worked as well in variety houses as in the parlor and had more appeal for younger people. And Berlin's rhythmic ballads, blending the vitality of syncopated dance music with erotic, teasing lyrics, were also written for a venue other than the home circle—the legitimate theater, on Broadway. Unlike his early songs for vaudeville, which like David Quixando's "American Symphony" in *The Melting-Pot* had been written for his fellow "new immigrants—those who have known the pain of the old world and the hope of the new"[4]—these pieces (and others also written for the legitimate stage) were no longer addressed to an audience of his peers but were written for the entertainment of people of social strata above his own; as I have pointed out in Chapter One, only some 2 percent of the audience for the legitimate theater was made up of members of the working class, and recent immigrants were likewise conspicuous by their absence.

Berlin was by no means the first Tin Pan Alley songwriter to write for the legitimate stage. Lew Fields and Joe Weber "[took] variety out of the Bowery beer saloons and [brought] it to Broadway"[5] when they opened their Broadway Music Hall in 1896, and Florenz Ziegfeld and other producers followed their example in the first decade of the new century with their Folies and Revues and Passing Shows, all of which were essentially variety-style entertainments dressed up with more elaborate and lavish costumes, sets, and music than would have been possible in vaudeville houses. The music for such shows sometimes imitated that of European operetta and at other times drew on one or another of the styles of American vernacular music. One show might feature a score evoking Strauss or Lehar, another might be filled with Tin Pan Alley-style ragtime songs and dances, and another might mix the two.

This was not true of book musicals performed on these same Broadway stages through the first decade of the twentieth century; their scores were invariably written in a style derived from European light opera, whether the composer happened to be European or American. Even George M. Cohan's perky, extroverted music, which struck some listeners on both sides of the Atlantic as characteristically American, evoked marches and social dances that had originated in the Old World, and it sounded perfectly at home in British music halls.

Berlin continued to write for the vaudeville stage after 1911, when his songs began to be interpolated into musical comedies and revues with some frequency and often a great deal of success, but his overriding ambition by then was to write the music for a complete musical comedy, which finally happened in late 1914 with *Watch Your Step*. Like other Broadway shows, it "attract[ed] the elite of 'sassiety' to the New Amsterdam," where it played;[6] it was reviewed enthusiastically in the *New York Times* and other journals that paid little or no attention to vaudeville or to the affairs of the people who patronized that sort of entertainment; the stars of the show, Irene and Vernon Castle, were the darlings of New York's cafe society; scenes were set in a law office, in the Metropolitan Opera House, and aboard a Pullman sleeper, locations not much frequented by working-class immigrants or first-generation Americans. Any of Berlin's pals from the Lower East Side attending the show would have felt out of his element.

There are no ethnic characters in *Watch Your Step*, or in most of Berlin's individual songs written in 1913 and 1914. The increasing stylistic homogeneity of his music of this period, strikingly evident when these pieces are compared to his earlier songs, is not the result of a process of "melting and reforming," however. Berlin was absorbing more and more of the style of the mainstream Euro-American popular musical stage at this time, as can be seen in his increasing use of melodic sequence and other devices common to nineteenth-century classical music and light opera. One would be hard put to find any trace of the musical style of Italian, German, or Jewish novelty songs in these pieces, and dialect is absent from the lyrics.

A recent book by Allen Forte "offer[s] a detailed and in-depth study of a small number of fine songs composed [between 1924 and 1950] in the vernacular of American popular music."[7] The author, offering his book as "a small contribution to our understanding and, if I may presume, our appreciation of a significant repertoire of beautiful music that will remain forever popular,"[8] makes use of "modern music-analytical techniques" derived from the writings of the German music theorist Heinrich Schenker. As he explains the "essential process [of] *analytical reduction*" underlying his work: "Two principles govern the reductive analysis of tonal music—and they apply to the American popular ballad just as they apply to classical tonal music: 1) *the principle of harmonic-contrapuntal definition;* and 2) *The principle of melodic-structural distinction* between notes that represent large-scale voice-leading continuity and those that are entirely of local significance."[9]

Six songs by Berlin are analyzed according to a completely text-based methodology, as are all songs considered in the book. Melodic, harmonic, and structural details as found in the published sheet music are examined with no reference to factors of performance or reception. I doubt that this approach can tell us anything about the quality of these songs or suggest why audiences responded to them, but since the underlying analytical techniques were devised by European scholars in an attempt to deal with pieces of modern European classical music as autonomous objects,[10] Forte manages to establish a connection between these six songs by Berlin and the latter repertory by demonstrating that both can be analyzed in the same way. He dismisses Berlin's earliest songs as "indescribably bad,"[11] apparently because they don't yield their secrets to this sort of analysis. I've just suggested that Berlin began incorporating more elements drawn from European classical music and operetta into his songwriting technique from 1912 on, and I'm sure that his songs of this period could be analyzed according to the methodology used by Forte for slightly later pieces, thus verifying my suggestion.

Returning to *Watch Your Step,* writers who have had trouble reconciling the show's enthusiastic reception with what they take to be its deficiencies of plot and the weaknesses of its overall musical structure have overlooked the fact that it was the first full-length book musical with a score written throughout, from overture to last-act finale, in the style of syncopated dance music. It was advertised as a "syncopated musical show," and a critic in Boston expanded on this: "[T]he program calls it a 'syncopated' show. It is nothing else. It is an apotheosis of syncopation. The 'plot' is syncopated. It starts; it hesitates; it is lost; it is caught up again without warning in the whirl and then disappears entirely."[12]

Berlin put a personal stamp on the music of *Watch Your Step* by his use of pervasive syncopation. Even though syncopation of one sort or another had been used in much of the classical and popular music of nineteenth-century Europe, Berlin's syncopated patterns in his music of this period were perceived, with a certain amount of historical accuracy, as being derived from African American styles. And here we have a problem with Zangwill's vision of the "Melting-Pot." European himself, with limited firsthand experience with the realities of American life, his play is concerned with the "races of Europe" in the New World. There are no black characters in his drama, and no intimation of the role that African Americans might play in shaping "the Republic of Man and the Kingdom of God" despite resistance not only from America's "nativists" but from recent immigrants as well. Tellingly, David Quixando expresses his vision of the

United States in one of the classic forms of European high art, the symphony, while Berlin wrote popular songs and a musical comedy.

The musical style of *Watch Your Step*, combining pervasive syncopation with Berlin's newly gained control of the techniques of European-based composition, was new to the American musical theater. It proved to be a decisive influence on the next several decades of musical comedy; thus, Berlin's *Watch Your Step* can be seen as a seminal work, more so than any other piece from that period.

National and ethnic traits of turn-of-the-century immigrants, and also of those people who had been in America much longer, proved to be stubbornly persistent, if malleable. Berlin's earliest songs celebrate the distinctive cultures of people who had come to America from various lands without mixing them together. *Watch Your Step*, on the other hand, mixing elements of Euro-American light opera with rhythmic impulses derived (even if only at second or third hand) from African American cultural practices, demonstrated that a multicultural society needn't force one to mix every strand available in such an environment but instead opens up the possibility of endless mixtures and options.

Zangwill had it wrong. The emerging twentieth-century American character and culture didn't develop as a "melting and re-forming" of elements from European lands alone. What actually happened was not, in the end, a process of homogenization, and it didn't result in a generic American people and culture.

Appendix 1

Published Songs of Irving Berlin, 1907–1914

Listed below are the titles of all songs copyrighted and published between 1907 and the end of 1914 for which Berlin wrote all or some of the lyrics, music, or both. Each title is given as it appears on the first page of the published sheet music and on the copyright entry card in the Library of Congress rather than on the sheet music cover, since cover artists were sometimes given incorrect or incomplete information.

Numbers in brackets after each title refer to the order in which the song appears in Charles Hamm, *Irving Berlin: Early Songs, 1907–1914*, 3 vols. (Madison: A-R Editions, published for the American Musicological Society, 1994).

The second line of each entry gives copyright information: the E number, assigned to each copyrighted item of printed music, and the date on which copyright was assigned. The third line identifies Berlin's collaborator(s) on the song; if there is no third line, the song is attributed to Berlin alone.

Abie Sings An Irish Song [155]
    E311248—15 May '13
After The Honeymoon [78]
    E262636—31 Aug '11
Alexander And His Clarinet [40]
    E232639—19 May '10
        Ted Snyder
Alexander's Bag-Pipe Band [101]
    E278333—24 Feb '12
        E. Ray Goetz, A. Baldwin Sloane

Alexander's Ragtime Band [60]
      E252990—18 Mar '11
Along Came Ruth [177]
      E335767—1 May '14
Always Treat Her Like A Baby [185]
      E347212—24 Aug '14
Angelo [A2]
      E229420—13 Apr '10
Anna 'Liza's Wedding Day [141]
      E304024—15 Jan '13
Antonio [107]
      E284515—13 May '12
Apple Tree And The Bumble Bee, The [146]
      E305272—7 Mar '13
At The Devil's Ball I [130]
      E293434—14 Nov '12
At The Devil's Ball II [133]
      E299488—18 Dec '12
At The Devil's Ball III [139]
      E301125—8 Jan '13
At The Picture Show [140]
      E301409—20 Jan '13
            E. Ray Goetz
Becky's Got A Job In A Musical Show [112]
      E285627—6 June '12
Before I Go And Marry, I Will Have A Talk With You [25]
      E221856—31 Dec '09
Best Of Friend Must Part, The [3]
      E175845—6 Feb '08
Bring Back My Lena To Me [55]
      E241527—20 Oct '10
            Ted Snyder
Bring Back My Lovin' Man [89]
      E271161—16 Nov '11
Bring Me A Ring In The Spring And I'll Know That You Love Me [92]
      E271969—5 Dec '11
Business Is Business [67]
      E255849—21 Apr '11
Call Again! [116]
      E285990—17 June '12
Call Me Up Some Rainy Afternoon [36]
      E230607—23 Apr '10

Christmas-Time Seems Years And Years Away [22]
    E219710—2 Dec '09
        Ted Snyder
Colored Romeo [48]
    E239224—14 Sept '10
        Ted Snyder
Come Back To Me, My Melody [122]
    E296703—8 Oct '12
        Ted Snyder
Cuddle Up [91]
    E271441—24 Nov '11
Daddy, Come Home [170]
    E328318—16 Dec '13
Dat's-A My Gal [58]
    E248729—14 Jan '11
Dear Mayme, I Love You! [34]
    E229542—18 Apr '10
        Ted Snyder
Do It Again [123]
    E296722—9 Oct '12
Do Your Duty Doctor! (Oh, Oh, Oh, Oh, Doctor) [12]
    E213051—6 Aug '09
        Ted Snyder
Dog Gone That Chilly Man [83]
    E266709—30 Sept '11
Don't Leave Your Wife Alone [135]
    E300049—20 Nov '12
Don't Put Out The Light [71]
    E257470—6 May '11
        Edgar Leslie
Don't Take Your Beau To The Seashore [82]
    E266385—22 Sept '11
        E. Ray Goetz
Dorando [5]
    E203814—11 Mar '09
Down In Chattanooga [169]
    E323417—21 Nov '13
Down In My Heart [129]
    E298127—30 Oct '12
Down To The Folies Bergere [69]
    E255928—24 Apr '11
        Vincent Bryan, Ted Snyder

Draggy Rag [33]
    E229419—13 Apr '10
Dreams, Just Dreams [53]
    E240951—12 Oct '10
        Ted Snyder
Elevator Man Going Up, Going Up, Going Up, Going Up!, The [118]
    E288757—5 July '12
Ephraham Played Upon The Piano [74]
    E260178—20 June '11
        Vincent Bryan
Everybody's Doing It Now [88]
    E269369—2 Nov '11
Fiddle-Dee-Dee I [115]
    E285805—12 June '12
        E. Ray Goetz
Fiddle-Dee-Dee II [117]
    E286188—27 May '12
        E. Ray Goetz
Follow Me Around [131]
    E298601—13 Nov '12
Follow The Crowd [172]
    E330624—30 Jan '14
Furnishing A Home For Two [187]
    E347984—8 Oct '14
God Gave You To Me [180]
    E338500—29 Apr '14
Good-bye, Girlie, And Remember Me [13]
    E213052—6 Aug '09
        George W. Meyer
Goody, Goody, Goody, Goody, Good [137]
    E300412—11 Dec '12
Grizzly Bear [35]
    E230452—19 Apr '10
        George Botsford
Happy Little Country Girl [149]
    E309806—21 May '13
Haunted House, The [182]
    E339657—5 May '14
He Promised Me [93]
    E272255—12 Dec '11
Herman Let's Dance That Beautiful Waltz [50]
    E240313—24 Sept '10
        Ted Snyder

He's A Devil In His Own Home Town [175]
 E331516—14 Mar '14
  Grant Clarke
He's A Rag Picker [186]
 E347874—28 Sept '14
He's So Good To Me [138]
 E300853—4 Jan '13
Hiram's Band [125]
 E297549—21 Oct '12
  E. Ray Goetz
How Can You Do It, Mabel, On Twenty Dollars A Week? [96]
 E272549—19 Dec '11
I Beg Your Pardon, Dear Old Broadway [65]
 E254307—28 Mar '11
I Didn't Go Home At All [4]
 E203451—13 Mar '09
  Edgar Leslie
I Just Came Back To Say Good Bye [24]
 E220879—8 Dec '09
I Love To Quarrel With You [174]
 E330900—10 Feb '14
I Love You More Each Day [39]
 E232638—19 May '10
  Ted Snyder
I Want To Be In Dixie [98]
 E275297—18 Jan '12
  Ted Snyder
I Want To Go Back To Michigan (Down On The Farm) [183]
 E343400—30 July '14
I Was Aviating Around [158]
 E311257—16 May '13
  Vincent Bryan
I Wish That You Was My Gal, Molly [19]
 E217169—14 Oct '09
  Ted Snyder
If All The Girls I Knew Were Like You [132]
 E298624—15 Nov '12
If I Had You [178]
 E335768—1 May '14
If I Thought You Wouldn't Tell [18]
 E217168—14 Oct '09
  Ted Snyder

If That's Your Idea Of A Wonderful Time (Take Me Home) [184]
    E345233—22 June '14
If The Managers Only Thought The Same As Mother [30]
    E226408—15 Feb '10
        Ted Snyder
If You Don't Want Me (Why Do You Hang Around) [167]
    E322040—24 Sept '13
If You Don't Want My Peaches You'd Better Stop Shaking My Tree [179]
    E338500—29 Apr '14
I'm A Happy Married Man [38]
    E231098—2 June '10
        Ted Snyder
I'm Afraid, Pretty Maid, I'm Afraid [109]
    E284616—6 Feb '12
I'm Going On A Long Vacation [54]
    E240952—12 Oct '10
        Ted Snyder
In My Harem [143]
    E304585—1 Feb '13
Innocent Bessie Brown [52]
    E240647—5 Oct '10
International Rag, The [161]
    E315561—12 Aug '13
Is There Anything Else I Can Do For You? [46]
    E237829—8 Sept '10
        Ted Snyder
It Isn't What He Said, But The Way He Said It! [173]
    E330899—11 Feb '14
I've Got To Have Some Lovin' Now [104]
    E279448—4 Mar '12
Jake! Jake! The Yiddisher Ball-Player [160]
    E314881—2 July '12
        Blanche Merrill
Just Like The Rose [9]
    E211289—2 July '09
        Al Piantadosi
Keep Away From The Fellow Who Owns An Automobile [120]
    E289979—9 Aug '12
Keep On Walking [152]
    E310336—14 Apr '13
Ki-I-Youdleing Dog, The [151]
    E314106—4 Apr '13
        Jean Schwartz

Kiss Me My Honey, Kiss Me [47]
    E238127—3 Aug '10
        Ted Snyder
Kiss Your Sailor Boy Goodbye [162]
    E315602—15 Aug '13
Lead Me To That Beautiful Band [106]
    E283517—18 Apr '12
        E. Ray Goetz
Little Bit Of Everything, A [124]
    E297194—18 Oct '12
Marie From Sunny Italy [1]
    E150811—12 Oct '07
        Mike Nicholson
Meet Me To-Night [94]
    E272256—12 Dec '11
Million Dollar Ball, The [110]
    E285079—6 May '12
        E. Ray Goetz
Molly-O! Oh, Molly! [72]
    E257638—13 May '11
Monkey Doodle Doo, The [156]
    E311249—15 May '13
My Melody Dream [86]
    E268592—14 Oct '11
My Sweet Italian Man I [128]
    E298124—31 Oct '12
My Sweet Italian Man II [144]
    E305080—21 Feb '13
My Wife's Gone To The Country (Hurrah! Hurrah!) [8]
    E209740—18 June '09
        Ted Snyder, George Whiting
Next To Your Mother, Who Do You Love? [20]
    E218110—26 Oct '09
        Ted Snyder
No One Could Do It Like My Father! [6]
    E204479—2 Apr '09
        Ted Snyder
Oh How That German Could Love [31]
    E226408—15 Feb '10
        Ted Snyder
Oh, That Beautiful Rag [42]
    E235374—7 July '10
        Ted Snyder

Oh! Where Is My Wife To-Night? [15]
      E214570—16 Sept '09
            Ted Snyder, George Whiting
Oh, What I Know About You [10]
      E211292—2 July '09
            Joseph H. McKeon, Harry M. Piano, W. Raymond Walker
Old Maids Ball, The [153]
      E310412—16 Apr '13
One O'Clock In The Morning I Get Lonesome [80]
      E266077—16 Sept '11
Opera Burlesque [102]
      E279162—24 Feb '12
Piano Man [51]
      E240646—5 Oct '10
            Ted Snyder
Pick, Pick, Pick, Pick On The Mandolin, Antonio [97]
      E274520—2 Jan '12
Pullman Porters On Parade, The [154]
      E311090—16 Apr '13
            Maurice Abrahams
Queenie [2]
      E175522—29 Feb '08
            Maurice Abraham
Ragtime Jockey Man, The [113]
      E285800—11 June '12
Ragtime Mocking Bird [100]
      E275605—25 Jan '12
Ragtime Soldier Man [119]
      E288879—12 July '12
Ragtime Violin! [84]
      E266996—6 Oct '11
Run Home And Tell Your Mother [77]
      E260540—29 June '11
Sadie Salome (Go Home) [7]
      E204481—2 Apr '09
            Edgar Leslie
San Francisco Bound [147]
      E398422—13 Mar '13
She Was A Dear Little Girl [16]
      E216226—5 Oct '09
            Ted Snyder
Snookey Ookums [145]
      E305082—21 Feb '13

Society Bear [105]
    E282261—1 Apr '12
Sombrero Land [90]
    E271198—17 Nov '11
        E. Ray Goetz, Ted Snyder
Some Little Something About You [17]
    E217166—14 Oct '09
        Ted Snyder
Somebody's Coming To My House [157]
    E311250—15 May '13
Someone Just Like You [27]
    E222372—22 Dec '09
        Ted Snyder
Someone's Waiting For Me (We'll Wait, Wait, Wait) [11]
    E211293—2 July '09
        Edgar Leslie
Spanish Love [68]
    E255927—25 Apr '11
        Vincent Bryan, Ted Snyder
Spring And Fall [103]
    E279163—24 Feb '12
Stay Down Here Where You Belong [188]
    E349008—20 Oct '14
Stop That Rag (Keep On Playing, Honey) [21]
    E219550—24 Nov '09
        Ted Snyder
Stop, Stop, Stop (Come Over And Love Me Some More) [49]
    E239367—17 Sept '10
Sweet Italian Love [41]
    E234395—9 July '10
        Ted Snyder
Sweet Marie, Make-a Rag-a-Time Dance Wid Me [29]
    E224516—18 Jan '10
        Ted Snyder
Take A Little Tip From Father [99]
    E275357—20 Jan '12
        Ted Snyder
Take Me Back [163]
    E315974—8 Sept '12
Telling Lies [28]
    E223314—14 Jan '10
        Henrietta Blanke-Belcher

"Thank You, Kind Sir!" Said She [44]
    E237664—31 Aug '10
        Ted Snyder
That Dying Rag [59]
    E250877—18 Feb '11
        Bernie Adler
That Kazzatsky Dance [56]
    E245819—19 Dec '10
That Mesmerizing Mendelssohn Tune [26]
    E222371—22 Dec '09
That Monkey Tune [63]
    E254260—25 Mar '11
That Mysterious Rag [79]
    E265636—31 Aug '11
        Ted Snyder
That Opera Rag [37]
    E230794—28 Apr '10
        Ted Snyder
That's How I Love You [108]
    E284516—13 May '12
That's My Idea Of Paradise [189]
    E352071—10 Oct '14
There's A Girl In Arizona [166]
    E320280—17 Sept '13
        Grant Clarke and Edgar Leslie
There's A Girl In Havana [81]
    E266188—19 Sept '11
        E. Ray Goetz, A. Baldwin Sloane
They're On Their Way To Mexico [181]
    E338892—2 May '14
They've Got Me Doin' It Now [159]
    E311999—17 June '13
They've Got Me Doin' It Now Medley [164]
    E318425—11 July '13
This Is The Life I [171]
    E330482—26 Jan '14
This Is The Life II [176]
    E334172—21 Feb '14
Tra-La, La, La! [168]
    E322040—24 Sept '13
True Born Soldier Man, A [111]
    E285201—15 May '12

Try It On Your Piano [43]
    E235475—7 July '11
Virginia Lou [61]
    E253397—20 Mar '11
        Earl Taylor
Wait Until Your Daddy Comes Home [134]
    E299526—19 Dec '12
We Have Much To Be Thankful For [150]
    E309808—21 May '13
Welcome Home [142]
    E304275—23 Jan '13
When I Lost You [127]
    E297996—8 Nov '12
When I'm Alone I'm Lonesome [64]
    E254261—25 Mar '11
When I'm Thinking Of You [121]
    E296287—27 Sept '12
When It Rains, Sweetheart, When It Rains [70]
    E257181—29 Apr '11
When It's Night Time In Dixie Land [190]
    E349951—5 Dec '14
When Johnson's Quartette Harmonize [114]
    E285801—11 June '12
When The Midnight Choo-Choo Leaves For Alabam' [126]
    E297717—2 Nov '12
When You Kiss An Italian Girl [73]
    E259700—16 June '11
When You Play That Piano, Bill [32]
    E228389—16 Mar '10
        Ted Snyder
When You're In Town [66]
    E254667—11 Apr '11
Whistling Rag, The
    E253962—31 Mar '11
Wild Cherries [14]
    E213300—12 Aug '09
        Ted Snyder
Wishing [57]
    E246503—17 Dec '10
        Ted Snyder
Woodman, Woodman, Spare That Tree! [76]
    E260385—27 June '11
        Vincent Bryan

Yankee Love [95]
    E272387—15 Dec '11
        E. Ray Goetz
Yiddisha Eyes [45]
    E237828—8 Sept '10
Yiddisha Nightingale [85]
    E268019—7 Oct '11
Yiddisha Professor [136]
    EE300175—23 Nov '12
Yiddle, On Your Fiddle, Play Some Ragtime [23]
    E220516—30 Nov '09
You Picked A Bad Day Out To Say Good-bye [148]
    E309405—25 Apr '13
You've Built A Fire Down In My Heart [75]
    E260179—20 June '11
You've Got Me Hypnotized [87]
    E269368—2 Nov '11
You've Got Your Mother's Big Blue Eyes! [165]
    E319799—12 Sept '13

Appendix 2

Unpublished Songs by
Irving Berlin, Before 1915

The following explanations are keyed to the entries in this appendix.

1. Lyrics in IBC-LC
2. Titles from song lists by Berlin in IBC-LC
3. Performed, but never published
4. Lead sheets and lyrics in IBC-LC
5. Recorded, but not published
6. Sketched for *Watch Your Step,* material in IBC-LC

All Aboard For Mattawan[1]
All That I Want[2]
Answer Me[3]
     alternate title for "Keep A Taxi Waiting, Dear"
At The Acrobat Ball[1]
Beautiful Chorus Girls[1]
Beautiful Photograph, A[1,2]
Big Chief Ephraham[2]
Brains[1]
Call Of My Broken Heart, The[1]
Cuddle Up To Any Other Girl[1,2]
Curly Hair[2]
Dinner Bells[2]
Don't Be Stingy[6] (lead sheet)
Don't You Remember Mary Brown[1]

Don't Wait Until Your Father Comes Home[3] (sung by Berlin on a bill at
    Hammerstein's Victoria Theatre, Sept. 1911)
Down On Uncle Jerry's Farm[4]
Drink, Brothers Drink (with Vincent Bryan)[1]
Eight Little Song Writers[1]
Evening Exercise[1]
Ever Since I Met You I'm A Nut (with Grant Clark & Jean Schwartz)[1]
Funny Little Melody, The[5]
Good Bye, Becky Cohen[3] (sung by Fannie Brice in *Ziegfeld Follies of 1910*)
Happy Little Chorus Girl[1]
Has Anybody Seen That Beautiful Lady[2]
He Never Comes Home At All[1]
He Sympathized With Me[3] (written for May Irwin in *Mr. Jim,* title of
    show changed to *Getting A Polish* before first performance)
He's Just That Kind Of Man[1,2]
He's Only My Husband[2]
Home Town[6] (lead sheet)
How Can You Love Such A Man?[5]
Hummin' Rag, The (melody and lyric published in *The Daily Mail,* Lon-
    don, in June 1913)
Husbands and Wives[6] (lyric sheet, piano-vocal score)
I Could Live On Love And Kisses[4]
I Don't Care For Long Haired Musicians[6] (lyric sketch)
I Felt That Something Was Going To Happen[2]
I Know That Lady[1]
I Love A Small Town[1]
I Love The Voice Of A Cello[2]
I Might Go Home To Night (with Vincent Bryan)[1]
I Want A Harem Of My Own[2]
If It Wasn't For My Wife And Baby[1]
If They Were All Like You[6] (lyric sheet, lead sheet)
I'll Be A Mother To You[2]
I'll Make It Warm For You[1,2]
I'm Getting Strong For You[1]
It Was Good Enough For Grandfather[2]
It Was Good Enough For Your Father[1]
It's Really None of My Affair (lyric sheet in collection of James Fuld)
I've Got A Lot Of Love For You[4]
I've Got To Catch A Train Goodbye[4]
I've Written Another Melody[1]
I've Written Another Song[1]
Keep A Taxi Waiting, Dear[3] (performed in *Hell,* 1911)
Kiss Me Good Night[2]

Let Me Love You Just A Little Bit [1,2]
Mary O'Hooligan [5]
Midnight Eyes [1,2]
Midnight Sons, The [3] (title listed in *Variety,* 27 May 1911, for a program
    by The Alley's Old Timers)
Million Dollar Girl [1]
Musical Mose [2]
My Father Was An Indian (with Edgar Leslie) (lyric sheet in possession of
    James Fuld)
My Gal Down Home [2]
My Gal In Italy [1]
My Once-In-A-Century Girl [1]
My Old Sweetheart [1]
My Tango Man [1]
My Wife Bridget [3] (written for May Irwin in *Mr. Jim,* title of show
    changed to *Getting A Polish* before first performance. Rights sold to
    Irwin.)
Old Fashioned Serenade [2]
Paint Me A Picture Of The Man I Love [1,2]
Piano Bugs [1]
Play A Little Sentimental Music [2]
Poor Little Chamber Maid [1]
Revival Day [5]
Samuel Brown (The Operatic Waiter) [1]
Save A Little Bit For Me [1]
Sell My Shak In Hackensack [1]
Show Me [2]
Since I Married Julius Krause [2]
Somewhere (But Where Is It?) [4]
Spooning In The New Mown Hay (with Vincent Bryan) [1]
Sweet Sixteen [2]
Take Me Back To Your Garden Of Love (parody) [1]
Tatooed Man, The [4]
Tell Me Again That You Love Me [2]
That's The Reason I'm In Love With You [2]
That's How I Love You Mike [1]
That's Just Why I Love You [1]
There's A Fire Burning Down In My Heart (Put It Out—Put It Out—
    Put It Out) [6] (lyric sketch)
There's A Girl On My Mind [1,6] (lyric sheet and lead sheet)
They're Dancing Teachers [6] (lyric sheet and lead sheet)
(My Sweetheart) They All Came With You [1,2]
They All Took A Drink Of It [1,2]

'Till I'm M-A-double-R-I-E-D To Y-O-U [1]
Tip The Waiter [1]
Under The Palms [1]
Until [1]
Wait Until I Get You Home [2]
We Had A Wonderful Time [1]
What Am I Gonna Do? [5]
What's Good Enough For Your Father Is Good Enough For You [1]
When I Get Back To My Home Town [1]
When I'm In Love [6] (lyric sheet, lead sheet)
Wife And Baby [2]
The Yiddisha Ball [1]
Yiddisha Wedding [1] (lyric sheet in possession of James Fuld)
You're Goin' To Lose Your Baby Some Day [4]

Appendix 3

Period Recordings of Early Songs by Irving Berlin

COMPILED BY PAUL CHAROSH

The information below was compiled to assist readers who wish to locate period recordings of the songs discussed in this book. All citations are of records made or released in the United States under the catalogue numbers shown and are vocal performances unless otherwise indicated. Irving Berlin does not always receive composer credit; sometimes it is extended only to his collaborators. Their names appear in Appendix I.

Some recordings were assigned more than one catalogue number and issued under more than one label. Zonophone masters were sometimes released as Oxford Records. Columbia sold or leased masters to other firms (e.g., manufacturers of talking machines and department stores) that sold pressings under their own labels. Climax, Harmony, Lakeside, Oxford, Silvertone, Standard, and United are examples of such labels. These are not listed here; the discography cites only the original release data. Full documentation of the activities of some record companies during this period is unavailable, and their output is known only through surviving specimens and chronologically scattered catalogues and release lists. There are no comprehensive title indices for any of the companies, and citations of some recordings may be missing entirely.

Alternate titles appearing on records are cross-indexed in italics. Recordings of songs performed in *Watch Your Step* are documented at the end of the discography.

The records listed here may sometimes be located in sound archives and private collections where they may be grouped according to their form (i.e., cylinder or disc), the company that issued them and the associated catalogue numbers, and their size or playing time. Such data are included here, as are matrix numbers, release and recording dates, when known. The following abbreviations are used: cyl. = cylinder; min. = minute; mx. = matrix number (on Victor records this is followed by a dash and a take number); rec. = recording date; rel. = release date.

After The Honeymoon
Maurice Burkhart

Edison 932	4-min. cyl.			rel. Mar '12
Victor	10″ disc	mx. B11041-1	rec. 29 Sep '11	unissued

Harriette Keyes

Zonophone 5807	10″ disc		rel. Nov '11

Prince's Band

Columbia A1107	10″ disc	mx. 19651	rec. 4 Nov '11	rel. Mar '12
[part of "Medley of Snyder's Hits"]				

Walter Van Brunt

Columbia A1073	10″ disc	mx. 19547	rec. 1 Sep '11	rel. Dec '11

Alexander And His Clarinet
Arthur Collins

Edison 455	4-min. cyl.	rel. Jul '10

Arthur Collins and Byron G. Harlan

Columbia A831	10″ disc	mx. 4415	rel. Jul '10
Indestructible 3087	4-min. cyl.		rel. Jul '10

Alexander's Bag-Pipe Band
Billy Murray

Victor 17054	10″ disc	mx. 11585-3	rec. 12 Feb '12	rel. Apr '12
Zonophone 5877	10″ disc			rel. Apr '12

Alexander's Ragtime Band
Arthur Collins and Byron G. Harlan

Columbia A1032	10″ disc	mx. 19398	rec. 7 Jun '11	rel. Sep '11
Indestructible 3251	4-min.cyl.			rel. c. Sep'11
Phono-Cut 5093	10″ disc			rel. c. 1911
U.S. Everlasting 399	2-min. cyl.			rel. Sep '11
Victor 16908	10″ disc	mx. B10374-1	rec. 23 May '11	rel. Sep '11
Zonophone 5766	10″ disc			rel. Aug '11

Melville Ellis (piano)

Columbia A1160	10″ disc	mx. 19752	rec. 7 Feb '12	rel. Nov '12
[arrangement includes "Magic Fire Scene from *Die Walkure*"]				

Billy Murray

Edison 817	4-min. cyl.		rel. Nov '11
Edison 2048	4-min. cyl.		rel. Nov '13
Edison 10522	2-min. cyl.		rel. Nov '11

Pathé Military Band, Paris
    Pathé 7743   11-3/8″ disc   rel. c. 1915
Prince's Band
    Columbia A1107   10″ disc   mx. 19651   rec. 4 Nov '11   rel. Mar '12
    [part of "Medley of Snyder's Hits"]
    Columbia A1126   10″ disc   mx. 19716   rec. 8 Jan '12   rel. Apr '12
U.S. Military Band
    U.S. Everlasting 1437   4-min. cyl.   rel. c. 1912
    [part of "Medley of Popular Hits"]
Fred Van Epps (banjo)
    Edison 1002   4-min. cyl.   rel. May '12
    Edison 1864   4-min. cyl.   rel. Sep '13
    [title song in medley]
Victor Military Band
    Victor 17006   10″ disc   mx. B11008-1   rec. 17 Oct '11   rel. Jan '12
Victor Military Band with chorus
    Victor   10″ disc   mx. B11007-1   rec. 17 Oct '11   unissued
Victor Mixed Chorus
    Victor 31848   12″ disc   mx. C11071-2   rec. 9 Oct '11   rel. Dec '11
    [part of "Song Medley No. 1—Snyder Successes"]
Victor Orchestra
    Victor 16963   10″ disc   mx. B10851-3   rec. 11 Aug '11 rel. Nov '11
    [part of "Snyder Successes" medley]

Along Came Ruth

anonymous band
    Little Wonder 28   5-1/2″ disc   rel. 1914
    [part of "Medley of Popular Airs No. 2"]
anonymous baritone solo
    Little Wonder 21   5-1/2″ disc   rel. 1914
Arthur Fields
    Columbia A1612   10″ disc   mx. 39569   rec. 19 Sep '14   rel. Dec '14
    Indestructible 3346   4-min. cyl.   rel. c. 1914
    Victor 17637   10″ disc   mx. B15146-4   rec. 2 Sep '14   rel. Nov '14
Albert Campbell and Henry Burr
    Rex 5170   10″ disc   rel. c. 1914
Victor Military Band
    Victor 35414   12″ disc   mx. C15247-3   rec. 13 Oct '14   rel. Dec '14
    [part of "Michigan Medley"]
    Victor 35422   12″ disc   mx. C15327-1   rec. 5 Nov '14   rel. Jan '15
    [part of "Hits of 1915" medley]

Always Treat Her Like A Baby

Irving Kaufman
    Victor 17636   10″ disc   mx. B15158-3   rec. 4 Sep '14   rel. Nov '14

At The Devil's Ball
Arthur Collins and Byron G. Harlan
    Phono-Cut 5241   10″ disc   rel. c. 1913
Peerless Quartet
    Victor 17315   10″ disc   mx. B12968-1   rec. 5 Mar '13   rel. May '13
Peerless Quartette with Maurice Burkhart
    Columbia A1282   10″ disc   mx. 38546   rec. 10 Jan '13   rel. Apr '13
Victor Military Band
    Victor 35277   12″ disc   mx. C12851-2   rec. 27 Jan '13   rel. Apr '13
    [part of "When The Midnight Choo Choo . . . Medley"]
Victor Mixed Chorus
    Victor 35305   12″ disc   mx. C13363-2   rec. 28 May '13   rel. Aug '13
    [part of "Song Medley No. 6—Snyder Specials"]

Beautiful Rag—see **Oh, That Beautiful Rag**

Becky's Got A Job In A Musical Show
Maurice Burkhart
    U.S. Everlasting 1497   4-min. cyl.   rel. Oct '12

Before I Go And Marry, I Will Have A Talk With You
    [Title appears in Edison literature as "Before I Go and Marry, I Will Have a
    Word With You"]
Ada Jones
    Edison 10339   2-min. cyl.   rel. Apr '10

Bring Back My Lena To Me
Maurice Burkhart
    Columbia   10″ disc   mx. 19589   rec. 5 Oct '11   unissued
    Edison 1028   4-min. cyl.   rel. Jun '12
    Victor 16994   10″ disc   mx. B11040-2   rec. 29 Sep '11   rel. Dec '11

Bring Back My Lovin' Man
Amy Butler
    Zonophone 5827   10″ disc   rel. Dec '11
Ada Jones
    Victor 17052   10″ disc   mx. B11358-2   rec. 13 Dec '11   rel. Apr '12

Call Me Up Some Rainy Afternoon
Joe Brown
    Sonora 5057   10″ disc   rel. Dec '10
Ada Jones
    Columbia A855   10″ disc   mx. 4523   rel. Sep '10
    Edison 485   4-min. cyl.   rel. Aug '10
    Indestructible 1386   2-min. cyl.   rel. Aug '10
Ada Jones with American Quartette
    Victor 16508   10″ disc   mx. B8912-3   rec. 4 May '10   rel. Aug '10

Prince's Orchestra
    Columbia A951   10″ disc   mx. 4995   rel. Feb '11
    [part of "Medley of Ted Snyder Hits"]

Christmas-Time Seems Years And Years Away
Manuel Romain
    Edison 10351   2-min. cyl.   rel. May '10

Come Back To Me My Melody
Walter Van Brunt
    Columbia A1237   10″ disc   mx. 38300   rec. 27 Sep '12   rel. Jan '13

Daddy, Come Home
Billy Murray
    Victor 17519   10″ disc   mx. B14167-3   rec. 31 Dec '13   rel. Mar '14

Dear Mayme, I Love You!
Henry Burr
    Columbia A836   10″ disc   mx. 4433   rel. Jul '10
    U.S. Everlasting 1046 4-min. cyl.   rel. c. 1910
Joe Maxwell
    Edison 491   4-min. cyl.   rel. Aug '10
National Promenade Band
    Edison 1121   4-min. cyl.   rel. Oct '12
    [part of "Take Me Back To The Garden Of Love Medley"]
Prince's Band
    Columbia A951   10″ disc   mx. 4995   rel. Feb '11
    [part of "Medley of Ted Snyder's Hits"]

Down In Chattanooga
Arthur Collins and Byron G. Harlan
    Columbia A1453   10″ disc   mx. 39098   rec. 14 Nov '13   rel. Feb '14
    Victor 17527   10″ disc   mx. B14097-1   rec. 13 Nov '13   rel. Mar '14
Pietro Deiro (accordion)
    Victor 17574   10″ disc   mx. B14637-1   rec. 14 Apr '14   rel. Jun '14
    [title song of medley]
Maxim's Cabaret Singers
    Columbia A1509   10″ disc   mx. 39166   rec. 29 Dec '13   rel. May '14
    [part of a sketch with music titled "Night Scene in Maxim's"]
Prince's Orchestra
    Columbia A1495   10″ disc   mx. 39179   rec. 9 Jan '14   rel. Apr '14
    [part of "Medley of Irving Berlin's Hits"]
Victor Military Band
    Victor 35384   12″ disc   mx. C14790-1   rec. 4 May '14   rel. Aug '14
    [part of "I Love The Ladies Medley"]

Dreams, Just Dreams
Frank Coombs
    U.S. Everlasting 1117   4-min. cyl.   rel. c. 1911
Indestructible Military Band
    Indestructible 3241   4-min. cyl.   rel. Aug '11
    [part of "Medley of Popular Hits"]
National Promenade Band
    Edison 1121   4-min. cyl.   rel. Oct '12
    [part of "Take Me Back To The Garden Of Love Medley"]
Prince's Orchestra
    Columbia A951   10" disc   mx. 4996   rel. Feb '11
    [part of "Medley of Ted Snyder Hits"]
James Reed (Reed Miller)
    Columbia A964   10" disc   mx. 19127   rec. 21 Nov '10   rel. Mar '11
W. H. Thompson
    Edison 10481   2-min. cyl.   rel. Mar '11
U.S. Military Band
    U.S. Everlasting 1437   4-min. cyl.   rel. c. 1912
    [part of "Medley of Popular Hits"]
Walter Van Brunt
    Indestructible 1504   2-min. cyl.   rel. Sep '11
Reinald Werrenrath
    Victor 5809   10" disc   mx. B9602-1,2   rec. 3 Nov '10   rel. Jan '11

Elevator Man, Going Up, Going Up, Going Up, Going Up!, The
    [Variant title on recording: *Going Up With the Elevator Man*]
Maurice Burkhart and Peerless Quartette
    Columbia A1188   10" disc   mx. 19925   rec. 7 Jun '12   rel. Sep '12

Everybody's Doing It Now
Arthur Collins
    Indestructible 3265   4-min. cyl.   rel. c. 1912
Arthur Collins and Byron G. Harlan
    U.S. Everlasting 445   2-min. cyl.   rel. Feb '12
    Victor 17020   10" disc   mx. B11292-2   rec. 22 Nov '11   rel. Feb '12
Columbia Quartette
    Columbia A1123   10" disc   mx. 19699   rec. 29 Dec '11   rel. Apr '12
Guido Deiro (accordion)
    Columbia A1294   10" disc   mx. 38182   rec. 5 Aug '12   rel. May '13
Empire Orchestra
    Pathé 5273, 30088   11-3/8" disc   rel. c. 1915
Indestructible Symphony Orchestra
    Indestructible 3250   4-min. cyl.   rel. late 1911
Premier Quartette
    Edison 1030   4-min. cyl.   rel. Jun '12
    Edison 10570   2-min. cyl.   rel. Aug '12

Prince's Orchestra
    Columbia A1165   10″ disc   mx. 19834   rec. 28 Mar '12 rel. Jul '12
    [part of "Ted Snyder's Hits, Medley No. 3"]
Arthur Pryor's Band
    Victor 17091   10″ disc   mx. B11848-1 rec. 10 Apr '12 rel. Jul '12
    [title song in medley]

Fiddle-Dee-Dee
    [Variant title on some recordings: *He Played It On His Fiddle-Dee-Dee*]
Lew Dockstader
    Columbia   10″ disc   mx. 19901   rec. 23 May '12 unissued
Lew Dockstader with quartette
    Columbia A1200   10″ disc   mx. 38120   rec. 8 Jul '12   rel. Oct '12
Ida Hamilton and Jack Charman
    Pathé 5324, 30096   11-3/8″ disc   rel. c. 1915
U.S. Concert Band
    U.S. Everlasting 1582 4-min. cyl.   rel. Dec '12
    [part of "Ted Snyder's 1912 Medley Overture"]
Walter Van Brunt and Maurice Burkhart
    U.S. Everlasting 502   2-min. cyl.   rel. Oct '12
    Victor 17150   10″ disc   mx. B12126-2 rec. 20 Jun '12 rel. Oct '12

Follow The Crowd
anonymous band
    Little Wonder 28   5-1/2″ disc   rel. 1914
    [part of "Medley of Popular Airs No. 2"]
anonymous baritone solo
    Little Wonder 17   5-1/2″ disc   rel. 1914
Irving Berlin
    Columbia   10″ disc   mx. 32229   rec. c. 1914   unissued
    [The same matrix number was assigned to "What Am I Gonna Do?"]
Ned La Rose and Peerless Quartette
    Columbia A1513   10″ disc   mx. 39263   rec. 24 Feb '14 rel. May '14
J. W. Myers
    Rex 5111   10″ disc   rel. c. 1914

Funny Little Melody, The
Maurice Burkhart
    Columbia   10″ disc   mx. 38306   rec. 1 Oct '12   unissued
Walter Van Brunt and Maurice Burkhart
    Victor 17213   10 ″ disc   mx. B12502-2 rec. 9 Oct '12 rel. Jan '13

Going Up With The Elevator Man—*see* **Elevator Man, Going Up, Going Up . . .**

Grizzly Bear
American Quartet

Victor 16681	10 " disc	mx. B9600-3	rec. 22 Nov '10	rel. Jan '11

Arthur Collins

Columbia A844	10" disc	mx. 4447	rel. Aug '10
Indestructible 1459	2-min. cyl.		rel. Feb '11
Sonora 5051	10" disc		rel. Dec '10

Stella Mayhew

Edison 479	4-min. cyl.	rel. Aug '10

Prince's Orchestra

Columbia A951	10" disc	mx. 4995	rel. Feb '11

[part of "Medley of Ted Snyder Hits"]

Arthur Pryor's Band

Victor 5802	10" disc	mx. B9466-1	rec. 20 Sep '10	rel. Dec '10

Maude Raymond

Victor	10" disc	mx. B8901-1,2	rec. 29 Apr '10	unissued
Victor	10" disc	mx. B8901-3	rec. 2 Dec '10	unissued

Fred Van Epps (banjo)

Edison 1864	4-min. cyl.	rel. Sep '13

[part of "Alexander's Ragtime Band Medley"]

Victor Military Band

Victor 35190	12" disc	mx. C10028-1	rec. 3 Mar '11	rel. Jul '11

[part of "Two Step Medley No. 10"]

Happy Little Country Girl
Elida Morris

Victor 17430	10" disc	mx. B13387-4	rec. 31 Jul '13	rel. Nov '13

Victor Military Band

Victor 35322	12" disc	mx. C13762-3	rec. 11 Sep '13	rel. Nov '13

[part of "Somebody's Coming To My House Medley"]

He Played It On His Fiddle-Dee-Dee—*see* **Fiddle-Dee-Dee**

Herman Let's Dance That Beautiful Waltz
Ada Jones

Indestructible 1470	2-min. cyl.	rel. May '11
Zonophone 5735	10" disc	rel. Jun '11

He's A Devil In His Own Home Town
Byron G. Harlan

Indestructible 3341	4-min. cyl.	rel. c. 1914
Pathé B5017, 30155	11-3/8" disc	rel. c. 1915
Rex 5117	10" disc	rel. c. 1914

Eddie Morton
    Columbia A1525   10″ disc   mx. 39288   rec. 18 Mar '14   rel. Jun '14
Billy Murray
    Victor 17576   10″ disc   mx. B14779-1   rec. 30 Apr '14   rel. Jul '14
Victor Military Band
    Victor 17617   10″ disc   mx. B15064-1   rec. 15 Jul '14   rel. Oct '14
    [part of "Croony Melody Medley"]

He's A Rag Picker
anonymous band
    Little Wonder 133   5-1/2″ disc   rel. 1915
    [part of "Medley of Popular Airs No. 3"]
anonymous quartette
    Little Wonder 23   5-1/2″ disc   rel. 1914
Peerless Quartet
    Columbia A1628   10″ disc   mx. 39572   rec. 23 Sep '14   rel. Jan '15
    Edison 2513   4-min. cyl.   rel. Feb '15
    Edison 50194   10″ disc   mx. 3361   rel. c. 1915
    Indestructible 3343   4-min. cyl.   rel. c. 1914
    Victor 17655   10″ disc   mx. B15208-3   rec. 21 Sep '14   rel. Jan '15
Victor Military Band
    Victor 35422   10″ disc   mx. C15327-1   rec. 5 Nov '14   rel. Jan '15
    [part of "Hits of 1915" medley]

Hey Wop
Rhoda Bernard
    Pathé 30396   11-3/8″ disc mx. E65434   rel. Jun '16
George L. Thompson
    Edison 2627   4-min. cyl.   rel. Jul '15
    Edison 50244   10″ disc   mx. 3679   rel. c. 1915
    Operaphone 1052   8″ disc   rel 1916

How Can You Love Such A Man?
Josie Sadler
    Edison 10420   2-min. cyl.   rel. Sep '10

I Just Came Back To Say Good Bye
Amy Butler
    Zonophone 5485   10″ disc   rel. Jun '09

I Love To Have The Boys Around Me—*see* songs from *Watch Your Step* after this section.

I Want To Be In Dixie
    [Variant title on some recordings: *I'm Going Back To Dixie*]
Arthur Collins and Byron G. Harlan
    Columbia A1112   10″ disc   mx. 19679   rec. 4 Dec '11   rel. Mar '12

Edison 948	4-min. cyl.			rel. Mar '12
Edison 1978	4-min. cyl.			rel. Oct '13
Indestructible 3255	4-min. cyl.			rel. c. 1912
U.S. Everlasting 453	2-min. cyl.			rel. Mar '12
Victor 17075	10″ disc	mx. B11293-2	rec. 22 Nov '11	rel. Jun '12
Zonophone 5879	10″ disc			rel. Apr '12

Guido Deiro (accordion)

Columbia	10″ disc	mx. 38184	rec. 6 Aug '12	unissued

Gene Greene

Pathé 536	11-3/8″ disc		rec. Mar '13	rel. c. 1915

National Promenade Band

Edison 1752	4-min. cyl.			rel. Jun '13

[part of "When The Midnight Choo Choo . . . Medley"]

Prince's Orchestra

Columbia A1165	10″ disc	mx. 19834	rec. 28 Mar '12	rel. Jul '12

[part of "Ted Snyder's Hits, Medley No. 3"]

Arthur Pryor's Band

Victor 17091	10″ disc	mx. B11848-1	rec. 10 Apr '12	rel. Jul '12

[part of "Everybody's Doing It Now Medley"]

I Want To Go Back To Michigan (Down On The Farm)

[Variant title on some recordings: *I Want To Go Back To The Farm* and *I'm Going Back To The Farm*]

anonymous duet

Little Wonder 60	5-1/2″ disc			rel. 1914

anonymous vocal solo

Little Wonder 47	5-1/2″ disc			rel. 1914

Morton Harvey

Victor 17650	10″ disc	mx. B15137-6	rec. 2 Oct '14	rel. Dec '14

Elida Morris

Columbia A1592	10″ disc	mx. 39496	rec. 17 Jul '14	rel. Nov '14
Indestructible 3339	4-min. cyl.			rel. c. 1914

Billy Murray and chorus

Edison 2507	4-min. cyl.			rel. Jan '15
Edison 50198	10″ disc	mx. 3365		rel. c. 1915

National Promenade Band

Edison 2471	4-min. cyl.			rel. Dec '14
Edison 50182	10″ disc	mx. 3284		rel. c. 1915

Pathé Dance Orchestra

Pathé 30242	11-3/8″ disc			rel. Oct '15
Pathé B8035, 70105	14″ disc			rel. c. 1915

U.S. Concert Band

U.S. Everlasting 1582	4-min. cyl.			rel. Dec '12

[part of "Ted Snyder's 1912 Medley Overture"]

Victor Military Band

Victor 35414	12″ disc	mx. C15247-3	rec. 13 Oct '14	rel. Dec '14

[part of "Michigan Medley"]

Victor 35422   12" disc   mx. C15327-1   rec. 5 Nov '14   rel. Jan '15
[part of "Hits of 1915" medley]

I Wish That You Was My Gal, Molly
Manuel Romain
Edison 414   4-min. cyl.   rel. May '10

If I Had You
Henry Burr
Columbia A1562   10" disc   mx. 39440   rec. 11 Jun '14   rel. Sep '14
Arthur Fields
Little Wonder 43   5-1/2" disc   rel. 1914

If That's Your Idea Of A Wonderful Time (Take Me Home)
Arthur Collins and Byron G. Harlan
Little Wonder 62   5-1/2" disc   rel. 1914
Ada Jones
Rex 5162   10" disc   rel. c. 1914
Victor 17630   10" disc   mx. B15097-2   rec. 29 Jul '14   rel. Dec '14

If You Don't Want Me (Why Do You Hang Around)
Prince's Orchestra
Columbia A1495   10" disc   mx. 39179   rec. 9 Jan '14   rel. Apr '14
[part of "Medley of Irving Berlin's Hits"]

I'm Afraid, Pretty Maid, I'm Afraid
Ada Jones and Billy Murray
Edison 1067   4-min. cyl.   rel. Aug '12
Zonophone 5913   10" disc   rel. Jun '12
Ada Jones and Walter Van Brunt
Columbia A1164   10" disc   mx. 19821   rec. 18 Mar '12   rel. Jul '12
U.S. Everlasting 1505 4-min. cyl.   rel. Aug '12

I'm Going Back To Dixie—see I Want To Be In Dixie

I'm Going Back To The Farm—see I Want To Go Back To Michigan

In My Harem
Guido Deiro (accordion)
Columbia   10" disc   mx. 38840   rec. 13 May '13   unissued
Billy Murray
Edison 1841   4-min. cyl.   rel. Sep '13
National Promenade Band
Edison 2139   4-min. cyl.   rel. Jan '14
[part of "International Rag Medley"]
Edison 50133   10" disc   mx. 2590   rel. c. 1914
[part of "International Rag Medley"]

Prince's Orchestra
> Columbia A1338   10" disc   mx. 38831   rec. 8 May '13   rel. Aug '13
> [part of "Medley of Snyder Hits"]

Walter Van Brunt
> Columbia A1302   10" disc   mx. 38646   rec. 24 Feb '13   rel. May '13
> Indestructible 3297   4-min. cyl.   rel. c. 1913
> Phono-Cut 5223   10" disc   rel. c. 1913
> U.S. Everlasting 1646   4-min. cyl.   rel. Oct '13

Victor Military Band
> Victor 17325   10" disc   mx. B13006-2   rec. 25 Mar '13   rel. Jun '13
> [title song in medley]

International Rag, The

Arthur Collins and Byron G. Harlan
> Columbia A1406   10" disc   mx. 38981   rec. 1 Aug '13   rel. Nov '13
> Indestructible 3304   4-min. cyl.   rel. c. 1913
> Victor 17431   10" disc   mx. B13716-1   rec. 3 Sep '13   rel. Nov '13

Pietro Deiro (accordion)
> Victor 17506   10" disc   mx. B14005-1   rec. 29 Oct '13   rel. Feb '14

Maxim's Cabaret Singers
> Columbia A1509   10" disc   mx. 39166   rec. 29 Dec '13   rel. May '14
> [part of a sketch with music titled "Night Scene in Maxim's"]

Billy Murray
> Edison 2078   4-min. cyl.   rel. Dec '13

National Promenade Orchestra
> Edison 2139   4-min. cyl.   rel. Jan '14
> [title song in medley]
> Edison 50133   10" disc   mx. 2590   rel. c. 1914
> [title song in medley]

Prince's Band
> Columbia A5532   12" disc   mx. 36839   rec. 19 Dec '13   rel. Mar '14

Prince's Orchestra
> Columbia A1495   10" disc   mx. 39179   rec. 9 Jan '14   rel. Apr '14
> [part of "Medley of Irving Berlin's Hits"]

Rex Military Band
> Rex D-5082   10" disc   rel. c. 1914

Victor Military Band
> Victor 17487   10" disc   mx. B13953-1   rec. 13 Oct '13   rel. Jan '14

Is There Anything Else I Can Do For You?

Ada Jones
> Columbia A909   10" disc   mx. 4830   rel. Nov. '10

Keep Away From The Fellow Who Owns An Automobile

Maurice Burkhart
> Columbia   10" disc   mx. 38175   rec. 2 Aug '12   unissued

Gene Greene
    Pathé 446, 30020   11-3/8″ disc mx. 92288   rec. c. Dec '12   rel. c. 1915
Ada Jones and chorus
    U.S. Everlasting 1594   4-min. cyl.   rel. Jan '13
Walter Van Brunt
    Columbia A1252   10″ disc   mx. 38396   rec. 6 Nov '12   rel. Feb '13

Keep On Walking
Walter Van Brunt
    Phono-Cut 5223   10″ disc   rel. c. 1913

Kiss Me My Honey, Kiss Me
Albert Campbell and W. H. Thompson
    U.S. Everlasting 357   2-min. cyl.   rel. c. 1911
Indestructible Military Band
    Indestructible 3241   4-min. cyl.   rel. Aug '11
    [part of "Medley of Popular Hits"]
Ada Jones and Billy Murray
    Edison 617   4-min. cyl.   rel. Feb '11
    Edison 1634   4-min. cyl.   rel. Mar '13
Elida Morris
    Victor 16807   10″ disc   mx. B9145-3   rec. 13 Sep '10   rel. Dec '10
    Columbia A906   10″ disc   mx. 4593   rel. Nov '10
    Indestructible 1439   2-min. cyl.   rel. Dec '10
Prince's Orchestra
    Columbia A951   10″ disc   mx. 4995   rel. Feb '11
    [part of "Medley of Ted Snyder Hits"]
Victor Mixed Chorus
    Victor 31848   12″ disc   mx. C11071-2   rec. 9 Oct '11   rel. Dec '11
    [part of "Song Medley, No. 1—Snyder Successes"]

Kiss Your Sailor Boy Goodbye
Pietro Deiro (accordion)
    Victor 17574   10″ disc   mx. B14637-1   rec. 14 Apr '14   rel. Jun '14
    [part of "Down in Chattanooga Medley"]

Lead Me To That Beautiful Band
Collins and Harlan
    Zonophone 5919   10″ disc   rel. Jul '12
Stella Mayhew
    Edison 1082   4-min. cyl.   rel. Aug '12
    Edison 2173   4-min. cyl.   rel. Feb '14
Billy Murray
    Victor 17078   10″ disc   mx. B11809-2   rec. 1 Apr '12   rel. Jun '12
Arthur Pryor's Band
    Victor 35240   12″ disc   mx. C12355-2   rec. 10 Sep '12   rel. Nov '12
    [part of "Snyder Successes No. 2" medley]

U.S. Concert Band
    U.S. Everlasting 1582   4-min. cyl.   rel. Dec '12
    [part of "Ted Snyder's 1912 Medley Overture"]
Walter Van Brunt and Maurice Burkhart
    Columbia A1172   10″ disc   mx. 19873   rec. 29 Apr '12   rel. Aug '12

Lucia Sextette Burlesque—see Opera Burlesque

Mary O'Hoolihan
Amy Butler
    Zonophone 5803   10″ disc   rel. Nov '11

Medley of Irving Berlin's Songs—see They've Got Me Doing It Now Medley

Melinda's Wedding Day
Collins and Harlan
    Columbia A1285   10″ disc   mx. 38597   rec. 27 Jan '13   rel. Apr '13
    Edison 1844   4-min. cyl.   rel. Sep '13
    Victor 17295   10″ disc   mx. B12872-1   rec. 5 Feb '13   rel. Apr '13
Victor Military Band
    Victor 17362   10″ disc   mx. B13251-2   rec. 8 May '13   rel. Aug '13
    [title song in medley]

Million Dollar Ball, The
Maurice Burkhart
    Columbia   10″ disc   mx. 38222   rec. 26 Aug '12   unissued
Billy Murray
    Victor 17172   10″ disc   mx. B12323-1   rec. 3 Sep '12   rel. Nov '12

Minstrel Parade, The—see songs from *Watch Your Step* after this section.

My Sweet Italian Man
Mike Bernard (piano)
    Columbia A1313   10″ disc   mx. 38473   rec. 4 Dec '12   rel. Jun '13
    [part of "Medley of Snyder Hits"]

My Wife's Gone To The Country (Hurrah! Hurrah!)
Arthur Collins and Byron G. Harlan
    Columbia A724   10″ disc   mx. 4137   rel. Sep '09
    Victor 5736   10″ disc   mx. B8115-2   rec. 16 Jul '09   rel. Sep '09
    Victor 16750   10″ disc   mx. B8115-3   rec. 16 Jul '09   rel. Nov '10
Edward M. Favor
    Edison 10218   2-min. cyl.   rel. Oct '09
Fred Lambert (Frank C. Stanley)
    Zonophone 5526   10″ disc   rel. Sep '09

Bob Roberts
　　Indestructible 1145   2-min. cyl.   rel. Sep '09
Zonophone Orchestra
　　Zonophone 5561   10″ disc   rel. Dec '09
　　[part of "Popular Chorus Medley Two-Step No. 5"]

No One Could Do It Like My Father!
Fred Lambert (Frank C. Stanley)
　　Zonophone 5526   10″ disc   rel. Sep '09

Oh How How That German Could Love
Irving Berlin
　　Columbia A804   10″ disc   mx. 4333   rel. Apr '10

Oh, That Beautiful Rag
　　[Variant titles on some recordings: *Beautiful Rag* and *That Beautiful Rag*]
Brown Brothers Saxophone Quintette
　　Columbia   10″ disc   mx. 19433   rec. 26 Jun '11   unissued
Arthur Collins
　　Columbia A853   10″ disc   mx. 4531   rel. Sep '10
　　Phono-Cut 5013   10″ disc   rel. c. 1910
　　Zonophone 5653   10″ disc   rel. Sep '10
Arthur Collins and Byron G. Harlan
　　Indestructible 1424   2-min. cyl.   rel. Nov '10
Stella Mayhew and Billie Taylor
　　Edison 10438   2-min. cyl.   rel. Nov '10
Prince's Orchestra
　　Columbia A951   10″ disc   mx. 4995, 4996   rel. Feb '11
　　[part of "Medley of Ted Snyder Hits"]

Oh, What I Know About You
Ada Jones
　　Columbia A800   10″ disc   mx. 4329   rel. Apr '10

Old Maid's Ball, The
Arthur Collins and Byron G. Harlan
　　Columbia A1345   10″ disc   mx. 38825   rec. 6 May '13   rel. Aug '13
Billy Murray
　　Victor 17354   10″ disc   mx. B13111-3   rec. 13 May '13   rel. Jul '13
National Promenade Band
　　Edison 2139   4-min. cyl.   rel. Jan '14
　　[part of "International Rag Medley"]
　　Edison 50133   10″ disc   mx. 2590   rel. c. 1914
　　[part of "International Rag Medley"]
Walter Van Brunt
　　Phono-Cut 5224   10″ disc   rel. c. 1913

Victor Military Band
  Victor 17375   10″ disc   mx. B14431-3   rec. 14 Jun '13   rel. Aug '13
  [part of "Snooky Ookums Medley"]

One O'Clock In The Morning I Get Lonesome
Gene Greene
  Pathé 446, 30020   11-3/8″ disc mx. 92287   rec. c. Dec '12   rel. c. 1915
Walter Van Brunt
  Columbia A1098   10″ disc   mx. 19632   rec. 1 Nov '11   rel. Feb '12
  Zonophone 5868   10″ disc   rel. Mar '12

Opera Burlesque
  [Variant title on recordings: *Lucia Sextette Burlesque* and *Opera Burlesque On Sextette From Lucia*]
Billy Murray and mixed chorus
  Edison 1107   4-min. cyl.   rel. Sep '12
Billy Murray and Vaudeville Quartet
  Victor 17119   10″ disc   mx. B11977-3   rec. 22 May '12   rel. Aug '12

Piano Man
Gene Greene
  Victor   10″ disc   mx. B10214-1   rec. 20 Apr '11   unissued
Billy Murray
  Edison 673   4-min. cyl.   rel. May '11

Pick, Pick, Pick, Pick On The Mandolin, Antonio
Billy Murray
  Victor 17045   10″ disc   mx. B11475-1   rec. 22 Jan '12   rel. Apr '12

Pullman Porters On Parade, The
William Halley
  Victor 17453   10″ disc   mx. B13419-3   rec. 30 Jun '13   rel. Dec '13
Al Jolson
  Columbia A1374   10″ disc   mx. 38901   rec. 4 Jun '13   rel. Oct '13
Victor Military Band
  Victor 17465   10″ disc   mx. B13937-1   rec. 9 Oct '13   rel. Dec '13
  [title song in medley]

Ragtime Jockey Man, The
Maurice Burkhart and Peerless Quartette
  Columbia A1188   10″ disc   mx. 19924   rec. 7 Jun '12   rel. Sep '12

Ragtime Mocking Bird
Dolly Connolly
  Columbia A1126   10″ disc   mx. 19721   rec. 8 Jan '12   rel. Apr '12

Ragtime Soldier Man
Mike Bernard (piano)

Columbia A1313	10″ disc	mx. 38473	rec. 4 Dec '12	rel. Jun '13
[part of "Medley of Snyder's Hits"]				

Arthur Collins and Byron G. Harlan

Columbia A1201	10″ disc	mx. 38100	rec. 1 Jul '12	rel. Oct '12
Phono-Cut 5087	10″ disc			rel. c. 1912
U.S. Everlasting 510	2-min. cyl.			rel. Nov. '12
Victor 17150	10″ disc	mx. B12198-2	rec. 17 Jul '12	rel. Oct '12

Gene Greene

Pathé 100, 30005	11-3/8″ disc	mx. 92179	rec. c. Oct '12	rel. c. 1915

Edward Meeker

Edison 1618	4-min. cyl.		rel. Feb '13

National Promenade Band

Edison 1752	4-min. cyl.		rel. Jun '13
[part of "When The Midnight Choo-Choo . . . Medley"]			

Arthur Pryor's Orchestra

Victor 35240	12″ disc	mx. C12355-2	rec. 10 Sep '12	rel. Nov '12
[part of "Snyder Successes No. 2" medley]				

Ragtime Violin!
American Quartet

Victor 17025	10″ disc	mx. B11380-2	rec. 15 Dec '11	rel. Feb '12

Maurice Burkhart

Columbia A1106	10″ disc	mx. 19590	rec. 5 Oct '11	rel. Mar '12

Arthur Collins

Indestructible 3261	4-min. cyl.		rel. c. 1912
Phono-Cut 5081	10″ disc		rel. c. 1912
U.S. Everlasting 446	2-min. cyl.		rel. Feb '12
Zonophone 5854	10″ disc		rel. Feb '12

Gene Greene

Pathé 5347, 30097	11-3/8″ disc	mx. 92134	rec. c. Sep '12	rel. c. 1915

Premier Quartette

Edison 966	4-min. cyl.		rel. Apr '12
Edison 1806	4-min. cyl.		rel. Aug '13
Edison 10560	2-min. cyl.		rel. Jun '12

Prince's Band

Columbia A1107	10″ disc	mx. 19651	rec. 4 Nov '11	rel. Mar '12
[part of "Medley of Snyder's Hits"]				

Arthur Pryor's Band

Victor 17091	10″ disc	mx. B11848-1	rec. 10 Apr '12	rel. Jul '12
[part of "Everybody's Doing It Now Medley"]				

Fred Van Epps (banjo)

Edison 1864	4-min. cyl.		rel. Sep '13
[part of "Alexander's Ragtime Band Medley"]			

Victor Band
   Victor 17044   10″ disc   mx. B11506-1   rec. 24 Jan '12   rel. Apr '12
   [title song of medley]

Revival Day
Al Jolson
   Columbia A1621   10″ disc   mx. 39568   rec. 19 Sep '14   rel. Jan '15

Run Home And Tell Your Mother
Molly Ames and Columbia Quartette
   Columbia A1042   10″ disc   mx. 19450   rec. 7 Jul '11   rel. Oct '11
Anna Chandler
   Edison 800   4-min. cyl.   rel. Oct '11
Helen Clark
   Zonophone 5795   10″ disc   rel. Oct '11
Victor Orchestra
   Victor 16963   10″ disc   mx. B10851-3   rec. 11 Aug '11   rel. Nov '11
   [part of "Snyder Successes" Medley]

Sadie Salome (Go Home)
Edward M. Favor
   Edison 10243   2-min. cyl.   rel. Nov '09
   Indestructible 1211 2-min. cyl.   rel. Nov '09
Bob Roberts
   Columbia A789   10″ disc   mx. 4294   rel. Mar '10

San Francisco Bound
Peerless Quartet
   Victor 17367   10″ disc   mx. B13166-2   rec. 18 Apr '13   rel. Aug '13

Settle Down In A One Horse Town—*see* songs from *Watch Your Step* after this section.

Simple Melody—*see* songs from *Watch Your Step* after this section.

Snookey Ookums
Arthur Collins and Byron G. Harlan
   Columbia A1317   10″ disc   mx. 38703   rec. 18 Mar '13   rel. Jun '13
   Edison 1796   4-min. cyl.   rel. Jun '13
   Indestructible 3296 4-min. cyl.   rel. c. 1913
   Phono-Cut 5192   10″ disc   rel. c. 1913
   Rex 5010   10″ disc   rel. c. 1913
Billy Murray
   Victor 17313   10″ disc   mx. B12948-1   rec. 26 Feb '13   rel. May '13
National Promenade Band
   Edison 2139   4-min. cyl.   rel. Jan '14
   [part of "International Rag Medley"]

Edison 50133   10″ disc   mx. 2590   rel. c. 1914
[part of "International Rag Medley"]
Victor Military Band
Victor 17325   10″ disc   mx. B13006-2   rec. 25 Mar '13   rel. Jun '13
[part of "In My Harem Medley"]
Victor 17375   10″ disc   mx. B14431-3   rec. 14 Jun '13   rel. Aug '13
[title song in medley]
Victor Mixed Chorus
Victor 35305   12″ disc   mx. C13363-2   rec. 28 May '13   rel. Aug '13
[part of "Song Medley No. 6—Snyder Specials"]

Society Bear
[Variant title on some recordings: *That Society Bear*]
Arthur Collins and Byron G. Harlan
Columbia A1163   10″ disc   mx. 19843   rec. 5 Apr '12   rel. Jul '12
Phono-Cut 5095   10″ disc   rel. c. 1912
Columbia Quartette
Columbia   10″ disc   mx. 19781   rec. 4 Mar '12   unissued
Walter Van Brunt
U.S. Everlasting 1515   4-min. cyl.   rel. Jun '12
Victor 17068   10″ disc   mx. B11739-1   rec. 14 Mar '12   rel. May '12
Zonophone 5896   10″ disc   rel. May '12

Somebody's Coming To My House
National Promenade Band
Edison 2139   4-min. cyl.   rel. Jan '14
[part of "International Rag Medley"]
Edison 50133   10″ disc   mx. 2590   rel. c. 1914
[part of "International Rag Medley"]
Walter Van Brunt
Edison 1941   4-min. cyl.   rel. Oct '13
Victor 17381   10″ disc   mx. B13463-2   rec. 20 Jun '13   rel. Sep '13
Victor Military Band
Victor 35322   12″ disc   mx. C13762-3   rec. 11 Sep '13   rel. Nov '13
[title song in medley]

Spanish Love
Andrea Sarto and male chorus
Columbia A1031   10″ disc   mx. 19396   rec. 7 Jun '11   rel. Sep '11
Elizabeth Spencer
Edison 766   4-min. cyl.   rel. Sep '11

Stay Down Here Where You Belong
anonymous baritone
Little Wonder 46   5-1/2″ disc   rel. 1914
Henry Burr
Victor 17716   10″ disc   mx. B15590-1   rec. 13 Jan '15   rel. Mar '15

Arthur Fields

| Columbia A1628 | 10" disc | mx. 39595 | rec. 26 Oct '14 | rel. Jan '15 |
| Indestructible 3344 | 4-min. cyl. | | | rel. c. 1914 |

Victor Military Band

| Victor 35422 | 12" disc | mx. C15327-1 | rec. 5 Nov '14 | rel. Jan '15 |

[part of "Hits of 1915" medley]

Stop, Stop, Stop (Come Over And Love Me Some More)

Arthur Collins

| Zonophone 5676 | 10" disc | | | rel. Jan '11 |

Mabel Howard

| U.S. Everlasting 1129 | 4-min. cyl. | | | rel. 1911 |

Elida Morris

Columbia A953	10" disc	mx. 4941		rel. Feb '11
Indestructible 1457	2-min. cyl.			rel. Feb '11
Victor 16687	10" disc	mx. B9146-2	rec. 13 Sep '10	rel. Jan '11

Billy Murray

| Edison 648 | 4-min. cyl. | | | rel. Apr '11 |
| Edison 10504 | 2-min. cyl. | | | rel. Jul '11 |

Prince's Orchestra

| Columbia A951 | 10" disc | mx. 4996 | | rel. Feb '11 |

[part of "Medley of Ted Snyder Hits"]

Victor Dance Orchestra

| Victor 35190 | 12" disc | mx. C10028-1 | rec. 3 Mar '11 | rel. Jul '11 |

[part of "Two Step Medley No. 10"]

Stop That Rag (Keep On Playing, Honey)

American Quartet

| Victor 16787 | 10" disc | mx. B8697-1 | rec. 11 Mar '10 | rel. Nov '10 |

Arthur Collins and Byron G. Harlan

| Columbia A829 | 10" disc | mx. 4416 | | rel. Jul. '10 |
| Edison 10363 | 2-min. cyl. | | | rel. May '10 |

Sweet Italian Love

Byron G. Harlan

| Columbia A896 | 10" disc | mx. 4563 | | rel. Oct '10 |

Billy Murray

Edison 10427	2-min. cyl.			rel. Oct '10
Victor 16790	10" disc	mx. B9382-1	rec. 29 Aug '10	rel. Nov '10
Zonophone 5670	10" disc			rel. Jan '11

Prince's Orchestra

| Columbia A951 | 10" disc | mx. 4996 | | rel. Feb '11 |

[part of "Medley of Ted Snyder Hits"]

Bob Roberts

| Indestructible 1409 | 2-min. cyl. | | | rel. Oct '10 |

Victor Dance Orchestra
  Victor 35190   12″ disc   mx. C10028-1   rec. 3 Mar '11   rel. Jul '11
  [part of "Two Step Medley No. 10″]

***Syncopated Walk, The—see* songs from *Watch Your Step* after this section.**

Take A Little Tip From Father
Lew Dockstader
  Columbia   10″ disc   mx. 19756   rec. 12 Feb '12   unissued
Carl Ely
  Indestructible 1512   2-min. cyl.   rel. c. 1912
Billy Murray
  Victor 17064   10″ disc   mx. B11474-3   rec. 22 Jan '12   rel. May '12
  Zonophone 5866   10″ disc   rel. Mar '12
Prince's Orchestra
  Columbia A1165   10″ disc   mx. 19834   rec. 28 Mar '12   rel. Jul '12
  [part of "Ted Snyder's Hits, Medley No. 3"]
Arthur Pryor's Band
  Victor 17091   10″ disc   mx. B11848-1   rec. 10 Apr '12   rel. Jul '12
  [part of "Everybody's Doing It Now Medley"]
W. H. Thompson
  U.S. Everlasting 505   2-min. cyl.   rel. Sep '12
U.S. Concert Band
  U.S. Everlasting 1582 4-min. cyl.   rel. Dec '12
  [part of "Ted Snyder's 1912 Medley Overture"]
Zonophone Concert Band
  Zonophone 5916   10″ disc   rel. Jul '12
  [title song of medley]

Take Me Back
Henry Burr
  Columbia A1438   10″ disc   mx. 39031   rec. 29 Sep '13   rel. Jan '14
  Victor 17507   10″ disc   mx. B14036-2   rec. 5 Nov '13   rel. Feb '14
Prince's Orchestra
  Columbia A1495   10″ disc   mx. 39179   rec. 9 Jan '14   rel. Apr '14
  [part of "Medley of Irving Berlin's Hits"]
Walter Van Brunt
  Edison 2118   4-min. cyl.   rel. Jan '14

Telling Lies
Ada Jones and Billy Murray
  Edison 10314   2-min. cyl.   rel. Feb '10

That Beautiful Rag—see **Oh, That Beautiful Rag**

That Kazzatsky Dance
Prince's Orchestra
  Columbia A951   10″ disc   mx. 4996   rel. Feb '11
  [part of "Medley of Ted Snyder Hits"]

That Mesmerizing Mendelssohn Tune
Arthur Collins and Byron G. Harlan
  Columbia A801   10″ disc   mx. 4328   rel. Apr '10
  Edison 50063   10″ disc   mx. 1054   rel. c. 1913
  Edison 395   4-min. cyl.   rel. Apr '10
  Indestructible 3065 4-min. cyl.   rel. May '10
  Victor 16472   10″ disc   mx. B8625-3   rec. 12 Feb '10 rel. Apr '10
  Zonophone 5659   10″ disc   rel. Nov '10
Frank Coombs
  U.S. Everlasting 1082 4-min. cyl.   rel. c. 1911
Prince's Orchestra
  Columbia A951   10″ disc   mx. 4996   rel. Feb '11
  [part of "Medley of Ted Snyder Hits"]
Arthur Pryor's Band
  Victor 16504   10″ disc   mx. B8874-1   rec. 21 Apr '10 rel. Aug '10
  [part of "Snyder Hits" medley]
Victor Dance Orchestra
  Victor 35190   12″ disc   mx. C10028-1 rec. 3 Mar '11   rel. Jul '11
  [part of "Two Step Medley No. 10"]

That Mysterious Rag
American Quartet
  Victor 16982   10″ disc   mx. B11011-2 rec. 26 Sep '11 rel. Dec '11
Arthur Collins and Albert Campbell
  Columbia A1086   10″ disc   mx. 19577   rec. 29 Sep '11 rel. Jan '12
  U.S. Everlasting 436 2-min. cyl.   rel. Jan '12
  Zonophone 5822   10″ disc   rel. Dec '11
Empire Orchestra
  Pathé 5273, 30088 11-3/8″ disc   rel. c. 1915
Byron G. Harlan
  Indestructible 1511 2-min. cyl.   rel. c. 1912
Premier Quartette
  Edison 893   4-min. cyl.   rel. Jan '12
  Edison 10539   2-min. cyl.   rel. Feb '12
Prince's Band
  Columbia A1124   10″ disc   mx. 19718   rec. 8 Jan '12   rel. Apr '12
U.S. Military Band
  U.S. Everlasting 1437 4-min. cyl.   rel. c. 1912
  [part of "Medley of Popular Hits"]

Victor Band
   Victor 17044   10″ disc   mx. B11506-1   rec. 24 Jan '12   rel. Apr '12
   [part of "Ragtime Violin" medley]

That Opera Rag
Bob Roberts
   Indestructible 3168   4-min. cyl.   rel. Dec '10
   Sonora 5062   10″ disc   rel. Dec '10
   U.S. Everlasting 457 2-min. cyl.   rel. Apr '12

That Society Bear—see Society Bear

There's A Girl In Havana
Helen Clark and Walter Van Brunt
   Indestructible 3260   4-min. cyl.   rel. c. 1912
James F. Harrison
   Edison 903   4-min. cyl.   rel. Feb '12
   U.S. Everlasting 1227 4-min. cyl.   rel. Feb '12
Lyric Quartet
   Victor 16985   10″ disc   mx. B11060-1   rec. 6 Oct '11   rel. Dec '11
Arthur Pryor's Band
   Victor 35240   12″ disc   mx. C12355-2   rec. 10 Sep '12   rel. Nov '12
   [part of "Snyder Successes No. 2" medley]
Caroline Vaughan and Henry Burr
   Columbia A1099   10″ disc   mx. 19624   rec. 27 Oct '11   rel. Feb '12
Victor Military Band
   Victor 17375   10″ disc   mx. B14431-3   rec. 14 Jun '13   rel. Aug '13
   [part of "Snookey Ookums Medley"]
Beulah Gaylord Young and Henry Burr
   Zonophone 5842   10″ disc   rel. Jan '12

They Always Follow Me Around—*see* songs from *Watch Your Step* after this section.

They're On Their Way To Mexico
American Republic Band
   Pathé 5004, 30142 11-3/8″ disc   rel. c. 1915
   Pathé 8006, 70079 14″ disc   rel. c. 1915
William J. Halley
   Columbia A1565   10″ disc   mx. 39443   rec. 12 Jun '14   rel. 1914
Heidelberg Quintette
   Victor 17599   10″ disc   mx. B14838-4   rec. 28 May '14   rel. Aug '14
Eddie Morton
   Columbia   10″ disc   mx. 39391   rec. 20 May '14   unissued
Victor Military Band
   Victor 17592   10″ disc   mx. B14904-1   rec. 26 May '14   rel. Aug '14

They've Got Me Doin' It Now
Elida Morris
    Victor   10″ disc   mx. B13385-1,2   rec. 5 Jun '13   unissued
Billy Murray
    Victor 17429   10″ disc   mx. B13626-2   rec. 23 Jul '13   rel. Jan '14
Eddie Weston
    Columbia A1358   10″ disc   mx. 38859   rec. 17 May '13   rel. Sep '13

They're Got Me Doin' It Now Medley
Mike Bernard (piano)
    Columbia A1386   10″ disc   mx. 38925   rec. 27 Jun '13   rel. Nov '13
    [Columbia catalogues and label copy list it as "Medley of Irving Berlin Songs"]
Eddie Morton
    Columbia A1381   10″ disc   mx. 38916   rec. 20 Jun '13   rel. Oct '13
Billy Murray
    Edison 2016   4-min. cyl.   rel. Nov '13

This Is The Life
American Republic Band
    Pathé B5050, 30188   11-3/8″ disc   rel. c. 1915
    Pathé B8023, 70096   14″ disc   rel. c. 1915
anonymous band
    Little Wonder 8   5-1/2″ disc   rel. 1914
    [part of "Medley of Popular Airs No. 1"]
Arthur Collins
    Pathé 30159, 29022   11-3/8″ disc   rel. c. 1915
Pietro Deiro (accordion)
    Victor 17574   10″ disc   mx. B14638-3   rec. 14 Apr '14   rel. Jun '14
    [title song of medley]
Billy Murray
    Victor 17584   10″ disc   mx. B14702-2   rec. 14 Apr '14   rel. Jun '14
Billy Murray and chorus
    Edison 2375   4-min. cyl.   rel. Aug '14
National Promenade Band
    Edison 2397   4-min. cyl.   rel. Sep '14
    [title song of medley]
Peerless Quartette
    Columbia A1509   10″ disc   mx. 39249   rec. 17 Feb '14   rel. May '14
Rex Military Band
    Rex 5089   10″ disc   rel. c. 1914
Bob Roberts
    Rex 5099   10″ disc   rel. c. 1914
Victor Military Band
    Victor 35384   12″ disc   mx. C14790-1   rec. 4 May '14   rel. Aug '14
    [part of "I Love The Ladies Medley"]

Tra-La, La, La!
Arthur Collins and Byron G. Harlan
Columbia A1453	10″ disc	mx. 39099	rec. 14 Nov '13	rel. Feb '14
Victor 17481	10″ disc	mx. B14010-2	rec. 29 Oct '13	rel. Jan '14

Billy Murray
Edison 2136	4-min. cyl.		rel. Jan '14

Prince's Orchestra
Columbia A1495	10″ disc	mx. 39179	rec. 9 Jan '14	rel. Apr '14

[part of "Medley of Irving Berlin's Hits"]
Victor Military Band
Victor 17487	10″ disc	mx. B13953-1	rec. 13 Oct '13	rel. Jan '14

[part of "International Rag Medley"]

Virginia Lou
Henry Burr
Columbia A998	10″ disc	mx. 19250	rec. 7 Mar '11	rel. Jun '11

Frank Coombs
U.S. Everlasting 1245	4-min. cyl.		rel. Jul '11

Charles King
Victor 5842	10″ disc	mx. B9959-2	rec. 17 Feb '11	rel. Jun '11

Wait Until Your Daddy Comes Home
Victor Military Band
Victor 17325	10″ disc	mx. B13006-2	rec. 25 Mar '13	rel. Jun '13

[part of "In My Harem Medley"]

We Have Much To Be Thankful For
Manuel Romain
Edison 2081	4-min. cyl.		rel. Dec '13

That Girl Quartet
Victor 17409	10″ disc	mx. B13610-2	rec. 18 Jul '13	rel. Oct '13

Walter Van Brunt and chorus
Edison 50114	10″ disc	mx. 2423	rel. c. 1914
Phono-Cut 5225	10″ disc		rel. c. 1913

Welcome Home
Anna Chandler
Edison 1784	4-min. cyl.		rel. Aug '13

Peerless Quartet
Victor 17322	10″ disc	mx. B12859-1	rec. 30 Jan '13	rel. Jun '13
Columbia A1285	10″ disc	mx. 38566	rec. 18 Jan '13	rel. Apr '13

Victor Military Band
Victor 35277	12″ disc	mx. C12851-2	rec. 27 Jan '13	rel. Apr '13

[part of "When the Midnight Choo Choo . . . Medley"]

What Am I Gonna Do?
Irving Berlin
    Columbia   10″ disc   mx. 32229   rec. c. 1914   unissued
    [Columbia assigned the same matrix number to Berlin's recording of "Follow The
      Crowd."]

When I Lost You
Henry Burr
    Victor 17275   10″ disc   mx. B12787-2   rec. 10 Jan '13   rel. Apr '13
Irving Gillette (Henry Burr)
    Edison 1738   4-min. cyl.   rel. Apr '13
Charles D'Almaine (violin)
    Edison 2131   4-min. cyl.   rel. Jan '14
Maxim's Cabaret Singers
    Columbia A1509   10″ disc   mx. 39166   rec. 29 Dec '13   rel. May '14
    [part of a sketch with music titled "Night Scene in Maxim's"]
Prince's Orchestra
    Columbia A1338   10″ disc   mx. 38831   rec. 8 May '13   rel. Aug '13
    [part of "Medley of Snyder Hits"]
Manuel Romain
    Columbia A1288   10″ disc   mx. 38469   rec. 3 Dec '12   rel. May '13
Victor Mixed Chorus
    Victor 35305   12″ disc   mx. C13363-2   rec. 28 May '13   rel. Aug '13
    [part of "Song Medley No. 6—Snyder Specials"]
Victor Military Band
    Victor 35308   12″ disc   mx. C13253-1   rec. 8 May '13   rel. Aug '13
    [title song of medley]

When I'm Alone I'm Lonesome
American Quartet
    Victor 16884   10″ disc   mx. B10386-2   rec. 26 May '11   rel. Aug '11
Anna Chandler
    Edison 784   4-min. cyl.   rel. Sep '11
    Edison 10523   2-min. cyl.   rel. Nov '11
Adeline Francis
    Columbia A1039   10″ disc   mx. 19390   rec. 29 May '11   rel. Oct '11
Prince's Band
    Columbia A1107   10″ disc   mx. 19651   rec. 4 Nov '11   rel. Mar '12
    [part of "Medley of Ted Snyder Hits"]
Walter J. Van Brunt
    Zonophone 5762   10″ disc   rel. Aug '11
Victor Mixed Chorus
    Victor 31848   12″ disc   mx. C11071-2   rec. 9 Oct '11   rel. Dec '11
    [part of "Song Medley No. 1—Snyder Successes"]

When It Rains, Sweetheart, When It Rains
Manuel Romain

Columbia A1217	10″ disc	mx. 38135	rec. 12 Jul '12	rel. Dec '12
Indestructible 3309	4-min. cyl.			rel. c. 1913
U.S. Everlasting 1549	4-min. cyl.			rel. Nov '12

When It's Night Time In Dixie Land
[Written for *Watch Your Step* but deleted before the Broadway premiere]
American Republic Band

Pathé 30232	11-3/8″ disc		rel. Oct '15

anonymous orchestra

Little Wonder 153	5-1/2″ disc		rel. 1915
[part of "Medley No. 4"]			

anonymous tenor solo

Little Wonder 137	5-1/2″ disc		rel. 1915

Elizabeth Brice and Charles King

Columbia	10″ disc	mx. 46330	rec. 11 Jan '16	unissued
[part of medley]				

Jaudas Society Orchestra

Edison 50311	10″ disc		rel. Feb '16
[part of "My Bird of Paradise Medley"]			

When The Midnight Choo-Choo Leaves for Alabam'
Mike Bernard (piano)

Columbia A1313	10″ disc	mx. 38473	rec. 4 Dec '12	rel. Jun '13
[part of "Medley of Snyder's Hits"]				

Arthur Collins and Byron G. Harlan

Columbia A1246	10″ disc	mx. 38383	rec. 28 Oct '12	rel. Feb '13
Edison 1719	4-min. cyl.			rel. Apr '13
Indestructible 3289	4-min. cyl.			rel. c. 1913
Phono-Cut 5192	10″ disc			rel. c. 1913
U.S. Everlasting 1637	4-min. cyl.			rel. Oct '13
Victor 17246	10″ disc	mx. B12566-1	rec. 5 Nov '12	rel. Feb '13

Pietro Deiro (accordion)

Columbia A1323	10″ disc	mx. 38652	rec. 25 Feb '13	rel. Jul '13

Burt Earle and Anglo-American Orchestra

Pathé 5535	11-3/8″ disc		rel. c. 1915

Gene Greene

Pathé 536	11-3/8″ disc		rec. Mar '13	rel. c. 1915

National Promenade Band

Edison 1752	4-min. cyl.		rel. Jul '13
[title song of medley]			

Prince's Orchestra

Columbia A1338	10″ disc	mx. 38831	rec. 8 May '13	rel. Aug '13
[part of "Medley of Snyder's Hits"]				

Victor Military Band
    Victor 35277   12″ disc   mx. C12851-2   rec. 27 Jan '13   rel. Apr '13
    [title song of medley]
Victor Mixed Chorus
    Victor 35305   12″ disc   mx. C13363-2   rec. 28 May '13 rel. Aug. '13
    [part of "Song Medley No. 6—Snyder Specials"]

When You Kiss An Italian Girl
Maurice Burkhart
    Columbia A1046   10″ disc   mx. 19441   rec. 5 Jul '11   rel. Oct '11

When You're In Town
Henry Burr and Elise Stevenson
    Columbia A1021   10″ disc   mx. 19331   rec. 4 May '11   rel. Aug '11
    U.S. Everlasting 1264 4-min. cyl.   rel. Aug '11
    Victor 16898   10″ disc   mx. B10625-2   rec. 28 Jun '11   rel. Sep '11
    Zonophone 5747   10″ disc   rel. Jul '11
Indestructible Military Band
    Indestructible 3241   4-min. cyl.   rel. c. 1911
    [part of "Medley of Popular Hits"]
Ada Jones and Billy Murray
    Edison 859   4-min. cyl.   rel. Dec '11
Prince's Band
    Columbia A1107   10″ disc   mx. 19651   rec. 4 Nov '11   rel. Mar '12
    [part of "Medley of Ted Snyder Hits"]
Victor Mixed Chorus
    Victor 31848   12″ disc   mx. C11071-2   rec. 9 Oct '11   rel. Dec '11
    [part of "Song Medley, No. 1—Snyder Successes"]
Victor Orchestra
    Victor 16963   10″ disc   mx. B10851-3   rec. 11 Aug '11 rel. Nov '11
    [part of "Medley of Ted Snyder Hits"]

Whistling Rag, The
Gene Greene
    Pathé 167   11-3/8″ disc mx. 92225   rec. c. Nov '12 rel. c. 1915

Wild Cherries (Coony, Spoony Rag)
anonymous band
    Indestructible 3130   4-min. cyl.   rel. Oct '10
    [part of "Ragtime Medley No. 1"]
Arthur Collins
    Indestructible 1310   2-min. cyl.   rel. Apr '10
Edward Meeker
    Edison 10291   2-min. cyl.   rel. Jan '10
Eddie Morton
    Columbia A737   10″ disc   mx. 4151   rel. Oct '09
    Victor 16792   10″ disc   mx. B9326-2   rec. 27 Jul '10   rel. Nov '10

Arthur Pryor's Band
   Victor 16504   10″ disc   mx. B8874-1,2   rec. 21 Apr '10   rel. Aug '10
   [part of "Snyder Hits" medley]
Maude Raymond
   Victor   10″ disc   mx. B8025-1,2   rec. 5 Jun '09   unissued
A. Schmehl (xylophone)
   Indestructible 1147   2-min. cyl.   rel. Sep '09
Victor Orchestra
   Victor 16472   10″ disc   mx. B8554-2   rec. 15 Jan '10   rel. Apr '10
Zonophone Orchestra
   Zonophone 5496   10″ disc   rel. Jun '09

Wishing
Manuel Romain
   Edison 750   4-min. cyl.   rel. Aug '11

Woodman, Woodman, Spare That Tree!
Arthur Collins
   U.S. Everlasting 1333   4-min. cyl.   rel. Oct '11
   Zonophone 5774   10″ disc   rel. Sep '11
Bob Roberts
   Edison 837   4-min. cyl.   rel. Nov '11
   Victor 16909   10″ disc   mx. B10801-3   rec. 17 Jul '11   rel. Sep '11
Bert Williams
   Columbia A1321   10″ disc   mx. 38539   rec. 7 Jan '13   rel. Jul '13

Yiddisha Nightingale
Maurice Burkhart
   U.S. Everlasting 487   2-min. cyl.   rel. Aug '12
   Victor 17028   10″ disc   mx. B11042-3   rec. 29 Sep '11   rel. Feb '12

Yiddisha Professor
Maurice Burkhart
   Edison 1643   4-min. cyl.   rel. Mar '13

You've Got Me Hypnotized
Arthur Collins and Byron G. Harlan
   Columbia A1125   10″ disc   mx. 19703   rec. 29 Dec '11   rel. Apr '12
   Phono-Cut 5093   10″ disc   rel. c. 1912
   U.S. Everlasting 1420   4-min. cyl.   rel. Apr '12
Ada Jones and Billy Murray
   Edison 991   4-min. cyl.   rel. May '12

You've Got Your Mother's Big Blue Eyes
Lillian Davis
   Victor 17482   10″ disc   mx. B13946-5   rec. 27 Oct '13   rel. Jan '14

Prince's Orchestra
    Columbia A1495   10″ disc   mx. 39179   rec. 9 Jan '14   rel. Apr '14
    [part of "Medley of Irving Berlin's Hits"]
Victor Military Band
    Victor 35322   12″ disc   mx. C13762-3 rec. 11 Sep '13   rel. Nov '13
    [part of "Somebody's Coming To My House Medley"]

The Following Songs Were Performed in *Watch Your Step*

I Love To Have The Boys Around Me
anonymous orchestra
    Little Wonder 158   5-1/2″ disc   rel. 1915
    [part of "*Watch Your Step* Medley"]
Elizabeth Brice and Charles King
    Columbia   10″ disc   mx. 46330   rec. 16 Jan '16   unissued
    [part of medley]
Victor Military Band
    Victor 17727   10″ disc   mx. B15608-1 rec. 19 Jan '15   rel. Apr '15
    [part of "*Watch Your Step* Medley"]

I've Got-a Go Back To Texas
    [Interpolated into *Watch Your Step* during the New York run]
Elizabeth Brice and Charles King
    Columbia A1944   10″ disc   mx. 46317   rec. 6 Jan '16   rel. May '16

Minstrel Parade, The
anonymous duet
    Little Wonder 169   5-1/2″ disc   rel. 1915
Arthur Collins and Byron G. Harlan
    Victor 17783   10″ disc   mx. B15746-2 rec. 28 Apr '15   rel. Jul '15

My Bird Of Paradise
    [Sung in the 1915 London production of *Watch Your Step*]
American Republic Band
    Pathé 30250   11-3/8″ disc   rel. Oct '15
anonymous band
    Little Wonder 186   5-1/2″ disc   rel. 1915
    [part of "Medley No. 5"]
anonymous tenor solo
    Little Wonder 166   5-1/2″ disc   rel. 1915
Jaudas Society Orchestra
    Edison 50311   10″ disc   rel. Feb '16
    [title song in medley]
Peerless Quartette
    Columbia A1760   10″ disc   mx. 39979   rec. 23 Mar '15 rel. Jun '15
Prince's Band
    Columbia A5688   12″ disc   mx. 37290   rec. 19 May '15 rel. Aug '15

George Prescott
    Pathé 30246   11-3/8" disc   rel. Oct '15
Victor Military Band
    Victor 35457   12" disc   mx. C16002-2   rec. 16 May '15   rel. Jul '15
    [title song of medley]

Settle Down In A One Horse Town
Elizabeth Brice and Charles King
    Columbia   10" disc   mx. 46330   rec. 11 Jan '16   unissued
    [part of medley]
Frances Fisher and Henry Burr
    Columbia A1700   10" disc   mx. 39799   rec. 27 Jan '15   rel. Apr '15
Ada Jones and Billy Murray
    Victor 17708   10" disc   mx. B15556-2   rec. 30 Dec '14   rel. Mar '15
Prince's Band
    Columbia A5660   12" disc   mx. 37168   rec. 11 Feb '15   rel. May '15
Victor Military Band
    Victor 35432   12" disc   mx. C15550-1   rec. 12 Jan '15   rel. Mar '15
    [part of "*Watch Your Step* Medley"]

Simple Melody
anonymous tenor duet
    Little Wonder 308   5-1/2" disc   rel. 1916
Elsie Baker
    Victor   10" disc   mx. B17587-1,2 rec. 2 May '16   unissued
Billy Murray and Edna Brown (Elsie Baker)
    Victor 18051   10" disc   mx. B17588-1   rec. 2 May '16   rel. Jul '16
Walter Van Brunt and Mary Carson
    Edison 2607   4-min. cyl.   rel. May '15

Syncopated Walk, The
anonymous band
    Little Wonder 241   5-1/2" disc   rel. 1916
Peerless Quartet
    Victor 17748   10" disc   mx. B15733-2   rec. 24 Feb '15   rel. May '15
Prince's Band
    Columbia A5632   12" disc   mx. 37094   rec. 11 Dec '14   rel. Mar '15
Victor Military Band
    Victor 35432   12" disc   mx. C15501-1   rec. 12 Jan '15   rel. Mar '15
    [part of "*Watch Your Step* Medley"]

They Always Follow Me Around
Elizabeth Brice and Charles King
    Columbia   10" disc   mx. 46330   rec. 11 Jan '16   unissued
    [part of medley]

What Is Love
Elizabeth Spencer and chorus

Edison 2628	4-min. cyl.		rel. Jun '15
Edison 50239	10″ disc		rel. c. 1915

When I Discovered You
anonymous orchestra

Little Wonder 158	5-1/2″ disc			rel. 1915

[part of "*Watch Your Step* Medley"]
Elizabeth Brice and Charles King

Columbia	10″ disc	mx. 46330	rec. 11 Jan '16	unissued

[part of medley]
Victor Military Band

Victor 17727	10″ disc	mx. B15608-1	rec. 19 Jan '15	rel. Apr '15

[part of "*Watch Your Step* Medley"]

Additional recordings, made in England by members of the cast of the London production of 1915, are cited by Jack Raymond in *Show Music* (Washington: Smithsonian Institution Press, 1992), 61.

Sources consulted: period catalogues and supplementary lists of records issued by the various companies; release lists appearing in *Edison Phonograph Monthly* and in a trade monthly, *The Talking Machine World;* Major H. H. Annand (compiler), *The Complete Catalogue of the United States Everlasting Indestructible Cylinder, 1908–1913* (privately published, 1966) and *The Indestructible Record Company, Albany, New York, United States, 1907–1922* (privately published, Middlesex, England, 1970); Duane D. Deakins, M.D., *Edison Blue Amberol* and *Edison Standard Index* (privately published, late 1950s); Allen Koenigsberg, *Edison Cylinder Records, 1889–1912* (New York: APM Press, 1969); Brian Rust and Allen G. Debus, *The Complete Entertainment Discography (second edition)* (New York: Da Capo, 1989); numerical matrix lists prepared at Columbia Records during the 1950s by Helene Chmura; unpublished compilations prepared from primary sources by discographers Tim Brooks, William R. Moran, and Ted Fagan.

The compiler thanks Tim Brooks, Martin Bryan, and William R. Moran for their thoughtful and valuable assistance.

Notes

Preface

1. Israel Zangwill, *The Melting-Pot* (New York: Macmillan, 1909). First produced at the Columbia Theatre, Washington, D.C., on 5 October 1908.

2. Zangwill, *The Melting-Pot,* p. 36.

3. Ibid., p. 144.

4. Ibid., pp. 198–99.

5. Alexander Woollcott, *The Story of Irving Berlin* (New York: Putnam, 1925). Later biographies include Michael Freedland, *Irving Berlin* (New York: Stein & Day, 1974) and *A Salute to Irving Berlin* (London: W. H. Allen, 1986); Ian Whitcomb, *Irving Berlin and Ragtime America* (London: Century Hutchinson, 1987); and Laurence Bergreen, *As Thousands Cheer: The Life of Irving Berlin* (New York: Viking, 1991). See also Charles Hamm, "Irving Berlin's Early Songs As Biographical Documents," *Musical Quarterly* 77/1 (Spring 1993): 10–34 and Vince Motto, *The Irving Berlin Catalog* (*Sheet Music Exchange* 6, no. 5 (October 1988) and 8, no. 1 (February 1990).

6. According to research conducted recently by Berlin's daughters. See Mary Ellin Barrett, *Irving Berlin: A Daughter's Memoir* (New York: Simon & Schuster, 1994), pp. 98–99.

7. Bergreen, *As Thousands Cheer,* p. 11.

8. Woollcott, *The Story of Irving Berlin,* p. 21.

9. Ibid., p. 27.

10. Ibid., pp. 49–50.

11. Unpublished typescript, "Story of Harry Von Tilzer's Career," Library of Congress, p. 123.

12. Robert Park, "Racial Assimilation in Secondary Groups," *American Journal*

of Sociology (1914): 607. See also Stephen Steinberg, *The Ethnic Myth: Race, Ethnicity, and Class in America* (New York: Atheneum, 1981), pp. 44–74.

Introduction

1. The original sheet music of these songs is preserved in both private and public collections. The most complete of these is that of James J. Fuld of New York City. The most comprehensive institutional collections are the Lester S. Levy Collection of Sheet Music, now housed in the Milton S. Eisenhower Library of John Hopkins University, and the copyright deposit material in the Music Division of the Library of Congress in Washington, D.C. and in the British Library in London. The Performing Arts Research Center of the New York Public Library, the Starr Collection at the University of Indiana, the Driscoll Collection at the Newberry Library in Chicago, the Museum of the City of New York, and the John Hay Collection at Brown University are other important sources for the original versions of these songs. A modern, critical edition of all these songs is Charles Hamm, ed., *Irving Berlin: Early Songs, 1907–1914,* 3 vols. (Madison, Wis.: A-R Editions, *MUSA* 2, 1994). Other recently published smaller collections are *The Songs of Irving Berlin,* 7 vols. (Boca Raton, Fla.: Masters Music Publications, n.d.), *The Songs of Irving Berlin,* 6 vols. (New York: Irving Berlin Music Company, 1991), and *Irving Berlin's Lower East Side Songbook* (New York: Irving Berlin Music Company, 1995).

2. Rennold Wolf, "The Boy Who Revived Ragtime," *Green Book Magazine* 10 (August 1913): 208.

3. Irving Berlin, "How To Write Ragtime Songs," *Ideas* (August 1913): 53.

4. From an interview with Frederick James Smith, an unidentified clipping found in the first of Berlin's scrapbooks, now in the Irving Berlin Collection in the Library of Congress (IBC-LC).

5. Ibid.

6. Wolf, "The Boy Who Revived Ragtime," p. 208.

7. This is one of many unpublished lyrics in IBC-LC.

8. Robert Kimball and Berlin's youngest daughter, Linda Emmet, are preparing a complete edition of his published and unpublished song lyrics.

9. These lists are in IBC-LC.

10. These volumes are now in the possession of Berlin's three daughters.

11. Quoted in Bergreen, *As Thousands Cheer: The Life of Irving Berlin* (New York: Penguin, 1990), pp. 57–58.

12. Alexander Woollcott, *The Story of Irving Berlin* (New York: Putnam, 1925), pp. 65–68.

13. Born 15 August 1881 in Freeport, Illinois, Snyder was a songwriter and music publisher until he retired in 1930 to open a restaurant in Hollywood. Other than "Wild Cherries Rag" (1908) and the songs he coauthored with Berlin, his greatest commercial success was "The Sheik of Araby," written in 1921 with Harry B. Smith and Francis Wheeler.

14. David J. Clark, writing in the *Telegraph* for Sunday 8 October 1911. The song was attributed to Berlin and Leslie upon publication.

15. Wolf, "The Boy Who Revived Ragtime," pp. 202–3.

16. In an unpublished letter to James Fuld, dated 23 November 1954.

17. *Green Book Magazine* (February 1915) cited in Bergreen, *As Thousands Cheer: The Life of Irving Berlin,* pp. 55–56.

18. *Green Book Magazine* (February 1915), cited in Bergreen, *As Thousands Cheer,* p. 57.

19. An unidentified clipping in Berlin earliest scrapbook, now in IBC-LC.

20. Wolf, "The Boy Who Revived Ragtime," p. 208.

21. *The Daily Mail* (London), 21 June 1913, p. 3.

22. A change toward much greater standardization and simplification of piano accompaniments began soon after Hess began working for Berlin.

23. Harry Ruby, quoted in Bergreen, *As Thousands Cheer,* p. 155.

24. Hamm, *Irving Berlin: Early Songs,* vol. 1, pp. xxiv.

25. Ibid., p. xxiv.

26. Ibid., p. xxv.

27. Irving Berlin, with Justus Dickinson, " 'Love-Interest' As a Commodity," *Green Book Magazine* vol. 13 (April 1916): 698.

28. The quotations in this paragraph are taken from an unidentified clipping of an article by Berlin in the second of Berlin's scrapbooks, now in IBC-LC.

29. For a general discussion of the musical style of these songs, see Hamm, *Irving Berlin: Early Songs,* vol. 1, pp. xxv–xxviii.

30. From a recording made in 1911 by Arthur Collins and Byron C. Harlan, released as Victor 16908.

31. Carl Dahlhaus, *Foundations of Music History,* trans. J. B. Robinson (Cambridge: Cambridge University Press, 1983), p. 150.

32. See Richard Middleton, *Studying Popular Music* (Milton Keynes & Philadelphia: Open University Press, 1990), particularly pp. 16–32.

33. Charles Hamm, review of *The Music of Stephen C. Foster: A Critical Edition,* ed. Steven Saunders and Deane L. Root, *Journal of the American Musicological Society* 45, no. 3 (1992): 525–26.

34. For a book-length discussion of the varied and changing meanings of Foster's songs, see William Austin, *"Susanna," "Jeanie," and "The Old Folks at Home:" The Songs of Stephen C. Foster from His Time to Ours* (New York: Macmillan, 1975).

35. See, for instance, Franco Fabbri, "A Theory of Musical Genres: Two Applications," in *Popular Music Perspectives,* vol. 1 (Gothenburg and Exeter: International Association for the Study of Popular Music, 1982), pp. 52–81.

36. In "Chopin and Genre," *Music Analysis* 8, no. 3 (October 1989): 214.

37. *Running with the Devil: Power, Gender, and Madness in Heavy Metal Music* (Hanover, N.H.: Wesleyan University Press, 1993), pp. 29, 31.

38. Hamm, *Irving Berlin: Early Songs,* vol. 1, pp. xxviii–xlvi.

39. Paul Charosh of Brooklyn College and Eric Bernhof of San Francisco generously furnished the tapes, dubbed from original cylinders and discs, on which my discussions of period recordings are based.

40. For instance, an ad for the Ted Snyder Company appearing in *Variety* for 4 November 1911 claims that fifty extra choruses for "After the Honeymoon" are available from the publisher. The Snyder Company offers "any amount of extra verses at your command" for "Fiddle-Dee-Dee" in *Variety* for 26 July 1912 and,

in *Variety* for 9 December 1911, lists seven songs for which "Professional Copies and Orchestrations [are available] in any key" and also "conversation versions" of various songs.

41. The orchestration of "Alexander's Ragtime Band" was copyrighted on 18 October 1911 (E272343) and that for "Spanish Love" on 18 Oct 1911 (E272344); both arrangements were by William Schultz. The manuscript orchestration of "Opera Burlesque" is in the Library of Congress. The only substantial collection of unpublished publisher's materials, to my knowledge, is in the Harry Von Tilzer Collection in the Library of Congress, which contains many manuscript lead sheets, piano/vocal versions, and some orchestrations.

42. To avoid the clumsiness of the repeated use of "she/he" or "(s)he," in what follows I'll refer to the songwriter in the masculine, whatever his or her actual gender, and to the performer of the song in the feminine.

43. Edward T. Cone, *The Composer's Voice* (Berkeley: University of California Press, 1974), pp. 20–40.

Chapter One

1. Bert Lowry, quoted in Charles W. Stein, ed., *American Vaudeville As Seen by Its Contemporaries* (New York: Knopf, 1984), pp. 6–8.

2. Robert W. Snyder, *The Voice of the City: Vaudeville and Popular Culture in New York* (New York: Oxford University Press, 1989), p. 4.

3. Gunther Barth, *City People: The Rise of Modern City Culture in Nineteenth-Century America* (New York: Oxford University Press, 1980), pp. 193–94.

4. From "Lillian Russell's Reminiscences," *Cosmopolitan Magazine* 72 (February 1922): 13–18 ff., quoted in Stein, *American Vaudeville*, p. 11.

5. Michael M. Davis, Jr., *The Exploitation of Pleasure: A Study of Commercial Recreations in New York City* (New York: Russell Sage Foundation, 1911), cited in Snyder, *The Voice of the City*, p. 199.

6. Snyder, *The Voice of the City*, p. 64.

7. *Equity News* 9 (November 1923), quoted in Stein, *American Vaudeville*, pp. 124, 128.

8. For a useful description of a variety of places of entertainment found in one small section of the Bowery in the early days of vaudeville, see Armond Fields and L. Marc Fields, *From the Bowery to Broadway: Lew Fields and the Roots of American Popular Theater* (New York: Oxford University Press, 1993), pp. 40–46.

9. Barth, *City People*, pp. 205–206.

10. *National Magazine* 9 (November 1908), quoted in Stein, *American Vaudeville*, pp. 17, 20.

11. As reported by Edwin Milton Royle, "The Vaudeville Theatre," *Scribner's Magazine* 26 (October 1899).

12. From an Artist's Contract drawn up by the Family Theatre Department of the United Booking Offices of America, as reported in *Variety*, 25 March 1911, p. 11.

13. Snyder, *The Voice of the City*, p. 154.

14. Douglas Gilbert, *American Vaudeville: Its Life and Times* (New York: Whittlesey House, 1940), pp. 243–50.

15. Isaac Goldberg, *Tin Pan Alley: A Chronicle of the American Popular Music Racket* (New York: John Day, 1930), p. 214.

16. *World of Our Father* (New York: Harcourt Brace Jovanovich, 1976), p. 402.

17. Snyder, *The Voice of the City*, p. 110.

18. Barth, *City People*, pp. 221–22.

19. Fields and Fields, *From the Bowery to Broadway*, pp. 49–50.

20. Snyder, *The Voice of the City*, pp. 110–11.

21. Unidentified clipping in the Robinson Locke Collection, New York Public Library series 2, vol. 30.

22. Fields and Fields, *From the Bowery to Broadway*, p. 52.

23. Stephan Thernstrom (ed.), *Harvard Encyclopedia of American Ethnic Groups*, (Cambridge, Mass.: Harvard University Press, 1980), p. 548.

24. Stephen Steinberg, *The Ethnic Myth: Race, Ethnicity, and Class in America* (New York: Atheneum, 1981), p. 141.

25. From an unidentified clipping, dated 12 September 1911, in one of Berlin's scrapbooks, now in IBC-LC.

26. The definition is taken from *The New Harvard Dictionary of Music* (Cambridge, Mass.: Harvard University Press, 1986), p. 836.

27. Berlin published two altogether different songs under the title of "My Sweet Italian Man"; both had the same sheet music cover as well. The song in question here is the second of these, copyrighted in February 1913; the title properly should have been "My Sweet Italian Gal," the first and last line of the chorus.

28. See Thernstrom, *Harvard Encyclopedia*, pp. 571–98.

29. For an excellent discussion of the music and theater of New York's Jewish population during this period, see Mark Slobin, *Tenement Songs: The Popular Music of the Jewish Immigrants* (Urbana: University of Illinois Press, 1982).

30. At one point Sadie "heard [Yiddle] drinking soup," but this lack of table etiquette is not ethnic-specific; several of Berlin's Italian novelty songs also make reference to audible eating habits.

31. Fields and Fields, *From the Bowery to Broadway*, p. 132.

32. Preserved in the Irving Berlin Collection now in the Library of Congress (IBC-LC).

33. See Slobin, *Tenement Songs*, pp. 182–97, for a discussion of this style.

34. As reported in *Variety* for 10 December 1910, p. 23.

35. Ibid.

36. *Variety*, 26 August 1911, p. 10.

37. As quoted in Slobin, *Tenement Songs*, p. 61.

38. Thernstrom, *Harvard Encyclopedia*, p. 410.

39. Fields and Fields, *From the Bowery to Broadway*, pp. 79–80.

40. Columbia A-804, recorded in 1909.

41. The references are to Berlin's song "That Mesmerizing Mendelssohn Tune" and to Florenz Ziegfeld's showgirl wife (Anna Held), who was widely held to be the most beautiful woman on the vaudeville stage.

42. A considerable emphasis on sex is present, however, once it's understood that "walking" was a euphemism for sexual intercourse.

43. For a summary of these trends as they affected popular culture, see Charles

Hamm, "Irving Berlin's Early Songs As Biographical Documents," *Musical Quarterly* 77, no. 1 (Spring 1993): pp. 10–15.

44. The earlier lyric is preserved in IBC-LC.

45. The chorus of "In The Town Where I Was Born" (1914) by Dick Howard, Billy Tracey, and Al Harriman is typical of these pieces:

> There were no skyscrapers in my old hometown,
> There were no bright lights or no Broadways,
> And there were no taxis on the old main street,
> Or no midnight Cabarets,
> There were just plain people in that country town,
> Always up with the roosters in the morn,
> But if a fellow had a gal,
> He never had to watch his pal,
> In the town where I was born.

46. Evan Hunter, *Criminal Conversation* (New York: Warner, 1994), p. 262.

47. Unidentified newspaper clipping from about 1913, in the first of the scrapbooks kept by Irving Berlin, now in IBC-LC.

48. E. M. Wickes, *Writing the Popular Song* (Springfield, Mass.: Home Correspondence School, 1916), pp. 27–28.

49. *Variety,* 27 June 1913, p. 5.

50. This lyric, titled "Samuel Brown (The Operatic Waiter)," is preserved in IBC-LC.

51. For a fuller account of these songs, see Charles Hamm, "Irving Berlin's Early Songs As Biographical Documents," pp. 16–24.

52. These lyrics are preserved in IBC-LC.

53. *The Songs of Irving Berlin,* 6 vols. (New York: Irving Berlin Music Company, 1991).

Chapter Two

1. Michael Rogin, "Blackface, White Noise: The Jewish Jazz Singer Finds His Voice," *Critical Inquiry* 18, no. 3 (Spring 1992): 437.

2. Eric Lott discusses the relationship between blacks and Irish-Americans in nineteenth-century America, and the critical role played by the latter in the minstrel show, in *Love and Theft: Blackface Minstrelsy and the American Working Class* (New York: Oxford University Press, 1993), pp. 95–96 and 148–49.

3. Irving Howe, *World of Our Fathers* (New York: Harcourt Brace Jovanovich, 1976), p. 563.

4. Rogin, "Blackface, White Noise," pp. 419, 421.

5. Ibid., pp. 417, 439.

6. Ibid, p. 439.

7. Ian Whitcomb's phrase, from *Irving Berlin and Ragtime America* (New York: Limelight Editions, 1988), p. 81.

8. Charles Hamm, "Genre, Performance and Ideology in the Early Songs of Irving Berlin," *Popular Music* 13, no. 2 (May 1994): 146.

9. It was made into an equally popular parlor song in 1837 by the singer-songwriter Henry Russell, although there is no reference to this piece in Berlin's song.

10. For a summary of this practice, see Katherine K. Preston, *Opera on the Road: Traveling Opera Troupes in the United States, 1825–60* (Urbana: University of Illinois Press, 1993): pp. 312–14.

11. *Variety*, 19 November 1910, p. 21.

12. "Scott Joplin's *Treemonisha* Years," *American Music* 9, no. 3 (Fall 1991): 267–69.

13. Reported in Reid Badger, *A Life in Ragtime: A Biography of James Reese Europe* (New York: Oxford University Press, 1995), pp. 287–88.

14. In Charles Hamm, "Irving Berlin's Early Songs As Biographical Documents," *Musical Quarterly* 77, vol. 1 (Spring 1993): 20–23, and also in Chapter Three of this book.

15. New York: Knopf, 1950.

16. David A. Jasen and Trebor Tichenor, *Rags and Ragtime: A Musical History* (New York: Dover, 1978), p. 1.

17. Blesh and Janis, *They All Played Ragtime* (New York: Knopf, 1950), pp. 5, 220.

18. *Ragtime: A Musical and Cultural History* (Berkeley: University of California Press, 1980), p. 2.

19. "Ragtime Songs," *Ragtime: Its History, Composers, and Music,* ed. John Edward Hasse (New York: Schirmer Books, 1985), p. 70.

20. E. M. Wickes, *Writing the Popular Song* (Springfield, Mass.: Home Correspondence School, 1916), p. 33.

21. For a discussion of this feature, see Edward A. Berlin, *Ragtime: A Musical and Cultural History,* pp. 130–34.

22. Scott DeVeaux and William Howland Kenney, eds., *The Music of James Scott* (Washington, D.C.: Smithsonian Institution Press, 1993), pp. 37–38.

23. Julian Johnson, "Irving Berlin—A Restless Success," *Theatre Magazine* (February 1915): 97.

24. Edison Wax Amberol 479, recorded 19 April 1910.

25. Piano rags don't necessarily "have to do with" African American culture, either, aside from whatever musical ties they might have with black music. Even though some pieces, Ray Ruddy's "Little Sticks O' Licorice" (1911) for instance, have titles and/or covers making reference to black people and their culture, most rags by either black or white composers claim no such connection and even go to pains to distance themselves from such a notion. James Scott's "Grace And Beauty" (1909), subtitled "A Classy Rag," has a cover portrait of a stylish white woman dressed in furs and velvet, posing with a well-bred dog, for instance, and none of Scott Joplin's rags make reference to African American culture in their titles or cover illustrations.

26. Victor 16982-B, 1912.

27. Part of this had to do with changing marketing strategies, as publishers and songwriters realized that it was to their advantage not to "type" a given song too precisely but to advertise that it could be sung by a variety of performers and in different styles. Typically, Berlin's "When I'm Alone I'm Lonesome" was described

in *Variety* for 4 November 1911 as "a wonderful ballad, or can be used as a 'coon' song."

28. *Ben Harney's Rag Time Instructor* (Chicago: Sol Bloom, 1897).

29. Wickes, *Writing the Popular Song,* p. 33.

30. Edward A. Berlin, *King of Ragtime: Scott Joplin and His Era* (New York: Oxford University Press, 1994), p. 183.

31. Berlin, *King of Ragtime,* p. 184.

32. Quoted in ibid., p. 172.

33. DeVeaux and Kenney, *The Music of James Scott,* pp. 13, 16.

34. Quoted in Berlin, *King of Ragtime,* p. 103.

35. Isaac Goldberg, *The Story of Irving Berlin* (New York: Putnam, 1925), pp. 320–21.

36. On Indestructible Columbia Cylinder 3289.

37. This verse is included in the performance on *Popular Music in Jacksonian America* (Musical Heritage Society MHS 834561, 1962) by The Yankee Doodle Society under the direction of Joseph Byrd.

38. Irving Howe, *The Immigrant Jews of New York 1881 to the Present* (London: Routledge & Kegan Paul, 1976), p. 362. Zangwill's *The Melting-Pot* was dedicated to Roosevelt "in respectful recognition of his strenuous struggle against the forces that threaten to shipwreck the Great Republic which carries mankind and its fortunes."

39. *Irving Berlin: The Ragtime Years* (Nonesuch).

40. Benjamin Sears and Bradford Conner, *Come On and Hear! Early Songs by Irving Berlin, 1909–1915* (Oakton Recordings CD ORCD0001, 1994).

41. This sequence also appears in the film *Mammy* (1930).

42. The script of *Mister Bones* was copyrighted on 10 September 1928; a copy is in the Music Division of the Library of Congress.

Chapter Three

1. Laurence Bergreen, *As Thousands Cheer: The Life of Irving Berlin* (New York: Viking, 1990), p. 65.

2. Irving Berlin, as quoted in *Stereo Review,* February 1988.

3. Alexander Woollcott, *The Story of Irving Berlin* (New York: Putnam, 1925), p. 86.

4. Ibid., p. 85.

5. *A History of Popular Music in America* (New York: Random House, 1948), p. 376.

6. Alec Wilder, *American Popular Song: The Great Innovators, 1900–1950* (New York: Oxford University Press, 1972), p. 94.

7. Bergreen, *As Thousands Cheer,* p. 60.

8. This phrase is taken from E. M. Wickes, *Writing the Popular Song* (Springfield, Mass.: Home Correspondence School, 1916), p. 33.

9. See Edward A. Berlin, *Ragtime: A Musical and Cultural History* (Berkeley: University of California Press, 1980), pp. 107–11, and Scott DeVeaux and William Howland Kenney, eds., *The Music of James Scott* (Washington, D.C.: Smithsonian Institution Press, 1992), p. 37.

10. Edward Berlin, *Ragtime,* particularly pp. 1–20.

11. Wilder, *American Popular Song,* p. 94.

12. Irving Berlin, with Justus Dickinson, " 'Love-Interest' As a Commodity," *Green Book Magazine* vol. 13 (April 1916): 698.

13. Kay C. Thompson, "Lottie Joplin," *Record Changer* 9 (October 1949): 8, 18.

14. Edward A. Berlin, *King of Ragtime: Scott Joplin and His Era* (New York: Oxford University Press, 1994), p. 267.

15. From an interview with Trebor Tichenor, reported in Berlin, *King of Ragtime,* p. 267.

16. *They All Played Ragtime* (New York: Knopf, 1950).

17. Edward A. Berlin, "Scott Joplin's *Treemonisha* Years," *American Music* 9, no. 3 (Fall 1991): 260–76.

18. Ibid., p. 269. Berlin also discusses this issue in *King of Ragtime,* pp. 210–12.

19. Berlin, *King of Ragtime,* p. 211.

20. Charles Hamm, *Irving Berlin: Early Songs, 1907–1914,* vol. 1 (Madison, Wis.: A-R Editions, 1994. *MUSA 2*), p. xxv.

21. Ian Whitcomb, *Irving Berlin and Ragtime America* (New York: Limelight Editions, 1988), p. 81.

22. Irving Berlin, " 'Love-Interest' As a Commodity," p. 695.

23. Charles Hamm, "Irving Berlin's Early Songs As Biographical Documents," *Musical Quarterly* 77 (Spring 1993): 10–34.

24. Milton "Mezz" Mezzrow and Bernard Wolfe, *Really the Blues* (New York: Random House, 1946), pp. 4, 18.

25. See Jim Walsh, "Alexander's Recorded History," *Hobbies* 87 (January 1983): 64.

26. Woollcott, *The Story of Irving Berlin,* p. 87.

27. Whitcomb, *Irving Berlin and Ragtime America,* pp. 71, 75.

28. Bergreen, *As Thousands Cheer,* p. 60.

29. *Green Book Magazine* (February 1915), as quoted in Bergreen, *As Thousands Cheer,* p. 57.

30. Rennold Wolf, "The Boy Who Revived Rag-time," *Green Book Magazine* 10 (August 1913): 201–9. The emphases are mine.

31. Julian Johnson, "Irving Berlin—A Restless Success," *Theatre Magazine* 21 (February 1915): 67.

32. Michael Freedland, *A Salute To Irving Berlin* (London: W. H. Allen, 1986), p. 43.

33. Bergreen, *As Thousands Cheer,* p. 61.

34. Freedland, *A Salute,* pp. 43–44.

35. Wolf, "The Boy Who Revived Rag-time," p. 204.

36. *Philadelphia Telegraph,* 22 July 1914.

37. Billy Murray's version, recorded for the Edison Blue Amberol cylinder series. See Walsh, "Alexander's Recorded History," p. 67.

38. A conflation of the titles of two different songs by Berlin in Carus's set, "When I'm Alone I'm Lonesome" and "When You're In Town." See footnote 40.

39. The "Kelly" song mentioned is "Has Anybody Here Seen Kelly!" (1909) by C. W. Murphy and Will Letters, published in London and featured by Nora Bayes in the musical comedy *The Jolly Bachelors* (1910).

40. As noted by reviewers, "When I'm Alone I'm Lonesome" was another; the song's cover has a banner similar to that found on "Alexander," reading "Successfully Introduced by Emma Carus." The *New York Journal* for 17 June reports that the other three songs in Carus's set were Berlin's "When You're In Town," "Hands Up" by Joseph Lamb and J. Fred Helf, and an unidentified "Mary Ann."

41. Undated clipping in the Museum of the City of New York.

42. Wolf, "The Boy Who Revived Rag-time," p. 201.

43. Ibid., pp. 202–3.

44. Ibid., pp. 203–4. The program for the opening night gives the title of the song as "Answer Me," but reviews of the show make it clear that the piece in question was "Keep A Taxi Waiting." All subsequent programs list the number under the latter title.

45. Ibid., p. 204.

46. *American Song: The Complete Musical Theatre Companion* (New York: Facts On File Publications, 1985), p. 298. Programs and reviews of the show identify Arthur Lipson and Taylor Holmes as the principals in the prize fight segment, in which Dreadnaught Drexel is pitted against Battling Beresford.

47. Wolf, "The Boy Who Revived Rag-time," p. 204.

48. The song in question was Berlin's "Ephraham Played Upon The Piano," not copyrighted and published until 20 June.

49. "Irving Berlin's Career," unidentified clipping in The Museum of the City of New York.

50. *Variety,* 19 August 1911.

51. "Some Of These Days" was written by Shelton Brooks, one of the handful of black songwriters whose songs enjoyed success in vaudeville.

52. From the clipping "Irving Berlin's Career."

53. *Variety* for 20 October 1954. The zobos, kazoo-type instruments, were to become a regular feature of subsequent performances of the song.

54. *Variety,* 24 June 1911.

55. *Variety,* 9 September 1911.

56. Reid Badger, *A Life in Ragtime: A Biography of James Reese Europe* (New York: Oxford University Press, 1994), p. 263, n. 43.

57. The information in this section is taken mostly from Jim Walsh, "Alexander's Recorded History," pp. 62–67, 70, 75.

58. Ibid., p. 70.

59. The most complete list of recordings of "Alexander" made through the 1960s is found in Dave Jay, *The Irving Berlin Songography, 1907–1966* (New Rochelle: Arlington House, 1969), pp. 13–14. The most recent recording, as this is written, is a CD entitled *Come On and Hear!* (Oakton Recordings ORCD00001, 1993), performed by Benjamin Sears and Bradford Connor.

Chapter Four

1. The first-mentioned voucher is now in the Museum of the City of New York; the second was reported in Alexander Woollcott, *The Story of Irving Berlin* (New York: Putnam, 1925), p. 68.

2. Arthur Loesser, *Men, Woman and Pianos: A Social History* (New York: Simon and Schuster, 1954), p. 521.

3. Ibid, p. 503.

4. (Chicago: Smith & Simon Publishing Company, 1895), pp. iii–iv.

5. (Philadelphia & Chicago: J. H. Moore, 1895), pp. i–ii.

6. Gilbert Chase, *America's Music From the Pilgrims to the Present* (New York: McGraw-Hill, 1955), p. 165.

7. Daniel Walker Howe, "Victorian Culture in America," in Howe, ed., *Victorian America* (Philadelphia: University of Pennsylvania Press, 1976), pp. 12, 17.

8. Mary R. Melendy, *Ladies' Home Companion: A Book Giving Full Information on All the Mysterious and Complex Matters Pertaining to Women* (Chicago: H. J. Smith, 1901), pp. 64, 67.

9. Ibid, p. 65.

10. Rev. Hubbard Winslow (Boston: Crocker & Brewster, 1837), pp. 313–22, *passim*.

11. Lawrence W. Levine, *Highbrow/Lowbrow: The Emergence of Cultural Hierarchy in America* (Cambridge, Mass.: Harvard University Press, 1988), p. 120.

12. For a discussion of this repertory, see Charles Hamm, *Yesterdays: Popular Song in America* (New York: W. W. Norton, 1979), pp. 162–200.

13. "Poet's love or composer's love?" in Steven Paul Scher, *Music and Text: Critical Inquiries.* (Cambridge: Cambridge University Press, 1992), p. 179.

14. This argument is developed at length in "Whose life? The gendered self in Schumann's *Frauenliebe* songs," in Scher, *Music and Text,* pp. 219–40.

15. Hamm, *Yesterdays,* pp. 46, 58.

16. For a discussion of mixed modes of transmission in popular music, see John Spitzer, " 'Oh! Susanna': Oral Transmission and Tune Transformation," *Journal of the American Musicological Society* 47, no. 1 (Spring 1994): 90–136.

17. For a fuller discussion of these pieces, see Hamm, *Yesterdays,* pp. 210–19.

18. William W. Austin, *"Susanna," "Jeanie," and "The Old Folks at Home": The Songs of Stephen C. Foster from His Time to Ours* (New York: Macmillan, 1975), p. 162. See also Susan Key, "Sound and Sentimentality: Nostalgia in the Songs of Stephen Foster," *American Music* 13, no. 2 (Summer 1995): 145–66.

19. Eric Lott, *Love and Theft: Blackface Minstrelsy and the American Working Class* (New York: Oxford University Press, 1993), p. 193.

20. Ibid., p. 190, paraphrasing Alexander Saxton, "Blackface Minstrelsy and Jackson Ideology," *American Quarterly* 27, no. 1 (1975): 3–28.

21. For an account of ballad concerts in England, see Derek B. Scott, *The Singing Bourgeois: Songs of the Victorian Drawing Room and Parlour* (Milton Keynes & Philadelphia: Open University Press, 1989), pp. 120–33, and Wilma Reid Cipolla, "Marketing the American Song in Edwardian London," *American Music* 8, no. 1 (Spring 1990): 84–94.

22. *Variety,* 6 May 1911, p. 20. Ernest Ball was a highly successful writer of popular ballads with Irish or Irish-American protagonists.

23. For information on this anthology, see my introduction to a reprint edition brought out by Da Capo Press (New York) in 1983.

24. *Heart Songs* (Boston: Chapple Publishing Company, 1909), p. vi.

25. As, for instance, in Henry Burr's performance of "When I Lost You" on Victor 17275-A.

26. Laurence Bergreen, *As Thousands Cheer: The Life of Irving Berlin* (New York: Viking, 1990), p. 84.

27. Woollcott, *The Story of Irving Berlin,* p. 104.

28. Bergreen, *As Thousands Cheer,* pp. 84–85.

29. In an interview entitled "Irving Berlin and Modern Ragtime," found in an unidentified clipping in the first of Berlin's scrapbooks in LC-IBC, Berlin is quoted as saying, "I can truthfully say that I have accomplished a number of things which were thought impossible. I have established the syncopated ballad. . . ."

30. Victor 17787 (9146), made on 13 September 1910.

Chapter Five

1. From an unidentified clipping in the Harvard Theater Collection, Harvard University Library, Cambridge, Mass.

2. Unaccountably, some sources report that the show opened at the Globe Theatre.

3. Gerald Bordman, *American Musical Theatre: A Chronicle,* 2d ed. (New York: Oxford University Press, 1992), pp. 302–4.

4. Charles Hamm, "The USA: Classical, Industrial and Invisible Music," in Jim Samson, ed., *The Late Romantic Era: From the Mid-19th Century to World War I* (London: Macmillan, 1991), p. 314.

5. *Understanding Toscanini* (New York: Knopf, 1987), p. 37.

6. Lawrence W. Levine, *Highbrow/Lowbrow: The Emergence of Cultural Hierarchy in America* (Cambridge, Mass.: Harvard University Press, 1988), p. 102.

7. Armond Fields and L. Marc Fields, *From the Bowery to Broadway: Lew Fields and the Roots of American Popular Theater* (New York: Oxford University Press, 1993), p. 126.

8. Used by permission of the Museum of the City of New York.

9. According to Bordman, *American Musical Theatre.* However, Kurt Gänzl says says in *The Encyclopedia of The Musical Theatre,* vol. 1, (New York: Schirmer Books, 1994), p. 164, that the show opened on 2 November 1908 and ran for 104 performances.

10. I follow the practice of Bordman, in *American Musical Theatre,* and others of having each theatrical season begin in the summer rather than the fall.

11. The song was recorded commercially by Berlin himself on Columbia 804.

12. Fields and Fields, *From the Bowery to Broadway,* pp. 250–1.

13. This quotation, and much of the following description of the show, is taken from ibid., pp. 250–65.

14. Written in England by C. W. Murphy and Will Letters, the song became popular in the United States in an adaption by William C. McKenna.

15. *Variety,* 25 June 1910.

16. Billy Murray's period performance of "Sweet Italian Love" on Victor 16790 captures the heavy dialect with which this song, and others of the same sort, were performed.

17. For more information on Carle, see Gänzl, *Encyclopedia of the Musical Theatre,* vol. 1, pp. 224–5.

18. Dave Jay, *The Irving Berlin Songography 1907–1966* (New Rochelle: Arlington House, 1969), p. 12, and Steven Suskin, *Berlin, Kern, Rodgers, Hart, and Hammerstein: A Complete Song Catalogue* (Jefferson, N.C.: McFarland, 1990), p. 74.

19. Bordman, *American Musical Theatre,* p. 680.

20. *Cleveland Leader,* 3 November 1910. This item was kindly called to my attention by John Graziano.

21. This style may be heard in Williams's recording of the song on Columbia 1321.

22. Although Berlin's name doesn't appear on the published sheet music, his part in writing the song is acknowledged in copyright deposit documents in the Library of Congress.

23. Fields and Fields, *From the Bowery to Broadway,* p. 293.

24. Information taken from ibid., p. 295 ff.

25. Ibid., p. 313.

26. A third song listed on the cover, "Brand New," was not written by Berlin & Snyder, as claimed, but by Cecil Mack and Chris Smith, according to copyright entries.

27. A similar song is "Jake! Jake! The Yiddisher Ball-Player," written the following year.

28. Another sheet music cover has a large portrait of Laura Guerite, who "Successfully Introduced" it. She was not in the cast of the show.

29. Information and quote from Fields and Fields, *From the Bowery to Broadway,* p. 319.

30. Ibid., p. 320.

31. Berlin may have had input into two other songs in the show attributed to Goetz and Sloane, "Following The Girl Behind The Fan" and "Lonely Moon," although his name is nowhere associated with either.

32. Bordman, *American Musical Theatre,* p. 287.

33. Fields and Fields, *From the Bowery to Broadway,* p. 326.

34. Jay, *Irving Berlin Songography,* p. 25.

35. In this connection, it should be noted that he ended his collaboration with Ted Snyder, who had little experience or talent in writing for the musical stage.

36. This sketch is now in the Irving Berlin Collection in the Library of Congress (LC-IBC).

37. Rennold Wolf, "The Boy Who Revived Rag-time," *Green Book Magazine* 10, vol. 2 (August 1913): 209.

38. "How To Write Ragtime Songs," *Ideas* (an otherwise unidentified clipping in the earliest Berlin scrapbook, now in LC-IBC).

39. "Irving Berlin and Modern Ragtime," clipping in Berlin scrapbook. The "snatches" of the score mentioned here probably included "That Opera Rag" and "Opera Burlesque."

40. Wolf, "The Boy Who Revived Rag-time," p. 208.

41. Lyric in LC-IBC, used by permission of the Estate of Irving Berlin.

42. Lead sheet and lyrics in LC-IBC, published in *MUSA* 2, vol. 3, pp. 232–3.

43. This typescript is in the Museum of the City of New York in a folder of material pertaining to the *Ziegfeld Follies of 1912.*

Epilogue

1. See Charles Hamm, *Yesterdays: Popular Song in America* (New York: W. W. Norton, 1979), for a fuller discussion of these issues.

2. Edward Harrigan and David Braham, "McNally's Row Of Flats" (New York: William A. Pond, 1882).

3. Israel Zangwill, *The Melting-Pot* (New York: Macmillan, 1909), p. 198.

4. Zangwill, *The Melting-Pot,* p. 144.

5. Armond Fields and L. Marc Fields, *From the Bowery to Broadway: Lew Fields and the Roots of American Popular Theater* (New York: Oxford University Press, 1993), p. 123.

6. Unidentified clipping in the Harvard Theatre Collection, Cambridge, Mass.

7. Allen Forte, *The American Popular Ballad of the Golden Era 1924–1950* (Princeton: Princeton University Press, 1995), p. 4.

8. Ibid., p. 335.

9. Ibid., pp. 42–43.

10. I'm using the term "modern" here in its context of denoting an extended historical era in Western Europe extending from the Enlightenment and the Industrial Revolution to after the end of World War II.

11. Forte, *The American Popular Ballad,* p. 87.

12. Unidentified clipping in the Harvard Theatre Collection, Cambridge, Mass.

Index